The Lies We Believe In

China, Russia and the communist revolution in America

The Lies We Believe In

China, Russia and the communist revolution in America

JR Nyquist

May13
Books

2022

First edition: August 2022.

Cover art and layout by: Lucas Guse
Cover image by: Pete Linforth, Pixabay

May13 Books
Santa Catarina, Brazil

Summary

Across Shallow Swamps

09/24/2019

> — And I saw a great sadness descend on mankind. The best grew weary of their works. A doctrine appeared, accompanied by faith: 'All is empty, all is one, all is past!' And from all the hills it echoed: 'All is empty, all is one, all is past!' Indeed we have harvested: but why did all our fruit turn rotten and brown? What fell down from the evil moon last night? In vain was all our work; our wine has turned to poison; an evil eye has seared our fields and hearts. We have all become dry.... All our wells have dried up; even the sea has withdrawn. All the soil would crack, but the depth refuses to devour. 'Alas, where is there still a sea in which one might drown?' Thus are we wailing across shallow swamps.
>
> — Friedrich Nietzsche, Thus Spake Zarathustra

Our great shame — the shame of the present generation — is how we have been fooled: first, by the supposed collapse of communism; second, by our tolerance for the promises of socialist politicians who deny they are socialists; and third, into tolerating a bogus set of claims that should have been struck down as madness— like today's gender and race obsession, like the politics of climate change, like our culture's romance with the homosexual and the transsexual. It is, as Nietzsche intuited, a shallow swamp in which we hear the refrain, "Everything is empty, everything is one, everything is past." It is the crisis of European nihilism.

When the Soviet Union somehow vanished, we were told that communist subversion was a thing of the past. Then we elected communists domestically, though these people denied their Marxism and hid their subversive connections — some of us weren't fooled. But the public would not hear our warning. Socialism is advancing steadily, with an accelerating pace, insistently, militantly, with fang and claw at the ready. We are now locked into socialized medicine, which corrupts good medicine. The tax burden of "free" healthcare will effectively crowd out defense spending. No one dares to oppose tax money for grandma's surgeries (though socialized medicine is more likely to kill grandma than save her). For our compassion: say goodbye to carrier battlegroups, tank divisions and air wings. We don't need them anyway, right? The threat of totalitarian socialism ended in 1991.

But it didn't end, and they have us by the throat. And now we are boxed into one untenable position after another. Yes, they tricked us into socialized medicine, and they are tricking us into the global warming hysteria. Soon our society will be financially ruined, and our enemies will hold the balance of power in their hands. Our "mainstream" intellectuals, who dominate the government and the media, have already made sure that our nuclear arsenal has rotted away. There is no surviving these educated morons — people with huge brains, little minds, and no instincts whatsoever.

William F. Buckley famously said that he would "sooner live in a society governed by the first two thousand names in the Boston telephone directory than in a society governed by the two thousand faculty members of Harvard University." But Harvard has won, and Stanford and Yale, and….

I recently finished reading Stanford professor Michael McFaul's memoir of policymaking in the Obama administration. It was a tough read because McFaul is a politically correct enthusiast of the dullest, most repetitive, and exasperating type. He believes in feminism, climate change, world peace and democracy. He is a political fantasist ready to invest in a moonbeam farm if given half a chance. Here is a well-meaning bungler, an architect of Obama's Russia reset policy, who vaguely (kind of) admitted mistranslating the word "reset" on the button Hillary Clinton presented to Russian Foreign Minister Sergei Lavrov in 2009. McFaul has such blinding multicultural earnestness that he should never have been taught to read, or permitted to write. The inner disease that afflicts people of this kind was once described by H.L. Mencken as "the will to believe." As a policy-maker McFaul is dangerous at any speed; an intelligent simpleton whose advice must never be followed and whose prescriptions are fatal.

McFaul, of course, loathes President Trump; probably for the same reasons that Claire Berlinski loathes him; namely, on account of The president's decided non-intellectual bent, which rates in Claire's analysis as "illiteracy." We are told the president does not like to read. Trump's unfitness for high office begins here, precisely where the ruling class's autism begins. Oh yes, I know they read. But in my experience, they do not read with discernment, and they gravitate to the wrong books. It is an intellectualism permeated with self pity, dishonesty, and malice. One might say, in this matter, that our intellectuals are loathsome *because* they read.

Nietzsche knew there was a problem with intellectuals over 130 years ago. In *Thus Spake Zarathustra* Nietzsche wrote, "Another century of readers — and spirit itself will stink." In the next paragraph he explained, "Everyone being allowed to learn to read, ruins in the long run not only writing but also thinking."

Very few are capable of thinking, of keeping to the facts, of reserving judgement. Character is decisive here. The enthusiast immediately believes, enthuses, applauds. This is McFaul and the whole tribe of elite useful idiots. Covering his flank, and taking full advantage of his naïveté, is the tribe of the intellectual gangsters, the nihilists and revolutionary haters. I would take Trump's "illiterate" instincts over these people's "literate" nihilism any day.

It is not that Trump's distaste for reading is something to celebrate. I understand the limitations of someone who doesn't read good books. But still, Trump is better than the leftist literati who despise him. If he is evil, as Claire Berlinski suggests, then he is less evil than they are.

Manly virtue combined with strong instinct sometimes counts for more than reason in the life of man. As often happens, reason either prostitutes itself to justify the arrogance of the fragile ego, or it humbles itself before objective fact out of an abundance of inner strength. This latter case is relatively rare today. Therefore, it is fitting to be wary of intellectuals. And I say this as one who reveres intelligence, who believes in literacy, but who is disappointed in intellectuals as a class. I have seen too much unmanly wickedness in our literati to cherish any illusions about them. One must go further than Nietzsche in condemning these people. Granting literacy to the wicked is like giving a pedicure to a hyena.

Consider what our intellectual hyenas have done: False ideas are everywhere promoted. The new religion of the intellectuals is socialism, and it is taking hold on all sides. It devours the seed corn of the future. It deceives and corrupts the public. And once they get a sufficient hold on power, they will use violence against anyone who contradicts them. They are not interested in the rule of law. That is why the new religion of socialism has established so many totalitarian states across the globe — in Russia, China, Cuba, North Korea,

Vietnam, Venezuela, Nicaragua, Angola, Congo, Venezuela and more. People in those countries have no rights. They are chattel. And their socialist rulers always reveal themselves to be criminals, murderers, and destroyers. But all of them started out as intellectuals.

Do you see where we are headed?

Thomas Carlyle once observed that "man never yields himself wholly to brute Force, but always to moral Greatness." Here is the basis for a swindle: the imposition of a counterfeit moral greatness (a.k.a., Political Correctness). Thus, we have lost touch with real moral greatness.

The new religion of the intellectuals — socialism — is a doctrine that promises to bankrupt us, financially and intellectually. Those who have doubts, who disagree with the new doctrine, are immoral. They must be ignored, else they are labeled sexists, racists, or Nazis. We hardly consider what racism or sexism would be, if it were something other than a label used to destroy persons who disagree with specific policies — whether in family law, immigration, or national security.

A real racist isn't bothered by such labeling, and certainly isn't destroyed by it. Rather, it is his badge of honor. More commonly, the label of "racist" was designed with a different set of victims in mind; for it is entirely possible to conclude in favor of restricted immigration and the elimination of "abortion rights" on account of superior moral sense and prudence; not on account of a malicious disregard for women or aliens.

It is possible to oppose divorce, abortion and feminism without feeling animosity toward women. It is possible, indeed, that some of us are rightly concerned with the survival of our own kind, and our way of life, under a regime that insists that women should have careers instead of children. Might we admit that our forefathers, whose rulebooks we have thrown out, were wise and careful in preserving folkways that were sustainable? And now that we have inherited what their prudence and foresight obtained, we call their prudence racism and their foresight sexism.

Are we stupid?

The war that is really ongoing, in our time, is a war against our ancestors and against the Creator; a war of ingratitude — of monstrous, self-destructive, ingratitude.

Veronica Kamenskaya, a Moscow blogger, once commented on the decline of Western and post-Soviet civilization. She said that Christian civilization did not generally allow divorce. And then, we opened a virtual Pandora's Box. "As soon as divorce was legalized in France," Veronica wrote, "men started to divorce their wives to marry younger women." At first, 85-90 percent of divorces were initiated by men. France experienced a baby boom. Then, noted Veronica, "the pill came to France in 1969, and abortion was legalized in 1975. By the mid-80s a drastic change occurred." Before 1970 most French women, if they worked, were employed as small time clerks or secretaries — prior to marriage. Starting in the late 1960s, according to Veronica, "French women began to acquire professional standing, and they started to earn good money; so that marriage ceased being the best and only solution for the financial and sexual problems faced by French women."

Then and there, giving birth to children ceased to be inevitable. By 1987, 90 percent of French divorces were initiated by women. On this statistic Veronica reflected, "French men had brought it on themselves. They destroyed the family, which is the most precious of all institutions." Why would a woman seek security in marriage when her husband could discard her to marry a younger wife? Better for a woman, then, if she had a career instead of children. Veronica is not a social scientist, but she nonetheless sees some of the forces at work behind European degeneracy. Europe's birth rate has collapsed. The state has facilitated this collapse, with its no-fault divorce laws. Consequently, Europe has a shortage of people. And this brings us to the brink of an unprecedented crisis. To make up for this shortage of people, Europe has imported millions of Muslim workers; so many, in fact, that Europe is gradually turning into something called *Eurabia*.

Here we find a segue from "sexism" to "racism." Everyone, of course, has heard of the Constitution of the United States. It is the supreme law of the land. The first ten amendments to the Constitution are known as "the Bill of Rights." Americans today hear a great deal about "rights" and very little about the practical measures needed to ensure those rights. Many Americans have forgotten that you cannot have a constitution unless you have a country; and you cannot have a country unless you defend it against enemies, foreign and domestic. At bottom, every constitution must be construed so that the country's natural right to self defense is not canceled by a growing tangle of individual and minority rights that choke off the necessaries of national defense. So here we are, wrestling with the question: Do Muslims have a right to erect a Mosque near "ground zero" in Manhattan? Does the right of religious freedom, supposedly guaranteed by the Constitution, protect Muslims in the United States from discrimination? Does it protect them against barriers to immigration, against the distrust and dislike of the native population? Does it allow them to build a Mosque near the very place where Islamic "warriors" made a great gash in the skyline of America's greatest city?

Whatever we think of the Constitution, it cannot protect Muslims from the enmity which Islam generates wherever its standard has been raised. In fact, the Constitution was not written to protect the nation of Islam, or various colonies of that nation planted in our midst. The Constitution nowhere says that Muslims have the right to come to the United States, build mosques, or establish their own culture as part of a multicultural patchwork celebrated as a new kind of nation (which effectively negates what America once was). This is not why the Constitution was established. As stated in the Preamble, our Constitution was established "in Order to form a more perfect Union, establish Justice, insure domestic Tranquility, provide for the common defence, promote the general Welfare, and secure the Blessings of Liberty to ourselves and our Posterity…."

It is worth repeating that last phrase – "to ourselves and our Posterity." There is no reference to Muslims, explicit or implicit. They do not belong to our nation. They are not "ourselves and our Posterity." Furthermore, we should pay careful attention to the objectives of the Constitution. How does the presence of millions of Muslims in the United States make a "more perfect Union" or "insure domestic Tranquility"? Clearly, the presence of an alien colony in our midst serves to promote disunion and unrest.

How would the Arabs react if we built a Christian church in Mecca? Their violent reaction would be immediate and lethal. Are Muslims the enemies of America? It is presently inconvenient to say so; but insofar as Muslims are like Unitarians, they are no enemy. Insofar as they take the Koran and its teachings seriously, their enmity is established by their own precepts. If a person truly believes the Koran, they cannot be an American without making a mockery of that which Americans are. It is important to say once more: If a Muslim is only a nominal follower of the Prophet, there is no harm in him.

He might leave his faith, and become an American. On the other hand, if a Muslim is a Muslim in earnest, consistently and conscientiously following the teachings of the Prophet, then he cannot be a citizen of the United States in good faith. His allegiance is to Allah and to the Nation of Islam. He cannot serve two masters. Mohammed did not instruct his followers to "render unto Caesar the things that are Caesars...." The Muslim faith does not agree with this saying. For this and other reasons, Muslim culture cannot easily coexist with American culture.

The God worshipped by Muslims is different from the God worshipped by Americans. It is an error to think that Muslims and Americans can, in the end, live peacefully together in the same country. Such a project, if persisted in, will vouchsafe a religious war to our posterity. We might as well write a new Preamble for the Constitution "in Order to form a more perfect Disunion, establish Political Correctness, insure domestic Disorder, sabotage the common defense, promote general mayhem, and secure the Blessings of Military Dictatorship to ourselves and our Posterity." Then, at least, our words would better align with our policy. Of course, we are foolish and naive in our thinking, and hardly deserve our ancestors as we fail to consider the true situation of our posterity.

Few have the courage to point out the disastrous course we are following. Americans ought to read the history of Islam. Here they will find a religion spread by the sword; a militant zealotry that swept away the Roman Empire, conquered Africa, Spain and the Balkans. Here is a war that raged for centuries in which millions of Christians were slaughtered and enslaved. When exactly did Islam declare that their war against Christendom was over? When did the Muslims return those lands taken from the Christians?

Yet the doctrine of political correctness would have the West apologize to Islam for the legacy of colonialism. Given the history of Islam, and the history of the United States, only a fool would imagine that Islam and America could be safely blended together. But today we have this formula, invented and carried forward by the political left, called "multiculturalism." In fact, multiculturalism is merely a denial of American culture, and a rejection of the notion that immigrants *must assimilate* and become Americans.

In respect of this, a culture that is represented by all cultures, is not American. It is everthing but American. It would be like saying that everyone on earth is, in fact, an American; that every culture represents American culture. If this is accepted as true, then there can be no American culture and the whole of America's real heritage is wiped away at a single stroke. If this is not the objective of those promoting multiculturalism, then they have opened themselves up to a serious misunderstanding. For it appears that their project is to destroy the United States of America using multiculturalism as a weapon to disarm and disorient the American people, taking away the concept of "nation," replacing it with concepts that will allow them to play a game of "divide and conquer."

A nation is a group of people united during the course of generations by cultural and social ties, by language and history, by common values and folkways. It cannot be an amalgamation of every people and every culture, with tenuous connections and contrary folkways. Such is not a country or a culture, but a Tower of Babel. Yet we have been told to become this Tower of Babel, and thereby lose our unique national identity while engendering a civil war. This doctrine would eradicate America entirely, leaving nothing but a cratered landscape. To allow millions of Muslims into the United States, and say they are Americans, is a kind of insanity – *unless they are nominal Muslims.*

If a Muslim wants to become an American, it is certain that he must give up his religion in a fundamental sense, or else we should give up our country; for he cannot believe in Islam while faithfully swearing an oath of allegiance to the Constitution; for the Prophet Mohammed would not have approved of the U.S. Constitution. He would have called for its negation, and for the creation of a Caliphate, and many of his followers today understand this.

On the American side, it is clear that the Founding Fathers did not establish this country as a place for Mohammed's followers to colonize and subvert. This was not their intention, nor would they look favorably upon descendents who interpreted the Constitution as an instrument for the protection of an Islamic colony inside the United States. They would account any such interpretation as incredibly stupid, belonging to some new species of American idiot.

As may be readily apparent to the wise, it is backwards to imagine that a constitution comes first and a nation comes second, as if the nation was created for the constitution instead of the constitution for the nation. With this error comes the idea that individual rights trump national existence, so that we may push forward the concept of "rights" even if this concept leads to a general unraveling of national existence. There is no legitimate right which effectively disintegrates the nation that observes it; for it would be absurd to propose political principles which promise destruction to those who uphold them, as it would be absurd to propose laws that must lead to the negation of all law.

Not only does the individual have a right of self defense, but the nation also has a right of self defense. For if there were no nation, there could be no unit for organizing the effective defense of the individual. Furthermore, we should not pretend that national suicide is somehow an enlightened ideal. It is nothing of the kind. And those who despise the nation state are not progressive, but follow a path leading back to the Dark Ages. National patriotism is not a synonym for racism or collectivism. Love of America does not signify hatred against Muslims, or a campaign to denigrate them. Such love, properly considered, recognizes irreconcilable differences between the laws set down by the Prophet Mohammed, and the laws set down by our Founding Fathers. The two things cannot coexist in one nation, *under God*. For the Muslim and Christian conceptions of God are at variance, as well as our concept of law. A child can see this, and yet our politically correct authorities admit of no problem whatever.

If anyone should reproach the nation state with being the principle cause of war, they should reflect that wars have existed from the beginning of human history, and have occurred between city states, tribes, clans, and empires. It is a mistake to blame war on the nation state. War is part of the human condition. Men will fight each other whether or not they are organized under nation states or under feudal barons. It is an affliction of all states at all times, not peculiar to the nation state.

But haven't we evolved? Shouldn't we give up our petty nationalism? Aren't we all simply "citizens of the world"? If we embrace the Muslims, surely peace will follow. We are all human beings, and tolerance will prevail if we set the tone. Therefore, say the progressives, we need to embrace the oneness of humanity. It is the only alternative to destructive war.

Ask yourself: Why is America denied the right to defend its borders, its culture, and the very ground of its mourning (i.e., "ground zero")? Because the left dreams of a world without nations where war itself has been eradicated. This dream is the delusion fools and madmen. It is an excuse to wage an altogether more dreadful type of war — a war against civilization itself. In truth, there will never be a world without war, just as there will never be a world without poverty or death. To wage war against war is merely a pretext to pursue power for its own sake.

For those who want total power, the United States represents a barrier that must be knocked down; for it stands in the way of all those revolutionary lunatics dreaming of a brave new world. Oh yes, America stands in the way of the great socialist commonwealth of mankind — a butcher's block and a slaughterhouse. Here we see what kind of weapon multiculturalism is, and what it aims to achieve.

In this context, Islam merely serves as the "icebreaker of the revolution." Does a weapon, deployed against us by the revolutionary left, have rights? No. Does an enemy have rights? Only with regard to the agreed-upon rules of war. The American reader should ask himself, at the end of the day, what would happen if Islam or Communism had its way in America. What if Islam took over? What if a Communist regime came to power? In that case, wouldn't it be fair to describe America as a country occupied by an internal enemy? How is it, then, that we tolerate the open subversion of our country? How is it, then, that we are unable to name our enemies (excepting the ones hiding in distant caves)?

Don't we have the right to recognize those who are against us? Or are we already conquered? The reader may see, quite clearly, that all issues — from divorce and abortion to immigration and terrorism — are interconnected. What our ancestors accepted as wise and prudent we dismiss as sexism and racism. Therefore, we have embraced feminism to the detriment of our birth rate; and we have embraced multiculturalism to the detriment of our national security. Both feminism and multiculturalism belong under one and the same heading: **Collective Suicide**.

At bottom, the arguments in favor of Collective Suicide are hedonistic arguments. For it is hedonism which leads the man to divorce his wife, and the wife to choose a career. It is hedonism which embraces the pill and abortion. It is hedonistic to reject children in favor of a career, and to postulate oneself as the be-all and end-all of existence. It is hedonism that calls forth multiculturalism, because we are too busy shopping and having fun to notice that we have enemies.

It is, as Nietzsche foretold, a shallow swamp over which echoes the refrain, "Everything is empty, everything is one, everything is past."

Is Russia Secretly Communist?

09/27/2019

Many will not believe the truth. But here it is: The ruling clique in Russia is not nationalist. Real nationalist groups are persecuted in Russia. The leading political parties of the country are led by apparatchiks; that is to say, by "Soviet" persons.

A famous KGB defector once suggested that Russia's political parties are mere branches of the Communist Party, separated into sub-units to give the appearance of a democracy. If a truly independent party appeared in Russia the communists and their friends (who still control state security) would quickly infiltrate and take possession of it.

What we see today in Russia is a classic Soviet-style deception. The proof of this deception may be found in Putin's pro-Communist speech at the World Festival of Youth and Students in 2017, held in Sochi. Putin plainly stated his support for the young communists, saying they represent the future and he is behind them.

Russian support for communism today is more than mere lip service. The Russian government supports communist regimes around the world. Moscow is assisting the Marxist-Leninist regime in Nicaragua. Moscow has sent troops to defend communist Venezuela. Moscow has assisted North Korea with military technology, and they have also facilitated China's military buildup.

In what sense are these actions nationalist? Real nationalists do not support global communism. If we break this down carefully, going case by case, we will find that Russia is still part of the Communist Bloc and the Bloc is preparing for war.

In terms of pretending to be nationalist, Russia exploits our naïveté. Russian policy often predicates itself on a "scissors strategy" in which the Kremlin supports both sides of a local conflict. In this strategy one side is supported openly (and deceptively), as Putin appears to support Trump. Meanwhile, the opposite side receives clandestine guidance in hijacking the enemy's security process.

The Afghan wars (1979 – present) are an example of the scissors strategy as played by Moscow over four decades. Another example is the fight against

Muslim extremism more generally. But the boldest example is Russia's supposed support for nationalism even as Moscow's leftist agents of influence call nationalists "Nazis" and "traitors."

When the totalitarian left openly takes power in the United States, they might arrest all "class enemies" on the grounds that they are traitors colluding with Russia. And Putin will laugh — because Russia has always pinned its hopes on the American left, not the right. But almost nobody in the media understands the game.

Few pundits have a real understanding of Russia's sophisticated store of strategic tricks. Military historians do not understand many of the battles of the last century because they do not see the larger playing field on which battles are only a single aspect of something that involves seemingly unrelated areas of activity — from the corruption of language and culture to the eradication of God, family and country.

The problem is not entirely due to a failure of understanding, however. Much of recent history has been deceptively related by people who know they are lying, or don't care what the truth is. As Diana West wrote in her book, *American Betrayal*, "our true heroes were branded with the twentieth century's scarlet letter — *A* for anti-communist." Anyone who threatens the narrative of the new religion suffers what Eugene Lyons called "a species of intellectual ostracism."

Communism concealed itself after 1991, but it was more active than ever before — in the schools, in the media, in science and the arts. After 1991 the Communist Party Soviet Union went underground. This was not a new maneuver. The communists performed a similar disappearing act with the Comintern in May 1943. Those who thought Stalin had given up the idea of World Revolution were as wrong then as those who believe in the fall of communism today.

All these points should be perfectly obvious, yet people are unable to see past so many lies. These lies are now entrenched in the popular mind. We count ourselves clever for knowing all about Soviet "active measures" during the Cold War. Yet the alleged disappearance of these measures hides th

Well-informed communists know that the Soviet Union still exists, behind the facade of the Russian Federation. The USSR is still the Soviet motherland and "The General Staff" of the worldwide communist movement. Right now, the communist party is republishing the works of Lenin with help from Moscow's Progress Publishers. Yes, it is the same state-owned publishing house that was printing Soviet propaganda in the 1960s. Here we catch them out. Here the left is not lamenting the wicked nationalism of Putin. The American communists are working with the Russian state — right now, today, in promoting Marx and Lenin. How is this possible if Putin is a nationalist?

Of course, Putin is not a nationalist. And that is why he is building missiles and nuclear weapons as fast as he can. His goal is to smash capitalism, not to support nationalism. The United States may be very close to defeat as the moment of "one clenched fist" has arrived. Everyone missed the game, and now it is probably too late.

Good luck with supposing our domestic left have got where they are without Russian guidance. Our domestic communists are supporting the same active measures the Soviet Academy of Sciences procured for them in their sabotage and subversion operations of decades passed. Nothing has really changed since the 1930s, except that we have no anticommunist organizations such as the FBI or the Catholic Church. The anti-communist is an endangered species. And given what we see on every side, from the celebrity of Alexandria Ocasio-Cortez to belief in global warming, Western civilization is losing on every front.

Russia is still the motherland of socialism. Putin is not a nationalist, but a communist. The Kremlin did not want Trump to be president. They wanted Clinton, and they are building up AOC for the future. The Kremlin, in fact, lies about everything, even when there is no apparent reason to lie. In time, of course, the reasons will come into focus.

When Traitors Call Treason

10/22/2019

Recently I had a long conversation with Simona Pipko, who worked as a Soviet lawyer in the 1950s to early 80s. She said that Stalin devised the Soviet political and legal systems. "He told the communists to never admit any crime," she explained. "Always put the crime on the enemies of communism."

What happens when the traitors are calling "treason" and pointing fingers at the innocent? This is the political theater of our day; where traitors pretend to be against treason; where they prosecute — as traitors — anyone who stands in their way. And it is all in accordance with methods developed under J.V. Stalin, the infamous Soviet dictator.

If you are guilty of treason, accuse your political opponents of treason. If you are corrupt, say that they are corrupt. "I have heard Stalin speak in person. He was very clear, very logical," Pipko added. And obviously, Stalin's methods were effective, and were used at the famous show trials of the 1930s. Time and again Stalin's minions accused his political rivals of crimes. But who was the real criminal?

Simona said that House Speaker Nancy Pelosi and Rep. Adam Schiff were obviously cast in Stalin's mold. They are using Stalin's methods, she noted. One might say that homage to the method is homage to the end. For some of us, Pelosi's ideological agenda has been obvious for many years. After all, when you constantly support harmful policies, subversive agendas and narratives, then you are a subversive.

Last week House Speaker Nancy Pelosi accused Trump of working for Putin. During a meeting with the President she said, "With your foreign policy, all roads lead to Putin." She has previously called the president a traitor. Did Trump walk out? No, he hit back. Trump scandalized Pelosi and congressional Democratic leaders by saying Pelosi was a third-rate politician. But the real reason they stormed out may have been due to a more telling remark. It seems that Trump implied the Democratic leaders were communist sympathizers. He said there were communists involved in Syria "and you might like that."

Trump gave the Democrats a strong dose of their own medicine. How did they take it? Strange to say, they feigned outrage about unrelated slights.

The *New York Times* even omitted any mention of Trump's insinuation of Pelosi's communist sympathies. This strikes me as calculated.

Why should Trump's communist insinuation be glossed over by the *Times*? Given the advance of communism in the country, given the Democratic Party's subservience to the communist agenda, they didn't dare underscore the President's prescient observation.

Related to this, there is another point to be made — which few have dared to make. The defeat of communism in 1991 was neither final nor complete. Moscow's special services have advanced their agents into many U.S. leadership positions. Over the last three decades the communist penetration of the United States went from an epidemic to a pandemic after the election of Barack Obama. And this is why we are in the mess we see today.

Many will disagree with this analysis. But the reader should stop and think. Given their own past collusion with communist powers, why should Hillary Clinton and Nancy Pelosi accuse Donald Trump of collusion with Moscow? And why would *The New York Times* refrain from printing Trump's suggestion about Pelosi's ideological sympathies?

Because the remark was too close to the truth.

If Pelosi pretends to eschew Moscow and Beijing, we should not trust her. Her ideological record tells a very different story. Therefore, we must reiterate our question: What happens when the traitors are calling "treason" and pointing fingers at the innocent?

Watch carefully what happens next....

The "Impeachment" Fracas

10/29/2019

> No Apostle has ever doubted the future of his faith, and the socialists are persuaded of the approaching triumph of theirs. To the disciples of the new dogmas nothing appears more simple.
>
> — GUSTAVE LE BON

If socialism is a new kind of religion, if they must have power to save the downtrodden, if they are politically correct in word and deed, then they must have Donald Trump's head.

Donald Trump, as it turns out, is not a socialist. He is *not* the champion of the downtrodden. He is the champion of the United States of America. By precept he puts the American people ahead of the downtrodden. Consequently, he opposes the core principles of the new religion. He opposes the theory of anthropogenic global warming. The acolytes of the new religion therefore hate Donald Trump.

Since these people dominate the media, Trump's faults are amplified and exaggerated by the media. Since the socialists control the House of Representatives, the House begins a process of "impeachment." Since Marxists dominate education in America, they have educated the youth to vote for the party of socialism — against Trump.

The socialist plan is to remove Trump from office in order to consolidate socialist power. This power will be based on socialist concepts of governance, anti-capitalist economics, atheism and the social gospel. This is what is meant by the term "progressivism."

The socialists must conquer or die under the banner of impeachment. As their narrative evolves, Trump becomes a traitor by definition. As their narrative evolves, all who oppose socialism will also be listed as traitors. The new religion teaches that America itself is a kind of treason — a stain which must be blotted from the world map.

The socialists believe there should be no compromise with the outworn ideals of America's Founding Fathers. As soon as they can denounce the

Founding Fathers without negative consequences they will. If Russian missiles must destroy their targets in America, and Chinese troops must then appear in California, so be it. Such is the socialist faith. It hides its foreign allegiance behind the alibi of Trump-Russia collusion. Here is their political camouflage. Here they set an ambush for their countrymen.

The Socialist Utopia cannot be achieved as long as Trump is President. Remove Donald Trump and the way to paradise will be cleared. Remove Donald Trump and America will open its borders. Open the borders and the party of socialism will dominate forever. Achieving absolute control, they will disarm the country against its foreign enemies.

The world will then belong to Moscow and Beijing.

It's the Socialists, Stupid: A Note From Benjamin Gitlow

11/12/2019

The goal of the socialist is to consolidate political power. Only then can he build his ideal world by eradicating the "evils of capitalism." The socialists' cynical dislike of the existing system opens the way to the building of an even more cynical system — far from the ideal world they are trying to create. True-believing socialists can appear formidable, of course, even ferocious; or they can sound silly, even childish.

One of the most interesting socialists of the twentieth century was Benjamin Gitlow, who began as a true-believing communist and awoke to its immorality after a confrontation with Soviet dictator Joseph Stalin. In his introduction to Benjamin Gitlow's book, *The Whole of Their Lives*, Max Eastman described Gitlow as an ideal Marxist, and "the first man arrested in the United States for advocating communism."

> His trial occurred in 1919 in the midst of the famous 'red raids' of Attorney General Palmer. Clarence Darrow undertook to get him off by hushing the implications of the subversive things he had said. But Gitlow would have nothing to do with that. He was a revolutionist, and he insisted that Darrow defend him on the sole ground of the "right of revolution."

Because he advocated the overthrow of the U.S. Government, Gitlow was convicted and sentenced under New York's Criminal Anarchy statute of 1902. Gitlow made no attempt to hide his communist motives. During the trial, he denounced the U.S. political system as a "capitalist dictatorship." He addressed the jury as follows:

> The socialists have always maintained that the change from capitalism to socialism would be a fundamental change, that ... we would have a complete reorganization of society, that this change would not be a question of reform; that the capitalist system ...

> would give way to a new system of society based on a new code of laws, based on a new ethics, and based on a new form of government. For that reason, the socialist philosophy has always been a revolutionary philosophy and people who adhered to the socialist program … were always considered revolutionists, and … I am a revolutionist.

In its wisdom, the jury found him guilty. He served three years in Sing Sing Prison before being pardoned by Governor Al Smith. After leaving prison his revolutionary career was even more spectacular than before. Gitlow went on to occupy "every important post in the American Communist Party:" According to Eastman, Gitlow became editor-in-chief of the Communist Party's newspaper, he became a —

> member of its Political Committee, member of its Secretariat of Three, General Secretary of the party, director of its strike and trade union policy, secret leader of the Passaic textile workers strike, the biggest communist strike in our history, and twice the communist candidate for Vice President. He made his first trip to Moscow in 1927 at the special request of the Kremlin. An extended conversation with Stalin on the problems of the American movement ensured him the highest advancement. He became a member of the executive committee both of the Red Trade Unions International, and within the latter was elected to the Presidium, the inside ruling group of the world communist movement.

Gitlow was one of America's top communist leaders. But then something happened. He began to doubt the goodness and infallibility of Joseph Stalin, the number one boss in the worldwide communist movement. While attending the May 1929 session of the Presidium of the Communist International in Moscow, Stalin wanted to reshape the American party to his specifications. Therefore Stalin presented an "Address to the American Party" in which he denounced the American communist leaders as "right deviationists" and "unprincipled opportunists." In this way Stalin hoped to subordinate America's communist leaders to himself. In reaction, the American communists banded together, rebuking Stalin.

Like Moses coming down from Sinai, Stalin personally descended on the Presidium of the Communist International. He stepped up to the podium and laid down the law. He addressed the assembled communists as follows:

> ...the extreme factionalism of the leaders of the majority [of the American delegation] has driven them into the path of insubordination, and hence of warfare against the Comintern.... And now, the question arises: do the members of the American delegation, as communists, as Leninists, consider themselves entitled not to submit to the decisions of the Executive Committee of the Comintern on the American question?

The American delegation was terror-stricken by Stalin's statement. Being accused of factionalism and insubordination by Stalin, they imagined the worst. What would Stalin do to them? Were they safe? Would they be expelled from the Communist International? Characteristically, Stalin demanded that each member of the American delegation stand up and declare his position. One by one the American communists, frightened by the angry Soviet dictator, submitted. Gitlow was the last American to speak. He said,

> I cannot accept the demand put upon me to discredit myself before the American working class, for I would not only be discrediting myself and the leadership of the party, but the party itself which gave rise to such leadership.... Not only do I vote against the decision, but when I return to the United States I will fight against it!

A long whistle was heard from the crowd. Stalin strode back to the podium, enraged. The Soviet dictator spoke as follows:

> True Bolshevik courage does not consist in placing one's individual will above the will of the Comintern. True courage consists in being strong enough to master and overcome oneself and

> subordinate one's will to the will of the collective, the will of the higher party body.... And this is true not only in respect to individual parties and their central committees; it is particularly true in respect of the Comintern and its directing organs, which unite all parties of communists throughout the world.... They talk of their conscience and convictions.... But what is to be done if the conscience and convictions of the Presidium conflict with the conscience and convictions of individual members of the American delegation? What is to be done if the American delegation receives only one vote for their declaration, the vote of Comrade Gitlow, while the remaining members of the Presidium unanimously declared themselves against the declaration?

Such was Stalin's logic — the logic of political discipline. It is important to remember that the Communist International movement is and was ruled by consensus. Democracy in the communist movement did not mean voting your conscience. Democracy meant agreement, not dissent. In practice, collectivism requires consensus. It was so under Stalin, and it remains so in today's Russia (which is still secretly communist) and China (which is openly ruled by the Chinese Communist Party). Because he did not accept the communist consensus, Gitlow was booted out of the communist movement. According to Eastman,

> From being a high official in a power-structure supposedly on its way to take over the world, he became an obscure, penniless, professionless and well-nigh friendless person, walking the streets of New York looking for a job.

Gitlow was one of the chief organizers of the left in the United States. You could say he was one of the Founding Fathers of the so-called "progressive movement." As such he understood how the communist organization functioned in America — behind the scenes. He knew the strategic thinking of the Comintern. He knew everything the communists were doing in those days.

Because of his break with Stalin, Gitlow came to oppose communism and publicly warned of its methods. According to Gitlow it would be incorrect to view the Communist Party as a small and irrelevant faction of the left. Since the Russian Revolution the left in America and Europe has become, over time, a diverse group of political sects unwittingly dominated by a very small cadre of communists who are practiced in the arts of clandestine manipulation and control. Gitlow explained as follows:

> During the period in which the Communist Party operated as an underground organization, they injected themselves into practically every phase of American social and political life. In their activities the communists were guided by an all-inclusive policy based on the tactics of the United Front.

Lenin was the originator of "the tactics of the United Front," which placed communists inside various non-communist organizations for the purpose of gradually bringing those organizations into alignment with communist plans. In this way the left was reorganized and the communists provided focus to the whole. Gitlow wrote:

> By the skillful application of the United Front policy, the communists have become an important and often a decisive force in movements and actions, political and non-political, from which they would otherwise be excluded. The employment of United Front tactics forced the communists to learn how to deal with persons and movements not in their camp. Thus the communists developed into able negotiators and astute politicians. Once the communists got their toes into the narrow opening of a door to an organization, they usually succeeded in squeezing themselves bodily into the organization and either capturing the organization or dominating its affairs.

On the surface the casual observer sees no communists at all. There is only an apparently respectable organization working for a "good cause." On close inspection, however, many an organization will be found supporting policies that bring advantages to the communists. Take some cause which anyone might think legitimate, dress it up with slogans, and repeat those slogans thousands of times. Consequently, new laws will be adopted, new ways of thinking will be advanced. Who meanwhile notices that Marxist ideas are more and more taking root? — that capitalism is more and more hamstrung? The activists need only a cause, from the oppression of women or minorities to global warming or gay marriage. As Gitlow explained,

> The communists thereby create popular movements involving large masses of people, through which they can project their views publicly on a much broader basis than if they acted independently. Since the communists comprise the only closely knit , disciplined forces, they have relatively little difficulty getting the upper hand in the United Front. By playing on the vanity of prominent, influential persons, giving them honors, positions and places on committees with pompous-sounding names, and by cleverly exploiting United Front tactics, the communists, in recent years, have won for themselves the leadership of many causes of a progressive and humanitarian character.

Gitlow's statement, above, was first published in 1948, over seventy years ago. It is as true today as it was then. The communists were controlling or dominating various non-communist organizations in 1948. And yes, they are doing the same thing today, in 2019. We have been fooled into thinking there has been a "break with the past." We imagine there isn't a Comintern anymore. We imagine that communists in the United States no longer follow a strict party consensus established in Moscow or Beijing. Without understanding the United Front tactics of the communists, we are helpless to stop their advance. And they *are* advancing.

In decades past the communists infiltrated many organizations on the left. Today they also infiltrate the right, which has become incredibly soft. How is this possible? Because the communists were infiltrating the right from the outset, when the right was strong in numbers and conviction. Today it is child's play for them.

In 1921 the communists created a movement which came to be regarded as the most important anti-communist movement in the world. It was called the Monarchist Alliance of Central Russia. A Moscow bank served as its headquarters, and was for that reason informally known as the "Trust." Its agents linked arms with the White Russian diaspora, planning assassinations, issuing fake passports, infiltrating Soviet government ministries. All the intelligence agencies of Europe believed in the Trust's authenticity. They also relied on it for intelligence purposes.

Because of the Trust, the Soviet special services gained entry into anti-communist organizations around the world. Because of the Trust, communists got to know the weaknesses of the West's intelligence services. History books rarely mention the Trust for a very special reason: when Soviet intelligence revealed it was fake, the embarrassment was so great, and the humiliation so painful, everyone wanted to forget about it. So they did.

Under Lenin the communists learned to infiltrate everywhere, to pretend anything to anyone. There was no limit to the lies they would tell, no fraud too fantastic, no dupe too incredulous, no conspiratorial method too harebrained. They made the outlandish acceptable. And now, look at the politics of today. What is not outlandish?

I have just now given you the key, the explanation for it all.

What Will the Spider do?

11/05/2019

"In a wilderness of mirrors. What will the spider do [?]"

— T. S. ELIOT, "GERONTION", 1920

Twenty-five years ago a Soviet-era defector named Alex told me about a KGB office in the Soviet Union. They had all the desks arranged on the main floor, with one large desk in the middle of the office at which sat a nice, helpful, old man. He was everyone's friend. He listened sympathetically to the personal problems of the KGB staff. He gave them advice on all matters, and he smoothed things over with the boss, whose office door was always closed and dark. No one ever saw the boss except the old man. One day the old man retired and they had a party for him. It was at this party the old man announced he had been their boss all along. Alex finished the story by making his fingers into walking spider legs and said, "The spiders are everywhere." Then he winked.

Of course, it is true. The spiders are everywhere. They are set loose — as T.S. Eliot suggested — in a "wilderness of mirrors." Sometimes, in a wilderness of funhouse mirrors. Take, for example, the case of Brazilian congressman Alexandre Frota. Last Friday, in an interview with UOL (news), he charged several persons with unleashing a sophisticated disinformation campaign on Brazil. According to Frota, "[it is] run by the ... writer Olavo de Carvalho and journalist Allan Dos Santos, owner of Terça Livre TV, which is openly supportive of [President] Bolsonaro."

An intrepid detective, Frota's "investigation" has unearthed several tentacles of a vast "right wing" conspiracy:

> I began to learn of these digital militiamen, far-right militants, who are today dressed as parliamentary aides. With their credentials they are receiving good salaries, working inside government offices. We already have some positive suspicions of where they might be sheltered.

Congressman Frota alleged that a "dirty service" was being performed by someone behind the scenes. "Everybody knows it," he explained. There is a shadowy person "living there and supported by Filipe G. Martins [the special foreign affairs advisor to the President of the Republic]." It is someone who sits in a special room, near the President's office. It is someone who is respected by "the old man."

The journalist conducting the interview asked Frota the name of this shadowy figure; but he could not fully remember. The name was something like Jefferson or Jeffrey. "Yes," said Congressman Frota, "Jeffrey Richard Nyquist.... He is a person we are keeping our eye on.... He was often seen in the House [Chamber of Deputies], and to my surprise, his name was already connected with 'fake news.'"

According to Congressman Frota, Jeffrey Richard Nyquist has been loosed on Brazil's Chamber of Deputies, "providing services" with a charge of "between $15 and $20 thousand" to manipulate social networks, to mobilize "digital militiamen," to orchestrate a "far-right" revolution in Brazil.

Of course, Congressman Frota has named me — the author of this blog — of sitting at the center of a vast right-wing spiderweb. Indeed, T.S. Eliot was right to ask, "What will the spider do?" In the first instance, I challenge Congressman Frota to document these alleged Jeffrey sightings at the Chamber of Deputies. As a resident of America's Pacific Northwest region he will find me as difficult to catch as my political associate, Bigfoot Sasquatch. The thick forests around Brasilia provide us with ample cover. Don't be a little girl's blouse, Congressman Frota. Lead an expedition into the real wilderness. Step away from that funhouse mirror. Set aside your paranoid projections. My flying saucer is parked in a clearing, covered in camouflage netting. I dare you to find me!

"Happy hunting, Flota!"

The Swamp and its Creatures

11/08/2019

What is the swamp? In the 1950s, Senator Joseph McCarthy had a name for the swamp. He called it "the international communist conspiracy." He spoke of the communist penetration of government, the subversion of U.S. policy, the betrayal of our servicemen on faraway battlefields. He pointed to communism's nefarious domestic machinations. He wrote about our "retreat from victory," the legacy of General George C. Marshall — the gifting of Eastern Europe to Stalin, the betrayal of Nationalist China to Mao, and the loss of our atom bomb monopoly.

A chronically misinformed (or disinformed) reading public is sure to dismiss McCarthy as a fear-monger. "There was no communist conspiracy," say our mainstream pundits with a characteristic smirk. "McCarthy was engaged in a witch-hunt." Meanwhile these same pundits have promoted a *real* witch-hunt. They employ tactics falsely attributed to McCarthy in their unprecedented campaign of slander against President Trump.

Who dares to notice that a reversal has taken place? Those who might be identified as communist infiltrators or "fellow travelers" now dominate the mainstream media, the commanding heights of counterintelligence, and the criminal justice system. It naturally follows that the witches are now leading the witch-hunts. The communists themselves, thinly disguised as mainstream liberals, threaten anticommunists with fabricated criminal charges and process crimes.

This is exactly what is unfolding, though nearly everyone refuses to see it. We are now reaping what we have sown. Long ago the left managed to convince the country that McCarthy was a demagogue and a liar, that fear of communism was irrational, that no such infiltration of the government had occurred, that the Rosenberg (atomic spies) were innocent, that communist spy Alger Hiss was innocent. And today, if you look at a typical high school history textbook, McCarthy is the villain.

Think now, friends. Who wrote those textbooks? Don't you know? The communists took over education in this country, stealthily, patiently. This is why Johnny still can't read. This is why we awake one day to find that America's youth favor socialism over capitalism.

The communists have been taking over the country, bit by bit, little by little. Ask yourself why we built up communist China as an economic power. Why has our navy been shrinking? Why did we allow our nuclear deterrent to rot from old age? Why does the Democratic Party want to eradicate America's national border?

None of this is accidental. The policies that are urged on us from the left are calculated to disarm and destroy us from within. Look around you. What do we find? Do you really think they want to reduce your carbon footprint to save the planet, or is it an attempt to sabotage capitalism? Do you think they really care about homosexual marriage, or do you think it's a legal mechanism for persecuting the country's anticommunist core? — Bible believing Cristians?

Do you think everything has been culturally aligned with communist goals on accident? If so, I have some swamp land to sell you. And it is full of swamp creatures.

The Secrets of the Swamp

11/21/2019

The secret inner-workings of the swamp are found in the history of the revolutionary left. It is a history of treachery and greed, larceny and murder. The first secret of the swamp is hard for some to grasp; but here it is: the humanitarianism of the leftist revolutionary is a pose. His real creed is lust for power and wealth.

The first American revolutionary communist leader, Louis C. Fraina, received $386,000 from the Comintern to start a revolution in Mexico. What did he do? He spent the money on himself. The Comintern did not kill him for his bad faith, most likely because he had blackmailed other leading communists regarding their own improprieties and frauds.

American journalist John Reed was said to be a "great-souled" communist — honest and incorruptible. It is also said he died of a broken heart in Moscow because he finally realized that communism was a movement of thieves and murderers. His wife, Louise Bryant, wrote: "Jack died because of great personal disillusionment." She explained in greater detail in a letter to Benjamin Gitlow:

> Jack noticed how power and the lust for power affected the Bolshevik leaders.... He was terribly afraid of having made a serious mistake in his interpretation of an historical event for which he would be held accountable.... He blamed himself....

Reed was inconsolable. When illness gripped him, he had no desire to recover. His wife wrote, "I pleaded with him, for his own sake, not to give up. He didn't respond." Reed was sent to a Moscow hospital — where the care was indifferent at best. Louise wrote to Benjamin Gitlow:

> I spent horrible days and nights with him, days and nights I can never forget. He raved and he cried. He spoke constantly of being caught in a trap. They were terrifying words coming from Jack. You know the rest. He died three days later....

John Reed died on 17 September 1920. His story is a tragedy of idealism gone wrong. It reminds us that insincerity in politics is no small thing. Insincerity indicates weakness of character, a predilection for deceptive practices, which should only be reserved for enemies. What are we to think, then, of an all-encompassing fraudulence? — of a dishonesty which has no real regard for its own constituents? Here is a universal malevolence. Here is a politics that destroys the foundations of polity.

When we see the present machinations of the left in Washington, many are perplexed by the insincerity of its spokesmen. But actually, this is what we ought to expect. This is who they are. Honesty was not part of their training. Revolution has an altogether different ethic.

When Alexandria Ocasio-Cortez asks Bernie Sanders' supporters if they are "ready for revolution," she is talking about creating a new system of power, a reconfiguration of haves and have-nots. She is not proposing poverty and suffering for her own party and faction. She is championing Socialist Revolution as a means of self-enrichment, with the false promise of benefits to her listeners. But in that revolution some must be despoiled of their wealth. Some must be robbed. The capitalist system brought general prosperity to America because it is based on the protection of private property. This also coincides with the preservation of liberty; for in truth, there are no rights worth protecting if property is not protected. And there can be no basis of trust for real economic growth without property rights. This tells us, up front, that the socialist revolutionary is not about economic growth or general prosperity. The whole thing is about plunder and the enrichment of a faction.

This is another secret of the swamp. Plundering the commonwealth is what all true socialist states are about. And everyone, except those attached to the ruling clique, will be impoverished at the end of the process.

The true motivations of the socialist and communist leaders is a fascinating question. In his book, *The Whole of Their Lives*, Ben Gitlow described the Communist movement as a devilish machine for transforming idealists into criminals.

> In revolutionary politics the personal ambitions of leaders play an important role. The altruistic souls motivated by high ideals and principles are common in the rank-and-file and rare in the

> leadership. The struggle for power in the communist organization proceeds as bitterly as it does at royal courts.

The revolutionary demands political power to be concentrated in his or her hands. And what do the avatars of this new power do with it? The more power they have, the more they want. There is no end to their depredations. The more cynical their lies, the greater their greed, the more ready they are to destroy those who stand in their way, and steal from those who are disempowered.

They claim to be righteous, after all. They are champions of the downtrodden. All the evil they do is necessary for the sainted ends of socialism. Here is the justification for a political instrumentalism animated by zealotry; an evil admixture that can break the back of civilization and suffocate the human soul with the soft pillow of false humanitarianism. "We are saving the planet," they shout.

No. They will wreck the planet and demoralize mankind.

The corruption that accompanies socialist idealism stems from combining the naive socialist true-believer with the psychopathic socialist leader who sees socialism as the perfect vehicle for exploiting altruistic "useful idiots." Here is the secret formula for Hell on Earth.

The swamp is the vanguard of this Hell. Self-righteousness and corruption are its telltales. As the political battle in Washington unfolds, we can use these understandings to interpret what we are seeing, to form a clearer picture of the players.

Once you learn the secrets of the swamp, the motivation of the left comes into sharper focus. The reader need not take my word for it. The proof is in the pudding; — and what a pudding they are making of it!

The Surveillance State is Here, and the Left is Using it to Suppress Dissent

12/04/2019

Once upon a time the left worried about a surveillance state in America. Liberal judges ruled against the FBI monitoring or maintaining files on left wing subversive groups. But now, after these same subversive groups have taken control of the media and the intelligence agencies, a Democratic Congressman, in charge of the House Permanent Select Committee on Intelligence, is monitoring conservatives and (evidently) maintaining files on them.[1]

We might summarize what has happened since 2016 in the following way: The Democratic Party, in pursuit of power and political advantage, has weaponized U.S. intelligence and the House Intelligence Committee, to spy on a conservative President, a conservative congressman (Nunes), a journalist — and even to log the private phone calls of the president's lawyer (Rudy Giuliani).

This we learn from reading the Schiff Report (see previous blog post).[2] The arrogance of the report is only matched by its hypocrisy. The report ignores the principles of law used (in decades past) to neuter the counterintelligence functions of the FBI and CIA. Now the Democrats, who once loathed counterintelligence, move to reinstate it with a vengeance; only now the counterintelligence function will bear down on the opponents and critics of the left.

There can be no question, as of this moment, that the left is employing a strategy of intimidation. It openly uses the technical surveillance capabilities of the state to threaten conservatives, to allege secret crimes and conspiracies arising from the Republican side of the aisle, to allege collusion with hostile foreign powers, to attempt entrapment, to portray legal activities as illegal. Every Republican politician has been warned: — Your phone calls are recorded, your secret deals will be used against you. Resistance is futile. We can frame you for crimes on circumstantial evidence. We will call witnesses from our own ranks, suppress witnesses in your favor and — to top it off — we will try you

1 See https://www.scribd.com/book/438107041.

2 See *"The Schiff Report Document"*, 12/04/2019: https://jrnyquist.blog/2019/12/04/614/

in the media, make your guilt an accepted public fact, and reduce you to the status of a traitor or criminal.

Today the so-called liberals raise no protest against these abuses of power. It is now apparent that our left-of-center civil libertarians were not really interested in liberty. Their past arguments against the CIA and FBI only held while these organizations were fighting communism. Now that these institutions are under leftist management, they are openly weaponized against the conservatives.

Since conservatives are evil, and communists are good, the left has no qualms about violating a conservative's right to privacy. It was never okay to ask a communist, under oath, whether he was a member of the party. But today it is the left's position that conservatives are the enemies of the planet. Any or all measures, however extraordinary, must be employed to criminalize their political activity, to cripple their means of self-protection, and eliminate them from the country's political life.

That is the meaning of what we see today. The left has reached the conviction that they are not only right but righteous; that those who disagree with them should have no rights, no voice, no share in power. The events of today are a warning. The left is not going to be constrained by principle, by law, or decency. It has no regard for the truth. There are individuals on the left who may be principled, law abiding and decent; but the political powers of the left, which dominate our media and our government, have a totalitarian coloration.

The hypocrisy of what we are seeing is beyond anything we could have anticipated. How could Americans go along with this? How could they not see what has happened?

Whatever party you think you belong to, it's time to open your eyes. The enemy is inside the gate. The totalitarian countries, under the leadership of Russia and China, are building their forces for the coming war. The threads of external danger are woven together with threads of internal subversion.

Though it does not appear likely to the casual observer, all these threads belong to communism — an ideology which has shape-shifted, taking up various disguises; yet its revolutionary core remains the same. This serves to explain the totalitarian essence of the left's practices, narratives and aspirations.

The U.S. surveillance state and its operatives, now under the left, can only be understood if we view the whole process underway — in the growing fleets and armies of Russia and China, in the sly questioning of America's role in Europe, in Beijing's warnings to Australia, and the media's unwillingness to address the sudden reappearance of a renewed communist bloc, with many new member-states around the globe.

The Chinese and Western Classical Traditions: On Whether the End Justifies the Means

12/17/2019

The classical literature of ancient China, like that of ancient Greece and Rome, appears to emphasize moral goodness as the foundation of wisdom. But Chinese classical teachings on statecraft offer another perspective: one that places a special emphasis on deception, subversion, and secret agents.

In a book titled *The Tao of Spycraft,* Sun-tzu translator Ralph D. Sawyer describes classical Chinese texts in terms of their preoccupation with "craftiness"; first, in military strategy; second, as a method of softening up an enemy through false defectors and agents of influence. Early Chinese chronicles offer object lessons in "stealthy intrigues ... [and] perverse methods that should be denied the unrighteousness and kept from the dangerous," according to Sawyer.

The idea of using evil means for the advancement of good became firmly fixed at an early date in classical Chinese thought. The sages of the orient did not take precautions against the corruption of those exercising power; rather, Chinese despotism grew out of traditions which justified evil actions as indispensable to survival.

Adding cynicism to cynicism, Chinese autocracy gravitated toward the doctrine of "the Mandate of Heaven," which says that the acquisition of power (by whatever means) was proof of divine favor. According to this same logic, a ruler's overthrow was proof of his unworthiness. Thus, success by any means was morally justified. The cynical use of dishonesty and cruelty by those in power would thereafter prove unstoppable in a never-ending game of dog-eat-dog. Thus the Chinese era of the Warring States would become the focus of a classical curriculum rooted in deceit, cruelty and murder.

The idea of a constitutional process, with limited power under the rule of law, was alien to Chinese thought and practice. Chinese sages wrote about virtue, but developed no practical means of limiting evil rulers. There is no Lycurgus in Chinese history — no Marcus Junius Brutus, no Cato, no Cicero, no *practical* champions of liberty. China's advocates of practical wisdom were experts in the concentration of power, not experts in its limitation.

Of course, the ancient Greeks and Romans had their tyrants — like Dionysius of Syracuse and the Emperor Nero. These two figures received philosophical educations (Dionysius was taught directly by Plato, and Nero was a pupil of Seneca). Yet their behavior stood in opposition to the principles they were taught. The same cannot be said for the Chinese emperors and generals who learned Sun-tzu's *Art of War*, emphasizing falsehood and espionage, together with the ideas of Han Fei-tzu — the Machiavelli of ancient China.

If Dionysius and Nero turned their backs on Plato and Seneca, the Chinese rulers received positive intellectual encouragement to act contrary to the teachings of Confucius and Mencius. But even the teachings of Confucius would prove dubious, because he was understood as saying "anyone who abandons a perverse ruler to support... rebels claiming the Mandate of Heaven is a discerning defector, a hero rather than a traitor." [Sawyer] Confucius was cynically interpreted to say, in effect, that if rebels win, they are virtuous. If they lose, they are not. This produced in China a legacy rich in treason, a history overpopulated by defectors and betrayers whose opportunism became synonymous with "moral virtue."

The idea of using evil methods to defend the good was not effectively championed in Western thought until the Renaissance, when Machiavelli penned *The Prince*. Even then, Machiavelli was denounced by nearly everyone. Frederick the Great of Prussia wrote a book against Machiavelli's ideas, titled *Anti-Machiavel*, in which he stated: "I have always regarded The Prince as one of the most dangerous works which were spread in the world...." Frederick went on to say,

> ...it is a book which falls naturally into the hands of princes, and of those who have a taste for policy. It is all too easy for an ambitious young man, whose heart and judgment are not formed enough to accurately distinguish good from bad, to be corrupted by maxims which inflame his hunger for power.

Given the hyper-Machiavellian content of some Chinese classics, we can only imagine the anathemas Frederick would have poured out against the "sages" of the East. Undoubtedly he would have noted the dismal history of

China — a history of tyranny, betrayal and fatalism. Frederick wrote, by way of warning:

> The floods which devastate regions, the fire of the lightning which reduces cities to ashes, the poison of the plague which afflicts provinces, are not as disastrous in the world as the dangerous morals and unrestrained passions of the kings; the celestial plagues last only for a time, they devastate only some regions, and these losses, though painful, are repaired. But the crimes of the kings are suffered for a much longer time by the whole people.

Frederick added that "The true policy of kings is founded only on justice, prudence and kindness…." He characterized Machiavelli's philosophy as "full of horror…." — An effrontery to the public.

Though Frederick was an absolute king, he saw himself as subject to God, as owing duty to his people. He wrote his *Anti-Machiavel* on behalf of the Western philosophical tradition, which was grounded in the Old Testament prophets — informed by the Greek and Roman philosophers — and by the classical historians.

We read in Thucydides' *Peloponnesian War* the chilling "Melian dialogue," in which democratic Athens dictated terms to a neutral city which they arbitrarily exterminated. When the Melians argued for justice, the Athenians scoffed. Thucydides shows the wickedness and short-sightedness of Athenian policy. For Athens was courting destruction, even then, falsely imagining itself invincible and beyond the reach of justice. (Athens would lose the war.) Thucydides underscored the disastrous consequences of the "might makes right" philosophy of the Athenians, and the appalling cost to society when evil men attain high office.

In T*he Annals of Imperial Rome* Tacitus shows us how the despotism of the Caesars declined into the wickedness of abject tyranny, sexual deviancy, murder and madness. When Titus Livius wrote his *History of Rome* in the first century, he prefaced it with an appeal to the moral values of his country's forefathers — comparing ancient nobility to modern depravity.

In this vein Livy recounted the generalship of Marcus Furius Camillus before the walls of Fallerii. According to Livy, a Greek tutor had treacherously lured his young pupils, the sons of the town's leaders, into the Roman camp — offering these unsuspecting children as hostages with which to break the siege. Camillus had the Greek tutor stripped and scourged, handed the whip to the eldest pupil and let them return safely to their parents with their flayed and unfaithful teacher in tow. The people of Falerii were overawed by this noble act, and promptly surrendered to the Roman general out of gratitude, trusting their lives and property to him. Thus an enemy state was transformed, by honorable conduct, into a friend.

Likewise the Greek historian Polybius, in his famous commentary on the Roman constitution, praised the ancient Romans for their honesty and piety, to which he credited the success of their Empire. It was only afterwards, when success had spoiled them, that the Romans descended into moral degradation.

Plato, Aristotle, and Cicero upheld moral goodness and virtue — as did Confucius and Mencius. But the Chinese maintained, beneath the surface, an esoteric teaching that made Machiavelli look like a Boy Scout in comparison. So evil were the teachings of China's sages, that China's rulers saw them as dangerous in the wrong hands. Thus, in very ancient times these teachings were kept secret by the governments of successive kings. The dark underside of China's classical teachings were conceived as "the essence of our state" (as one high-level Chinese official explained). "Since the classics contain timeless methods for governing, they cannot be loaned to other people's."

According to ancient Chinese generals and administrators, wise rulers do not allow others to read the "military strategies and the books of the philosophers, with crafty techniques."

> So if the Han emperor was unwilling to show his beloved relative these books … how can we today hand over classics filled with such information to our nemesis, the Western barbarians?

In Sawyer's translation, one high official argues that the Western barbarians are sensitive and intelligent: "If they penetrate the Book of Documents, they will certainly know how to conduct warfare." Crafty methods and concepts were, in themselves, secret weapons in a cultural treasure-trove of secret weaponry.

It is prudent to know evil techniques — not because we ought to practice them, but to recognize when others are practicing them on us. What is certain, at this time in history, is that China and Russia, and the far left, consistently employ Machiavellian methods — and those taught by Sun-Tzu. We must be clear as to where we stand and what we believe about their use. Subversion and deception are activities that corrupt the practitioner. Like weapons of war they can only be used reciprocally, and not without risk to the user. Just as killing in war is a terrible thing, and not to be entered into lightly, lying to an enemy is also dangerous. The penalty which nature readily imposes on liars is known by history through the cognitive degeneration of the tyrant. He lies and threatens everyone, and everyone is obliged to delude *him* in return.

As anyone can see, the left's moral degeneracy is exemplified by a conceit so corrosive that moral idiocy and ideological sclerosis are immediately visible on every side. The ruling elites of the West, immersed in fables of their own making, can no longer recognize the truth. Less and less do they see or understand the situation they are in. Their tendency is to delude themselves; but how will that serve them? It must be the case, however invincible they seem, that they are doomed.

China and Russia, the two leading empires of the Sun-tzu legacy (and the legacy of Lenin), are awash in corruption and gangsterism. They are degenerate empires. The power they have accumulated can only be used for destruction, since they have no intrinsic moral worth. They will be damned by history, even as they attempt to deceive the historians.

If the legacy of Sun-tzu takes hold throughout the world, then history will everywhere conform to the laws and patterns of Chinese history. The West will then lie buried in its own rubble. Humanity will suffer a dark age — an age of blood and ignorance. Perhaps the human race will die of shame; for such an outcome would be, in truth, unendurably shameful.

Gnosticism as Metaphor for the Democratic Contenders

01/03/2020

> Gnosticism, thus, has produced something like the counter-principles to the principles of existence; and, in so far as these principles determine an image of reality for the masses of the faithful, it has created a dream world which itself is a social force of the first importance in motivating attitudes and actions of Gnostic masses and their representatives.
>
> — ERIC VOEGELIN, *THE NEW SCIENCE OF POLITICS*

The dreamworld of Voegelin's Gnostics may be glimpsed while watching the Democratic presidential debates. Listen to their absurd fantasies — of global warming and coastal flooding, of erasing national borders and spending trillions on programs to impoverish us all. Where indeed will the money come from? Indebted to the hilt, this can only accelerate the erosion of prosperity and bring about an unprecedented economic dislocation; but, hey, it's all good, because, from thereon and after we can blame capitalism and sexism and racism — and move forward in agreement to build real socialism, or communism, or the Green New NEW Deal, without airplanes or cows or cars or free speech. God help the poor fool who objects.

Yes. The Democrat candidates are all predicated on this same dreamworld. They are all Gnostics, in Voegelin's sense of the term. They are all dedicated to "counter-principles." How better to explain it?

Voegelin was a very learned man. He knew what he was talking about, even if his mode of expression was scholarly. He was trying to express insights which the unschooled have no words to express. So he invented his own vocabulary, borrowing the term "Gnostic" to relay his idea of the thing which is, even now, making war on the spiritual and intellectual underpinnings of the most advanced civilization ever built by humans.

Voegelin wrote:

> Gnosticism as a counter-existential dream world can perhaps be made intelligible as the extreme expression of an experience which is universally human, that is, of a horror of existence and a desire to escape from it.

Escapism can be a dangerous thing. A rich and successful society, made pathologically soft by decades of success, can take its permanence for granted; may mistake its neurotic impulses for the true order of things; may erect a false self-interpretation on an inheritance no longer understood; adopting instead a new pattern of conduct which promises to unravel the fabric of civilization itself.

What follows, by necessity, is a decline in civic morality, a blindness to obvious dangers, and — says Voegelin — a reluctance to meet those dangers with seriousness. He added: "It is the mood of late, disintegrating societies that no longer are willing to fight for their existence."

The Gnostic dream world on stage at the Democratic presidential debates reflects this same process of unraveling — of an unserious regard for dangers, of neuroticism and existential hubris. Voegelin wrote:

> In gnosticism the non-recognition of reality is a matter of principle; in this case, one would have to speak of an inclination to remain aware of the hazard of existence in spite of the fact that it is not admitted as a problem in the gnostic dream world; nor does the dream impair civic responsibility or the readiness to fight valiantly in case of an emergency. The attitude toward reality remains energetic and active, but neither reality nor action in reality can be brought into focus; the vision is blurred by the Gnostic dream. The result is a very complex pneumopathological state of mind...

Non-recognition of reality, he says, is the first principle of the Gnostic. Actions which the prudent consider morally insane are undertaken because they are considered "moral" by the dreamer. According to Voegelin, "The gap between intended and real effect will be imputed not to the Gnostic's immorality of ignoring the structure of reality," but to the immortality of those who do not share the same mad dream.

The method of the morally insane is to invert responsibility. Their failures are always someone else's fault. Thus, Stalin's economic failures were not blamed on socialism's faulty economic assumptions but on the moral guilt of wreckers, saboteurs and spies; that is, anyone who did not share in the Gnostic madness of communism. Therefore it is logical that Stalin's secret police would shoot the engineers and experts whose reports reflected knowledge and wisdom that the communist might find threatening.

Voegelin noted, "practically every great political thinker who recognized the structure of reality, from Machiavelli to the present, has been branded as an immoralist by Gnostic intellectuals…." The Gnostics have even made a "parlor game" out of labeling Plato and Aristotle "fascists." It should not surprise us, therefore, that the Gnostics decry the wisdom of the past as evil.

When dangers appear, you can bet the Gnostics will take the wrong course of action. They will engage in manifold "magical" operations — cursing the wicked, pronouncing anathemas, resolutions, appeals to mankind, etc. They might even outlaw war.

Are we laughing yet?

The Gnostic represents political insanity. Just listen for twenty minutes to Elizabeth Warren. Every time she opens her mouth, the judicious wince. "Gnostic politics," said Voegelin, "is self-defeating." More than that, he warned that it inevitably leads to continuous warfare. He stated:

> This system of chain wars can end only in one of two ways. Either it will result in horrible physical destructions and concomitant revolutionary changes of social order beyond reasonable guesses; or, with the natural change of generations, it will lead to the abandonment of Gnostic dreaming before the worst has happened.

Does this have a familiar ring? Do we remember Hillary Clinton's call for a "no fly zone" in Syria — against Russian air units! The dreamworld of the Gnostic does not merely invade social policy. It has interpenetrated national security policy, too.

We must not forget that each step in our overseas involvement empowers big government. It also empowers the transformation of liberalism into communism. Voegelin noted:

> If liberalism is understood as the immanent salvation of man and society, communism certainly is its most radical expression; it is an evolution that was already anticipated by John Stuart Mill's faith in the ultimate advent of communism for mankind.

Western society, warned Voegelin, "is ripe to fall for communism…." And who would deny our steady leftward progress? Look at the Democrats running for the White House.

May God have mercy on us.

The Apocalypse of Radical Stupidity

01/11/2020

"What are the symptoms of … the derailment of man?" asked Eric Voegelin in his book, *Hitler and the Germans.* Man has a particular nature. He is a spiritual being and a rational being. The West drew its reason from the ancient Greeks, its spiritual grounding from the ancient Israelites. This was our twofold heritage. Only now we have abandoned it for positivism and materialism. Consequently, Western Civilization is rapidly unraveling.

According to Voegelin, the Old Testament teaches that we have a share in what is divine. Man is "theomorphic," to use a Greek term, or made in "the image of God." Voegelin noted, "The specific dignity of man is based on this…." Yet we have kicked this to the curb, seeing ourselves in "the image of the monkey." Prevailing thought has debunked the idea of the "first cause," the divine creator, the maker of all things. This is the spiritual side of our radical stupidity. Voegelin wrote, "One cannot de-divinize oneself without dehumanizing oneself…."

The brutality of our daily thought, our disconnection from spirit, would be readily apparent to a medieval or ancient person. For our part, we hardly know what we have lost. Because of this we are imbibing anti-depressants at an astonishing rate. Despite our comparative wealth and comfort we are increasingly unhappy. We are, as one social scientists noted, "coming apart."

On every side the most brutal slogans resound. We are now the creatures of an ideological age. As noted by Carl Jung, we have succumbed to mass-mindedness. "There are no longer any gods we can evoke to help us," he wrote. We now lead "an ignominious existence among the relics of our past…."

We have largely closed ourselves off from the spiritual. Many religious leaders are frauds. Many of the "faithful" lack the discernment to detect imposters. It is a sickening situation all the way around. As for our reason, it is now grounded on erroneous propositions — disconnected from spirit, from the ground of being. Because of this, noted Voegelin, "there occurs a loss of reality, insofar as this divine being, this ground of being, is … reality too…."

This "loss of reality" leads some men to set themselves up as God. They promise to eliminate poverty, war, disease. Oh yes, and they can leap tall buildings in a single bound while lowering global temperatures. Such is the essence of the New Religion – the religion of our moral idiots, evolving day-by-day to the "tyranny of the radically stupid."

You see, the moral idiot thinks he is cleverer than God. He is fabulously intelligent in the most radically stupid way imaginable. Yet, the moral idiot doesn't know that he lost himself. As a deserter from reverence and truth, he tells irreverent lies and lives in a childish fantasy world. It is not only the fantasy world of CNN, but the fantasy world of Fox News.

According to Hesiod there are three kinds of men: (1) those who think things through; (2) those who listen to the thinkers; and (3) those who neither think nor listen and, consequently, are stupid and even dangerous. Today, persons of this latter type are everywhere. They are in charge of everything. Voegelin says our entire ruling elite is of this type.

Voegelin says it is "extremely difficult to understand that the elite of a society can consist of a rabble." Then he says, "[our elite] really does consist of a rabble." The proof is there, before our very eyes. There is something wrong with almost all of our leaders. They are not properly oriented. They are profoundly disoriented. According to Voegelin:

> Stupidity shall mean here that a man, because of his loss of reality, is not in a position to rightly orient his action in the world, in which he lives. So when the central organ guiding his action, his theomorphic nature and openness toward reason and spirit, has ceased functioning, then man will act stupidly.

He will murder millions in concentration camps, commit genocide against minorities, firebomb cities full of women and children, drop nukes when the enemy is already trying to surrender, hand over whole regions to slavery in order to keep a bargain with a mass murdering ally, etc. etc. Such is our latter-day history, "full of sound and fury," signifying betrayal.

In the Hebrew understanding, a fool is one who creates chaos and disorder because of his folly. In Plato's terminology, the fool "does not have the authority of reason and … cannot bow to it." Look to the left and look to the right. Where are the wise men? Who bows to reason?

Our descent into chaos is progressive and may accelerate at any moment. Stupidity follows stupidity, error follows error. We are killing unborn babies through abortion, importing aliens from hostile civilizations, teaching children the virtue of sodomy and Bedouins the virtue of democracy; marriage can now be between a man and a man, war is waged on the wings of sanctimonious chatter, to achieve unobtainable objectives. *Despair all ye who enter here.*

We live in the Age of Radical Stupidity in which the elite are the radically stupid – a rabble of intelligent nitwits passionately combating reality and common sense. Our bankruptcy advances from twenty trillion to twenty five trillion, to a hundred and fifty trillion. Nothing can stop the slide into universal chaos, except reason and spirit. But where can these qualities be found?

We think we are the good guys, that we know what we are doing. But we have no clue. We mistake goodness for self-righteousness. We mistake ideological slogans for knowledge and reason. We do not know our limitations, and do not like being told that we are vulnerable. It is only a matter of time before our radically stupid leaders cause a major derailment. When everything begins to fall apart, when we are dying by the tens of millions, will we find leaders of a different stripe? Where will they come from?

What are we doing to oppose the radical stupidity of our rulers?

The Scissors Strategy as Method for Agent Positioning

01/13/2020

In previous essays I have referred to "the scissors strategy," which is also known by other names. Many readers do not have a clear idea of how this strategy works, or why it is effective. It is therefore useful to present two or more hypothetical/historical examples to illustrate.

EXAMPLE ONE: AFGHANISTAN

In 1979 the Soviet Union wanted to accelerate its infiltration of the Islamic world. One objective of infiltration was to take control of Muslim groups and use them to create new means for attacking the West.

The best point of entry for this strategy was Afghanistan. Within the Soviet Union there were two Soviet "republics" ideal for launching operations in Afghanistan. The two countries were Tajikistan SSR and Uzbekistan SSR. (Please note: significant numbers of Tajiks and Uzbeks live in Afghanistan.)

Before 1979 the Soviet Union used ethnic Tajik and Uzbek agents to infiltrate Afghanistan. It was child's play for them to influence these groups inside the country. Meanwhile, young Afghan technocrats, being open to Marxist indoctrination, were also vulnerable to Soviet influence and recruitment by outright communist channels. Agents could also be recruited from other tribal groups through Soviet-infiltrated criminal networks (i.e., via Soviet dominance of regional heroin trafficking). A great many small operations had to be developed, originating in very different parts of Afghanistan, to make the strategy viable. The object in such long-term operations is always to infiltrate every important tribal group, criminal mafia, police organization, economic center and political party in the country. You cannot use a scissors strategy without placing agents in these (and other) key sectors. It goes without saying, of course, that the first target of infiltration is always enemy counterintelligence, so that nobody ever has the wherewithal to identify your agents or their modes of operation.

The next problem, as a Soviet strategist, is how to advance your agents into positions of power within their respective groups. Conflict is the best way, especially if the conflict is violent. In terms of drug trafficking you advance your agents in the police by giving them leads from your agents among the drug traffickers. The police under your control arrest only those traffickers who are not under your control, paving the way for you to strengthen your hold on organized crime. Ultimately your strategy leads to a convergence of the police and the mafia — so that the leaders of the police are your agents, and they are secretly aligned with the country's leading criminals, who are also your agents.

With your agents in the criminal underworld, and inside the police, you acquire access to information on corruption. Especially, you get information on corruption within the intelligence services, banking system and political parties. You can jail whomever you want. You also have the power to bribe or blackmail anyone you evaluate to be vulnerable or useful. Now your influence within the country is gradually taking shape.

The next problem is preparing the target country for invasion. At this stage you might ask: Why invade the country? There are many reasons, and you must be careful that the enemy does not suspect any of them. But the immediate reason for conflict is to advance your agents inside the country as a whole. (Whatever power you have is not enough, and it never will be.)

Ideally, as a Soviet strategist, you want a dolt in control of Afghanistan. Given the radical stupidity of the country's American-educated elite, this is not hard. You do many favors for the government, asking little in return. You build roads and airfields. You create the infrastructure for your future invasion. Then, you convince President Useful Idiot that the American imperialists are plotting to attack his country. You stage provocations through agents in tribal areas to frighten the government. Finally, President Idiot asks for you to intervene. Soviet troops enter the country. Now you have created a conflict ripe for exploitation.

Your agents within the tribal groups have long established their *bona fides* by posturing as anti-Soviet loudmouths. After Soviet troops commit specific outrages, these agents gain greater stature. The growing conflict between the Soviet occupiers and the tribes is the perfect setting for killing various leaders, opening new leadership slots for your agents within each tribal group.

Next comes talent spotting. From around the Muslim world fighters are recruited to join the jihad against Godless Communism. But you have prepared your chessboard well. With your agents firmly placed among the mujaheddin, you can direct military operations from both sides. You can thereby kill off fighters who are genuinely dangerous to Moscow while identifying promising young recruits from the Arab world. You can build new heroes within the anti-communist camp. And you can do this on America's dime. These new heroes will be your agents in future terrorist offensives aimed at the West.

The CIA moves to arm the Afghan rebels, even as you are getting control of the rebel groups by way of your agents. Soon the CIA will be arming and training groups that you effectively control (as well as groups that have momentarily eluded your control). The Americans will, with their own hands, build the organizations that you will use against them in the future.

The operation will have many ups and downs. It will not be without cost. You will lose many "good" people. In fact, everyone must believe you lost this war. You will pull your troops out of Afghanistan with great fanfare. The West will thump its chest. But you have filled the mujaheddin leadership with your creatures. You have simultaneously spent years assassinating your enemies within the Muslim world, infiltrating the militant ranks with your agents.

The culmination will come when terrorists, harbored by a tribal group you do not control, attack the World Trade Center and the Pentagon. At approximately the same time your proxies arrange the assassination of an Afghan leader to solidify your control over the anti-Taliban factions. Your patience is about to be rewarded. When the Americans attack Afghanistan from the air, your agents will be their allies on the ground — together with other tribal groups under your control. Now you have brought about a new kind of convergence. NATO occupies Afghanistan on your behalf and hardly anyone (excepting Mohammed Karzai) will guess the truth. NATO officers and generals are now in the crosshairs of another round of the scissors game.

If the Soviets were in Afghanistan for the better part of a decade, NATO will be there for the better part of two decades. Now the ire of the Islamic world is no longer focused on a jihad against Godless communism (which seems to have vanished altogether). Now the Jihad is against the Godless United States.

You may think that the outcome here is accidental. But no, it is the result of diligence, discipline, and superior intelligence tradecraft. Please do not misunderstand. Nothing here was easy for the Russian special services. They made tremendous sacrifices, and the strategic value of the outcome is stunning; for new games can now begin which are played from the winnings of the old game.

EXAMPLE TWO: CHECHNYA, ISIS AND BEYOND

Lithuanian researcher Marius Laurinavičius gave readers an invaluable glimpse inside Moscow's ongoing scissors strategy against the Muslim World five years ago in a multi-part series.[3]

Laurinavičius documented numerous linkages between Islamic terrorists trained by the Russian special services and ISIS. The Chechen War itself, in all its improbable details (like the Afghan War before it), is the stuff of Moscow-made legend. Like the "fake news" of today we had fake Islamic propagandists originating in places like Tajikistan and Uzbekistan — at the time of a supposed "Islamic revival" authorized by the Communist Party Soviet Union (again, *improbably*). This revival then spawned a number of Islamic ideologists, as Laurinavičius shows, in league with the KGB or FSB or Putin advisor Alexander Dugin.

The Laurinavičius narrative is bewildering in the extreme, unless we understand the pattern of infiltration and agent placement it represents. Here are the factual telltales of Moscow's scissors strategy. Here are the processes of the Afghan war repeated in the Caucasus, with an eye to stabilizing the region after intentional destabilization. Here we see terrorists filtering in and out of Russia and nobody is the wiser. Here is the explanation of Russian Defense Minister Pavel Grachev's bizarre claim that the North Caucasus Military District would be the site of a huge World War III exercise. This statement foretold the Chechen wars of the 1990s before anyone realized Russia was training the likes of Ayman al-Zawahri (the current head of al Qaeda). However good a deception may be, hints are always dropped from the lips of Russian generals or statesmen. (Note: Grachev had commanded the 103 Guards Airborne Division of the Soviet Army in Afghanistan from 1985-88.)

3 See Part 2: https://www.google.com/amp/s/m.delfi.lt/endelfi/article.php%3fid=66856642&=1

"The rise of Wahhabis [in Chechnya] provides a lot of pabulum to Russian propaganda and political games," noted Laurinavičius. If you read through the detailed cases presented by Laurinavicius, his conclusion appears obvious. As stated in Part Two of his series, "The rudiment of Wahhabism in Chechnya is apparently … related to … suspected KGB agents."

In recent years, with regard to ISIS, some of the usual suspects appear once more, "involved in recruiting new terrorists to [the] Islamic state," Laurinavicius explained. If it is ridiculous to propose a "conspiracy theory" in regard to the Syrian Civil War, Laurinavicius sets aside theory and delves directly into conspiracy as history.

To understand this history we must understand the scissor strategy. One blade of the scissors shreds the leader of one group. In retaliation the leader of an opposing group is eliminated; in each group the Russian agents rise in the ranks, fill the shoes of the dead leaders, and the Russians consolidate their position.

Think now of the ultimate concluding moves of such a game — as played from Kabul to Baghdad to Washington.

Think!

Magic and Destruction

01/21/2020

> He who does not have demonic seeds within him will never give birth to a new world.
>
> — DR. ERNST SCHERTEL

Such was an annotation found in Adolf Hitler's copy of Schertel's book, *Magic: History-Theory-Practice*. It seems that Hitler had no problem with "demonic seeds." And he wanted to "give birth to a new world" — as did Karl Marx and Vladimir Lenin.

Hitler annotated another passage from Schertel, which bears on the Nazi leader's cynicism. The will of the magician in relation to his "demon," says Schertel, creates power which "is completely left to his [the magician's] discretion." Hitler's annotation continues:

> The 'people' he might gather around himself ... represent an enlargement of his I-sphere. But it already has happened that a magician abandoned, shattered, or castigated his own people, if they did not seem reactive anymore.

Recall, if you will, pictures of Berlin and other German cities from May 1945. One sees an endless moonscape of bombed-out buildings. Such was the cost to Germany of enlarging the magician's I-sphere.

As it turned out, Hitler's demonic seeds were potent, sprouting into a world war, accompanied by the persecution, incarceration, and death of innocent millions. One might likewise say that Lenin's demonic seeds also sprouted into the killing and incarceration of millions by Stalin — who joined with Hitler to invade Poland in August 1939. This is what triggered World War II.

President Vladimir Putin is now attempting to deny Moscow's responsibility for the invasion of Poland, justifying Stalin's aggression in humanitarian terms. According to Putin, the West is to blame for Hitler. Neville Chamberlain's policy of appeasement, said Putin, was the real cause of the war. As for

Poland's innocence, Putin called Poland's 1939 foreign minister, Col. Józef Beck, "an anti-Semitic pig."

Here is yet another sprinkling of demon seeds to bring about a "new world." For that is the magical dream which Putin shares with Stalin and Hitler. Here again, the magician has no real concern for his own people. He is a revolutionary who seeks to overturn the existing order.

There is a quotation about revolutionaries which Eric Voegelin favored, from a book titled *The Demons*, by Heimito von Doderer. Here Doderer says a revolutionary is "someone who wants to change the general situation because of the impossibility of his own position…." Doderer also stated: "A person who has been unable to endure himself becomes a revolutionary, then it is others who have to endure him."

In some sense, wrote Doderer, the revolutionary abandons the "highly concrete task of his own life." The need then arises to falsify the past. From this, says Voegelin, there follows the need of all revolutionaries to systematically falsify history. If society succumbs to this falsification, then society itself "perpetuates the highest betrayal" imaginable. And there is a corollary to this betrayal. The false reality thereby established cannot accept anyone who talks truthfully about the past or present. Such persons are then labeled as traitors.

In Schertel's book on magic Hitler has underscored a passage which denies the existence of objective truth. He calls the "objective world" a "jugglery of fantasy." The idea behind magic is to "change the world according to our will." Then one can "create reality where no reality is."

And that reality? — a smoking ruin where once a city stood.

General Chi's Nasty Wuhan Soup: A Recipe for BioWar?

01/30/2020

> Only by using non-destructive weapons that can kill many people will we be able to reserve America for ourselves. There has been rapid development of modern biological technology, and new bio-weapons have been invented one after another. Of course, we have not been idle.... We are capable of achieving our purpose of 'cleaning up' America all of a sudden.
>
> GENERAL CHI HAOTIAN

In a secret speech given to high-level Party cadres nearly two decades ago, Chinese Defense Minister, Gen. Chi Haotian, explained a long- range plan for ensuring a Chinese national renaissance. He said there were three vital issues that must be grasped. The first was the issue of living space — because China is severely overpopulated and China's environment is deteriorating. The second issue, therefore, is that the Communist Party must teach the Chinese people to "go out." By this Gen. Chi meant the conquest of new lands in which a "second China" could be built by "colonization." From this arises the third vital issue: the "issue of America."

General Chi warned his listeners: "This appears to be shocking, but the logic is actually very simple." China is "in fundamental conflict with the Western strategic interest." Therefore America will never allow China to seize other countries to build a second China. America stands in China's way. Chi explained the problem as follows:

> Would the United States allow us to go out to gain new living space? First, if the United States is firm in blocking us, it is hard for us to do anything significant to Taiwan, Vietnam, India, or even Japan, [so] how much more living space can we get? Very trivial! Only countries like the United States, Canada and Australia have the vast land to serve our need for mass colonization.

"We are not as foolish as to want to perish together with America by using nuclear weapons," said the general. "Only by using non-destructive weapons that can kill many people will we be able to reserve America for ourselves." The answer is found in biological weapons. "Of course," he added, "we have not been idle, in the past years we have seized the opportunity to master weapons of this kind."

The ruling Chinese Communist Party considers biological weapons to be the most important weapons for accomplishing their goal of "cleaning up America." Chi credits Deng Xiaoping with putting biological weapons ahead of all other weapon systems in the Chinese arsenal:

> When Comrade Xiaoping was still with us, the Party Central Committee had the perspicacity to make the right decision not to develop aircraft carrier groups and focus instead on developing lethal weapons that can eliminate mass populations of the enemy country.

It may seem difficult to believe, but Gen. Chi considered himself to be a "humanitarian" communist, and therefore admitted to mixed personal feelings on this matter: "I sometimes think how cruel it is for China and the United States to be enemies…." After all, he noted, America helped China in World War II. Chinese people remember that America opposed Japanese imperialism. But none of that matters now. "In the long run," said Gen. Chi, "the relationship of China and the United States is one of a life-and-death struggle." This tragic situation must be accepted. According to Gen. Chi, "We must not forget that the history of our civilization repeatedly has taught us that one mountain does not allow two tigers to live together."

According to Gen. Chi, China's overpopulation problem and environmental degradation will eventually result in social collapse and civil war. General Chi estimated that "more than 800 million" Chinese would die in such a collapse. Therefore, the Chinese Communist Party has no policy alternative. Either America is "cleaned up" by biological attacks, or China suffers national catastrophe. Chi makes the following argument:

> We must prepare ourselves for two scenarios. If our biological weapons succeed in the surprise attack, the Chinese people will be able to keep their losses at a minimum in the fight against the United States. If, however, the attack fails and triggers a nuclear retaliation from the United States, China would perhaps suffer a catastrophe in which more than half of its population would perish. That is why we need to be ready with air defense systems for our big and medium-sized cities.

In his speech, Gen. Chi provides us with a key for understanding China's development strategy. According to Chi, "Our economic development is all about preparing for the needs of war!" It is not about improving the life of Chinese people in the short run. It is not about building a consumer-oriented capitalist society. "Publicly, said Gen, Chi, "we still emphasize economic development as our center, but in reality, economic development has war as its center!"

The same can be said for China's intense interest in the biological sciences. The West has yet to grasp the underlying motive for China's ready participation in the West's P4 microbiology labs, where the world's most deadly microbes are studied, (i.e., pathogen lethality level 4 labs). This now bubbles to the surface in the Novel Coronavirus pandemic which has occurred in Wuhan, at the heart of China, just outside China's principle P4 virology lab (specializing in deadly viruses).

Not long after delivering his speech, General Chi stepped down as Defense Minister in 2003, the same year as the SARS (Coronavirus) outbreak in China. This was also (coincidentally) the same year Beijing decided to build the Wuhan P4 virology lab. Given Gen. Chi's speech, is the Novel Coronavirus outbreak in Wuhan an accident occasioned by weaponizing the virus at the city's P4 microbiology lab?

Three data points are worth considering. First, in 2008 Taiwan's top security official told lawmakers that "Taiwan had intelligence linking the SARS virus to research done in Chinese labs."[4] Given China's economic clout and political infiltration of Chinese language media, it is not surprising that National

4 "SARS a Chinese Weapon: Taiwan Official," https://www.smh.com.au/world/sars-a-chinese-weapon-taiwan-official-20081007-4vse.html

Security Bureau Director Tsai Chao-ming was forced to retract his statement, which had none of the usual features of a "gaff." Was Director Tsai forced to retract a statement that was true, since he could not reveal his intelligence sources inside China?

The second data point worth considering: The *Virology Journal* has an article by Gulfaraz Khan, published on February 28, 2013, outlining the discovery of the Novel Coronavirus in Saudi Arabia in June 2012.[5] Yes, it is the very same Novel Coronavirus with the following difference: when first discovered it could not be readily transmitted from humans to humans. Something changed in the virus since that time. Thus, the Wuhan version is labeled 2019-nCoV instead of simply NCoV. The latter is not contagious, while the former is spreading rapidly through China as these words are written. What do you suppose changed its transmissibility between 2012 and 2020? Random mutation or weaponization? If the current lethal outbreak had occurred in any other city than Wuhan, we might be inclined to believe in a random mutation. But Wuhan is ground zero for Chinese bioweapons. Should we credit such a coincidence?

The third data point worth considering: GreatGameIndia.com has published a piece titled "Coronavirus Bioweapon – How China Stole Coronavirus From Canada And Weaponized It."[6] The authors were clever enough to put Khan's *Virology Journal* article together with news of a security breach by Chinese nationals at the Canadian (P4) National Microbiology Lab in Winnipeg, where the Novel Coronavirus was allegedly stored with other lethal organisms. Last May the Royal Canadian Mounted Police were called in to investigate, by late July the Chinese were kicked out of the facility. The chief Chinese scientist was allegedly making trips between Winnipeg and Wuhan.

Here we have a plausible theory of the NCoV organism's travels: first discovered in Saudi Arabia, studied in Canada from whence it was stolen by a Chinese scientist and brought to Wuhan. Like the statement of Taiwan's intelligence chief in 2008, the GreatGameIndia.com story has come under intensive attack. Whatever the truth, the fact of proximity and the unlikelihood

5 "A novel coronavirus capable of lethal human infections: an emerging picture", de Gulfaraz Khan: https://www.ncbi.nlm.nih.gov/pmc/articles/PMC3599982/

6 "Coronavirus Bioweapon – How China Stole Coronavirus From Canada And Weaponized It": https://greatgameindia.com/coronavirus-bioweapon/

of mutation must figure into our calculations. It is highly probable that the 2019-nCoV organism is a weaponized version of the NCoV discovered by Saudi doctors in 2012. It is almost certainly part of the bioweapons program extolled by Gen. Chi Hàotián nearly two decades ago.

We must have an investigation of the outbreak in Wuhan. The Chinese must grant the world total transparency. The truth must come out. If Chinese officials are innocent, they have nothing to hide. If they are guilty, they will refuse to cooperate.

The real concern here is whether the rest of the world has the courage to demand a real and thoroughgoing investigation. We need to be fearless in this demand, and not allow "economic interests" to play a coy and dishonest game of denial. We need an honest inquiry. We need it now.

Truth and Beauty

02/07/2020

We possess art lest we perish of the Truth.

NIETZSCHE

In his wandering meditations on German thinkers and artists, Erich Heller asks, "Has the ugliness of the ugly truth increased so drastically since Plato's time that now anyone associating truth with beauty commits a philosophical felony?"

The weak in spirit might say "yes" to Heller's question. But the right answer is "no." It is not that truth has become uglier; rather, it is the growing ugliness of today's ruling lies. Indeed, a doctrinaire falsification of reality prevails in our media and with our political elites. (Look at the Russia collusion hoax as a recent example.)

The doctrinaire falsifiers of our time are on the left. They believe, wrongly, in definitive solutions to man's social and political problems: poverty, war, disease and disorder. But there are no definitive solutions to these problems. Those who believe in such solutions end by setting up a worse problem; namely. The problem of arbitrary, despotic government.

Because we are mortals living in a universe bounded by death and tragedy, nobody gets out of this world alive. Poverty, war and injustice will always be with us. The solutions offered by the left are minted in false coin. Theirs is the demagoguery of impending tyranny. And tyranny solves nothing. It merely increases man's share of poverty, war and injustice. The human condition can only be mitigated by political prudence, by checks and balances that hinder prospective centers of absolute power. But the left seeks to build those centers of power, decrying every check on its utopian ambitions. .

The left adheres to socialism — vaguely defined — as a flexible and secular dogma with shape-shifting tactical propensities. This dogma, like all dogmas, promotes intellectual laziness and dishonesty, moral degeneracy, economic decline and political despotism. History shows us this again and again. Yet we fail to learn from history as the intellectual disease metastasizes in our midst. We appear unable to stop its progression through our schools, our media and our government. Therefore we are continuously subjected to conceptual out-gassings of egalitarianism, Darwinism, scientism — the fashionable bilge that propels this degeneracy forward.

The ugliness of this worldview, which makes man into a kind of monkey, produces in its wake an ugly art and a cultural malaise. People are increasingly turning to antidepressants because the ugliness, triviality and faithlessness of the new materialist worldview, is depressing — and soul-rotting. So-called "scientific" socialism, of course, doesn't believe in the soul. It is soulless, despite its humanitarian pretensions. The wise see through the false good intentions of the leftist mainstream. The foolish cannot see, but participate by adding their genuine good intentions to something that is founded on fraud. Thus we have the confusing situation of good people backing an evil cause. It seems that this evil is not recognized because of the ignorance of what Nietzsche called "the many, too many."

The end product of all this is an ugly culture mediated by ugly pundits and uglier politicians. The ugliness here is spiritual, moral, and intellectual. The sycophants of "progressivism," are acolytes of the ugly. As opponents of truth, they end as purveyors of the ugly. In fighting them we also may become ugly, because enmity is reflective as well as reflexive.

Unlike the aristocratic order of previous centuries, the new order, infused with the psychopathies of the lumpen-proletariat, hasn't the wherewithal to prettify itself (however artfully it tries). The contemporary "artist" who joins with the social justice warriors, may overcome ugliness at moments; but the inner malaise of the whole cannot genuinely celebrate the beautiful silver lining in the dark cloud of reality — except as a canvas covered in vomit. Such is the artistic imperative of the subversive, the criminal, the revolutionary. Not merely an artistic revolt, but also *revolting*.

With the advent of Bolshevism, with the advance of the Big Lie, art became perverted. It has gradually turned toward a celebration of the vile and grotesque. Today's art galleries have shown us a crucifix in urine. In the topsy-turvy world of the Revolution, under the Epiphany of the Wicked, amid the woeful howling of nihilists, the faux artist joins the legion of the dammed. Here is the "pathologically closed consciousness" that Eric Voegelin warned against: the culture system of the deliberate betrayers, inverters, subverters — of human order.

How to Deal With the Chinese Communists

02/12/2020

First, you have to discover what the Chinese Communists think. From this you can piece together their agenda. Anyone who studies the Chinese Communist Party (CCP) and understands the thinking of President Xi Jinping, will also understand that communism is all about destroying capitalism, and destroying the leading capitalist power — America. Anyone who does not understand this, understands nothing.

The CCP wants America on its knees. They want to become the masters of the earth. They are ruthless in their methods, and do not care how many people will die. The CCP is a totalitarian party employing totalitarian methods. They have killed tens of millions in labor camps, with firing squads and other forms of capital punishment. The leaders of the regime are mass murderers who have trampled down the Chinese people.

Using common sense, would you have relations with these psychopaths? Would you have dealings with someone who wants to destroy you? Would you allow a poisoner to cook your food? Would you allow him to make your vitamins and your Medicines?

If you answer yes to any of these questions, then your prudence is at the same level as America's statesmen and business leaders. In general, they have answered yes to all these questions. Many American business leaders have formed close ties with the murderers in Beijing; for the entire Chinese economy is subject to the CCP. No business in China is truly independent of the government. As for American statesmen, it is shameful that they should clink glasses with CCP leaders. It is shameful to see them enable their country's most dangerous enemy. It is shameful that they are so stupid, so swindled, so blind to the enemy they are courting.

The best prescription for dealing with communists regimes goes something like this: Do not talk to them, they lie. Do not make deals with them, they cheat. Do not share scientific data with them, they will weaponize it. Do not trade with them, they will undercut your economy. Do not make arms control treaties with them, they will violate such treaties. Do not share deadly microorganisms with them, or you will catch a very bad flu.

It is suicide to snuggle up to a Communist. It is like the story of the man who found a frozen snake on the road, took pity on it, held it to his bosom if only to warm it back to life, and was fatally bitten. Why did he do it? Was it stupidity? Was it arrogance? A man cannot befriend a reptile. A capitalist cannot befriend a communist. The latter is a serpent whose sole intention is to sting.

In his book, *Deceiving the Sky*, Bill Gertz wrote, "No other Chinese leader since Mao has embraced the rigid orthodox Communist ideology more than Xi Jinping…" — So we shouldn't be fooled by the slick capitalist exterior of the Red Dragon. The CCP is not a capitalist organization. It is Communist. And they mean to do us harm.

No fooling.

American Reds

02/18/2020

By what process did the American Democratic Party become an alternative Communist Party? The answer is simple. After a century of subversion and infiltration, Marxists gradually gained the upper hand at the highest levels — all others driven out. The Marxists often succeeded by portraying themselves as moderates. Behind the scenes, however, as revealed by researcher Trevor Loudon, the leadership of the Democratic Party is anything but moderate. Theirs is a red network of radical groups — from Alinskyite "community organizers" and "Democratic" socialists, to Maoist and Kremlin stooges.

To show this is true (and not a figment of right-wing paranoid imagining), Trevor Loudon has written a book titled *White House Reds*, with citations and sources to prove his case. Loudon gives us the names of leading activists and their organizations. He shows us how the current crop of Democratic presidential candidates are all attached to the radical left.

A very sad situation now confronts the "land of the free," as our two party system must eventually tilt toward a Democratic victory in some future election. Meanwhile the Dem socialists have been chipping away at capitalism and the Constitution. Since the end of the Cold War, the Democratic Party has undermined the nation's defenses, weakened the economy, divided the people along racial lines, and blamed capitalism for the results of their own handiwork.

By exploding the false moderate images presented by the Dems, Loudon shows there is no viable right or center in the Democratic Party — except as a myth with which to smear the ever-leftward-moving Republicans as "right wing extremists." Loudon has grasped the underlying Marxist monoculture emerging out of the center-left facade of the Democratic Party. Loudon gives us a close-up view of the Democratic Party's presidential contenders, showing them to be fronts for a revolutionary and destructionist agenda.

Among the many tidbits in Loudon's book, we learn that Joe Biden became a Senator with help from Soviet agent Armand Hammer; that socialist Bernie Sanders had warm regard for the gulag-ridden Soviet Union; that Elizabeth Warren's radical anti-business agenda dovetails with her Maoist-left associations (not to mentions teach-ins with the likes of Francis Fox Piven); that Pete Buttigieg stands out as the son of a Marxist scholar and a longtime admirer of Soviet-lover Sanders.

Loudon also reveals how Julián Castro and Cory Booker integrated Marxism-Leninism with Chicano/black racial agendas at Stanford University — and were both promoted into politics by the "usual suspects." Last but not least, Loudon delivers the true *bona fides* of the grossly misperceived princess of the Dem "moderates," Tulsi Gabbard — shown to be a fellow-traveling Sanders-supporter — notoriously soft on Russia's communist allies in Venezuela and North Korea.

We must not forget that Bill Clinton and Barrack Obama long pretended to be centrists as they moved U.S. policy further and further to the left. Their party has gained such strength, and such a hold on bureaucracy and media there may be no turning back at this late stage in the game. It has even been suggested by President Donald Trump, that the 2020 election will be a contest between socialism and capitalism. Considering what Loudon has unearthed, the president appears to be right.[7]

7 For those who do not see the leftward drift of both political parties, please look at political scientist Tim Groseclose's book, *Left Turn* at https://www.amazon.com/dp/1250002761/ref=cm_sw_r_cp_api_i_HJhtEbG76A194

Paranoid Ideation in Political Discourse

02/19/2020

> ....I believe there is a style of mind that is far from new and that is not necessarily right-wing. I call it the paranoid style simply because no other word adequately evokes the sense of heated exaggeration, suspiciousness, and conspiratorial fantasy that I have in mind.
>
> RICHARD HOFSTADTER[8]

The prevalence of paranoid personality disorder in the general population has been estimated at around 4.5 percent.[9] In effect, the United States is home to over 14 million paranoids. But there is another category of persons, of indeterminate number, who indulge paranoid thoughts without being clinically paranoid. These are the people Richard Hofstadter described as evincing a "paranoid style" of political thought.

According to Hofstadter, "this term is pejorative, and it is meant to be; the paranoid style has a greater affinity for bad causes than good." In his Harper's article of November 1964, Hofstadter quotes three examples from American history: (1) a populist rant from 1855 claiming that monarchs and papists were plotting America's destruction; (2) an 1895 rant about "the secret cabals of the international gold ring"; and (3) a 1951 excerpt from Senator Joseph McCarthy's speech on the manipulation of U.S. foreign policy by Soviet agents.

We shouldn't be surprised that no evidence has emerged in subsequent years about the supposed 1855 monarchist/papist plot; neither did any evidence of such a plot emerged from memoirs or state archives, or histories; and the same can be said about the conspiracy of the alleged 1895 "gold ring"; and yet, whatever historians now allege against Senator Joseph McCarthy,

8 "The Paranoid Style in American politics": https://harpers.org/archive/1964/11/the-paranoid-style-in-american-politics/

9 "Paranoid Personality Disorder": https://www.therecoveryvillage.com/mental-health/paranoid-personality-disorder/#gref

intelligence archives show that hundreds of Soviet agents had, in fact, penetrated the U.S. Government in the 1940s.[10] Therefore, unlike the other two conspiracy theories cited by Hofstadter, the communist conspiracy was real; and its consequences are very much with us today.

The claim, then, that the anti-communist "hysteria" of the 1950s was the same as the anti-monarchist hysteria of the mid-nineteenth century, or populist hysteria against the gold standard in the 1890s, is to confound a reasonable fear with groundless paranoia. As Alexander Solzhenitsyn demonstrated in his three volume work, T*he Gulag Archipelago*, communism is anti-human in its homicidal inclinations — a taproot of tyrannous grandiosity and destructionism. Here we are not describing a "conspiracy theory." We are describing a conspiratorial political movement, outlined as such by Vladimir Lenin in his pamphlet, *What is to be Done?* — a movement that took power in the world's largest country (Russia), and the world's most populous country (China), and in more than a dozen other countries. It is a movement that has been led by psychologically abnormal persons, like Stalin, Mao, Pol Pot and Castro. It is a movement that has not relented, despite its many deceptions to the contrary, and even now continues to employ networks of subversives to realize a long-standing program of global conquest.

Was it right for Hofstadter, then, to characterize the anticommunism of Joseph McCarthy as partaking of a "paranoid style"? This pejorative characterization of anticommunism was the first major error in our postwar political understanding. It was an error that benefitted the communists, rehabilitating them as they flooded back into government during the 1960s. And we have been living with the consequences ever since.

The second error, thereafter, followed from the first, and from the Marxist-inspired dumbing-down of the public schools, which dimmed the wits of later generations. That second error was to mistake subsequent mass outbursts of sublimated fear as politically meaningless and irrational, thereby guaranteeing paranoia's future salience. With the decline of historical understanding,

10 On penetration of the U.S. Government by Soviet agents, see *The Venona Secrets: The Definitive Exposé of Soviet Espionage in America* (Cold War Classics): https://www.amazon.com/dp/1621572951/ref=cm_sw_r_cp_api_i_vTUrEbGM7ZJK1

Also see Diana West's *American Betrayal*: https://www.amazon.com/dp/1250055814/ref=cm_sw_r_cp_api_i_aVUrEbYZQ3QF8

in the midst of a growing philosophic and spiritual vacuum, people knew less and less how to interpret events. They were soon susceptible to "conspiracy theories," feeling intuitively that *something* was wrong, that something was out to "get them." As the general malaise of the times was not properly explained, and the nihilistic premises of the left were not generally understood to be a root cause, only the occult processes of the unconscious could perform the role of Public Oracle.

Human beings have an inborn hunger for the truth. If events cannot be rendered intelligible, if dialectical materialist explanations do not satisfy, imagination will make up the difference. The phantasmagoria of disoriented minds, afflicted with dreamlike metaphoric and symbolic "messages," have brought us to a grand *science fiction* melodrama; namely, to the flying saucer — what Carl Jung called "a modern myth of things seen in the sky." Here is an emerging subculture which ufologist Jacques Vallee has described as "the next form of religion." It is a subculture which grows, from year to year, to something that may usurp *all* culture. It has, with the controversy of its claims, reinvented a realm of superhuman beings. This time, not gods and demons, but interstellar reptiles from Zeta Reticuli, ultra-terrestrials, grays, and other space-faring or inter-dimensional humanoids.

There is a growing cult of believers for whom these beings are just as real as Thor and Odin were to the pagans of Scandinavia. And here, unsurprisingly, we find that Hofstatder's "paranoid style" has been readily grafted onto an ever-forming edifice, with stories of "men in black," government coverups, terrifying secrets, and an unseen galactic war between forces of good and evil.

A new mythology is being built, despite our scientific pretensions, of unseen worlds and hidden forces. *If The Invasion of the Body Snatchers* became the science fiction metaphor for a gradual communist takeover, the snatching of bodies via "alien abduction" would reflect an overall process of psychic transformation — of alien social engineers hijacking unsuspecting human subjects for long-term experimentation and social control.

The message in the metaphor is unmistakable. The hapless subjects do not take their experiences as metaphorical, however — and why should they? The decayed culture around them has lost the thread of its meaning. And one thing is certain about the new phenomenon: the subjects seem to believe in something intensely meaningful. According to the U.K. Guardian newspaper,

12 million Americans believe that "alien lizards" rule us.[11] It is absurd, of course — yet powerfully symbolic.

With no prior indication of mental illness, David Icke claims that shape-shifting reptilian aliens have taken over planet earth.[12] Icke was once a respected sports broadcaster in the United Kingdom, a former footballer. After hearing "messages" from the spirit world, his utterances became decidedly oracular, paranoid, bizarre — nevertheless attracting a large cult following. How is this to be explained?

If Alex Jones of Infowars refers to Earth as a "prison planet," and tells Joe Rogan in a recent podcast[13] of "alien beings" luring the global elite to indulge in ritual blood sacrifices, is there nonetheless a metaphorical truth in it? What we see across the spectrum of our diminishing awareness, is a growing hysteria from within. If we are now cut off from the truth by an all-pervading censorship, then the ersatz truth of the extraterrestrial reptile must suffice. It is all the masses have left as the darkness closes in on them; a symbol and reference-point for the experience of being poked and prodded by a power against which they are helpless.

Senator Joseph McCarthy attempted to warn America about a more literal kind of reptile: the *communist reptile*. McCarthy alluded to a national abduction by "alien" infiltrators. Their cold scientific cunning, their hostility to human life, and the drab grey Soviet "system" from which they hailed, earned them their diminutive stature as totalitarian "drones" — the faceless minions of world revolution.

I hope that no one is offended by this politically incorrect interpretation of "signs in the sky." Lest anyone pick up the cudgel of argument against me, remember *Nyquist's Law*: **Everyone believes something that someone else thinks is crazy.**

That does not exclude the possibility we're all nuts.

11 "Conspiracy craze: why 12 million Americans believe that alien lizards rule us": https://www.theguardian.com/lifeandstyle/2016/apr/07/conspiracy-theory-paranoia-aliens-illuminati-beyonce-vaccines-cliven-bundy-jfk

12 David Icke: https://en.m.wikipedia.org/wiki/David_Icke

13 Joe Rogan interview with Alex Jones: https://youtu.be/-5yh2HcIlkU

A Note on Antisemitism

02/25/2020

> The worst mistake I ever made was that stupid, suburban prejudice of antisemitism.
>
> EZRA POUND

There are three basic kinds of antisemitism. There is the antisemitism of the left — of Karl Marx and his essay on the Jewish question. There is the "antisemitism" of Muslims who want to drive Israel into the sea. There is the antisemitism of the National Socialists. Each antisemitic approach connects with a form of totalitarianism — a form of government that suppresses freedom of speech, freedom of the press, and economic freedom. But this is not all.

A German reader recently challenged me on antisemitism, suggesting my rejection of anti-Jewish conspiracy theory was due to Christian "brainwashing." I might have replied that his views were the result of "Nazi brainwashing," but that would have been to trade one insult for another. There is, of course, a large body of anti-Jewish conspiracy "literature." I found this "literature" to be animated by hatred — whatever it's pretenses to objectivity might be. The more you delve into the antisemitic "historians" and "theorists," the more you see irrational Jew-hatred peaking out from every page. There is an unfairness in the conclusions of antisemitic writers, a one-sidedness of evidence. After awhile, they leave the reader exhausted and irritated by their fanatical obsession with Jewish wickedness. All the outrages, all the crime, all the injustices of the world, lead them to a single group: the *Jews*.

Antisemitic discourse is a sorry, repetitive, pathological hammering at one people, one ethnic group, again and again and again. For the antisemite, nothing bad happens except the Jews are behind it. No disaster unfolds except the Jews are to blame. One may anticipate the antisemite's analysis on every subject, at any point in time. It is a monotonous, unvarying, humorless drumbeat — a clock that strikes the same hour continuously, a weather report on a drizzle that never ends, a broken record that repeats the same phrase, the same tone, the same sound. Antisemitism is *boring*. Yet the antisemite never tires of his obsession.

Antisemites are always burning to tell the world about Jewish bankers, Hollywood moguls, Masonic conspirators and the nine hidden Kabbalist's at the top. Their belief in *The Protocols of the Learned Elders of Zion* is unshakeable. They are impervious to evidence. (When Hitler was presented with proof that *The Protocols* was a forgery, he snarled that it didn't matter because the book was "true in principle" anyway.)

The cultural antisemite, like Kevin MacDonald, might dress his hobby-horse with the catchphrases of evolutionary science, but his conclusions are not far from Fritz Hippler's Nazi era film, *The Eternal Jew*, which claimed that "Jews sit at the junction of the world financial markets." Thereby the Jews have become "an international power" that "terrorizes the world stock exchanges, world opinion, and world politics." Such was the paranoia of Hitler and the Nazis. Such was a justification for their murderous rage.

Antisemitism continues to infect public discourse. The antisemite blames economic and social problems on the Jews. Modern decadence, they argue, is Jewish. Everything that has gone wrong within Christendom is attributed to Jewish sabotage. The antisemite forgets that civilizations become senile by way of prosperity. It is something that has happened before — to the Greeks and Romans of antiquity. Pagans of the fourth century lamented the death "Great Pan" just as Nietzsche lamented the death of God in the nineteenth. The Jews are not to blame. History is cyclical.

There are many factors contributing to our distress: materialism, atheism, urbanization, and the collapse of the family. Terrible inventions promise to undo us. The COVID-19 virus, which now threatens mankind, appears to be a Chinese creation — not Jewish. Our spendthrift lifestyle of indebtedness is everywhere supported and encouraged by a hedonistic shopping mall regime — *a thing as American as apple pie.*

Justifying his own ethnic malevolence, the antisemite is the very model of the degeneracy he pretends to oppose. His mottled insights are the result of an intellectual astigmatism. His sociological arguments and evolutionary "science" (like Kevin MacDonald's) rings hollow. It is the same old scapegoating formula. And since all groups and peoples share in the blame of latter-day corruption, evidence can always be produced to convict one among the others.

As we watch the cartoon-like characters running for high office in the United States, with the socialist contagion metastasizing in the background, the antisemite wants you to believe that it's all part of a Jewish plot. No serious student of history accepts this thesis. And for good reason. If Hitler had his way and exterminated every Jew in earth, our situation would be no different; for National Socialism was its own madhouse.

You cannot rely on antisemites. They are not the patriots they pretend to be. They will join with the communists in the end, because the communists will offer them a deal. And like all the other useful idiots, they'll end as serviceable fodder.

Unexpected Tidbits from a Russian Military Defector

03/05/2020

In late August 1998 I found myself sitting in a private meeting room at the Cosmos Club in Washington, D.C., flanked by two journalists. Pensively standing next to his chair on the other side of the table was former GRU Col. Stanislav Lunev, who had defected from the Russian Federation in March 1992. As we listened, spellbound by his brilliance, we learned of Russia's descent into corruption. But then he surprised us, quite unexpectedly, by saying that Russia's degradation had occurred as blowback after a decades-long KGB campaign to spread moral corruption in America.

Really? Why would Soviet Russia want to spread corruption in America? What purpose could it serve? "Because," he explained, "Americans were too honest. We could not effectively recruit your people as spies. We needed to soften you up."

He said that Soviet agents had given money to people in Hollywood with the idea of putting more sex and violence in movies. It was an attempt to coarsen the moral sensibilities of average Americans. Lunev said this policy had backfired. "We had gotten rid of religion in Russia so we had no protection. Our people lost all sense of right and wrong. Your country still believed in God, so the damage was not as great."

I then turned and asked, "What kind of people did you recruit as spies." He had a one-word reply that was unforgettable: "Journalists."

This perked the interest of the two journalists flanking me. "What is a journalist?" Lunev asked rhetorically. "A person who gathers information and makes reports."

Many people today think the United States is a leader in disinformation and propaganda. But this idea can be readily dismissed by the fact that the United States has long been infiltrated by, and influenced, to accept anti-American messages and themes as a matter of course. Our centers of learning are anti-American hotbeds. In fact, anti-Americanism is so pervasive it is no longer recognized as such — so that being against one's own country has been "normalized."

Since the government does not control the media in the U.S., the larger cultural narrative has long been up for grabs. If the country had not been infiltrated and partly taken over from within, the rhetoric of many politicians and newspapers today could by no means be explained.

Our reality, to a large degree, is a construction, painstakingly built, brick by brick, with elements conceived abroad. Americans have been persuaded, by countless artifices of rhetoric, by the Fool's Paradise of the shopping mall regime, that vigilance against the communist threat was paranoia, that Russia and China were not ruled by communists, that they were not using our openness and naïveté against us.

Then came the 9/11 attack. All of a sudden our military and intelligence resources were diverted from their Cold War-era targets to a new enemy. Islamic terrorists, hiding in caves, were the new threat. Russia was going to be our ally against this threat. We went to war with Baghdad and Kabul. We spent trillions. We wasted all our attention, all those years, all those resources, fighting people we had no real need to fight. The real threat was dismissed out of hand. The Chinese and Russians were now our partners. We forgot to maintain our nuclear weapons industry. The country's vigilance slipped to a new low. Marxists flooded into government under Obama.

In November 1998 I asked Col. Lunev how a successful nuclear attack against America could be carried out. He said, "If you ever hear that Arab terrorists have attacked an American city with nuclear weapons? Don't believe it."

"Why wouldn't I?"

"Because," he said, "it will be my people. It will be [Russian] Spetsnaz."

"What will happen after this [false flag] nuclear strike?" I asked.

"Some weeks or months later the missiles will come from Russia," he said.

I never did ask Lunev what was meant by an interval of "weeks or months" between a false flag attack and nuclear strikes from Russia. I went back and reread a number of Soviet military books, searching for clues.

Reviewing the literature I made the following list: (1) Marshal Sokolovskiy's book, *Soviet Military Strategy*, says that Russia must openly orient her people to make war on America before an attack is feasible; (2) this orientation would have to take place "in plain view," but in a way that Americans would not take alarm; (3) the first crippling waves of any attack on the United States, using weapons of mass destruction, could not be direct attacks; (4) Russia and

China would need a foolproof alibi (as suggested by Lunev's 1998 scenario involving a false-flag terrorist attack); (5) the mystery of Lunev's "weeks or months" interval has to do with the objective of collapsing the U.S. economy before the advent of war; (6) subsequent domestic unrest, with attending political divisions, would be more effectively inflamed; (7) financial collapse would negate early warning systems as well as command & control.

The seven points listed above might be called "The Sequence." That is to say, in strategic terms, a cascading series of catastrophic events leading to the negation of the West's defenses.

If we consider our current situation in light of "The Sequence," we find many points coming into alignment. With regard to the COVID-19 outbreak, there may have occurred (in this regard) an "evolution of intentions." Since the enemy intends to destroy the United States by means of "The Sequence," the accidental release of the COVID-19 pathogen in China provides the occasion for a spontaneous if unintended denouement. In other words, *why not roll with it?*

COVID-19 offers the perfect alibi for China. It also gives cover for war mobilization disguised as measures for fighting the virus. It is obvious that a COVID-19 outbreak will hit United States in the coming days. The resulting panic will cause an unprecedented financial contraction. American society, softened by decades of loose living, is ideologically divided. Worse yet, a significant percentage of the country believes the president is a Russian stooge.

Are the pre-conditions for unleashing "The Sequence" in place? Are China's intentions in relation to the COVID-19 virus "evolving"?

Socialism as Universal Solvent

03/06/2020

> **Solvent:** something that eliminates or attenuates something especially unwanted.
>
> — MERRIAM-WEBSTER DICTIONARY

Suppose we reject our God-given existence. What follows? The ungrateful creature, eager to thwart his Creator, would have to concoct an antidote to existence — *a universal solvent* — with which to dissolve Universal Being.

Dissolve every bit of it.

To achieve lasting results, your solvent might also aim at the dissolution of God. Therefore, include atheism in your solvent. Undermine belief in the supernatural. Declare that God is dead.

What if, in spite of your best efforts, God remained present — in faithful men?

Not a problem! Since nothing has been created that does not deserve oblivion, we may use Stalin's formula: "No man, no problem."

If you kill a man, no difficulty arises from his non-existence. (Assuming there is no afterlife.) The required solvent is therefore anything that kills the body. But why remove only *one* man to solve *one* problem? Aren't all men problematic? Therefore the required solvent is an elixir of *mass liquidation.*

Are you shocked? You shouldn't be. *Remember:* — The plan is to negate everything in the universe, including the Creator of that universe. The elixir, of course, has many corrosive ingredients. Its main ingredient, as history shows, has been "socialism."

This will surprise many people, but it's true.

Socialism was designed by the left — by the would-be negators of all that has been. As Marx's colleague, Frederick Engels, once wrote, "The … negation of the negation …. has in fact to serve here as the midwife to deliver the future from the womb of the past."

In country after country, for a hundred years, the socialism of Marx and Engels brought poverty, tyranny and corruption. The socialists claimed they were *dissolving* poverty, tyranny and corruption. They were — in Engels's words — "negating the negation." Why, then, did mankind lose by it? — in Stalin's USSR, in Mao's China, in Pol Pot's Cambodia, in Chavez's Venezuela?

Why?

Is the negation of the negation a matter of philosophic bungling? Or is it the malevolent outburst of a misfit? Is socialism, as dreamt of by the left, a logical impossibility? Or is socialism, as a solvent, a malicious project *by those who crave annihilation?*

No doubt, with the well-intentioned socialist, there is the bungle factor of the misbegotten idealist — an idealist who unwittingly opens the door to the psychopath's malevolent cunning. There is a sense in which, with the advent of socialism, the idealist and the psychopath become political co-dependents. The logical impossibility of socialist utopia guarantees that the bungler and the malefactor will attend its advent; thus, we see, its destructive course is assured by a "binary" milieu. *Here we see that two elements are needed to make a society implode.*

Destructive outcomes follow from destructive principles. And all the principles of socialism are made, consciously or unconsciously, for the liquidation of *essential things*. Consider what is placed before us under the socialist banner: It is an "ideal" which deprives man of his property rights, of his family, of his father, of his nationality, of his soul.

How does it work, in practice?

It employs environmental regulations, schools, family and administrative courts, to negate the *essence* of the individual nihilistically.

Here is a special malevolence. One may dress it up with fine phrases and noble poses, but the objective is not to create something new. The real objective is destruction for destruction's sake. And that is what we see in the communist passion for revolution. It is not a new tablet of values. It is the negation of all values — *of the possibility of values.*

If faith is a belief in God's goodness, then despair is a belief in God's malevolence. Revolutionary socialism is founded upon the latter. A truly religious person inevitably realizes that socialist revolution is an error. Salvation is not in it, but damnation aplenty.

Socialism boils down to one question: Is God's creation a gift, or something to rebel against? Whichever position you take, everything follows therefrom. Ask yourself, as a practical matter, which premise has made the world better? Which premise makes us better people? Which premise preserves? Which destroys?

Only one answer is right.

The Rise and Fall of a Fool's Paradise

03/09/2020

Twenty years ago, a reader sent me an email as follows: "I have read your most recent articles with interest and fascination." He then described himself as an expert "in biology, biotechnology, chemistry and biological weaponry." He was apparently troubled by my approach to the subject of biological war, and asked the following question: "Do you have any thoughts as to why many writers or various individuals focus on the threat and do not spend equal time on counter-strategy discussions?"

You raise a great question, I replied. The reason writers spend little time on counter-strategies is that a realistic adaptation to mass destruction weapons requires institutional changes that have long been politically unacceptable to Americans.

It was the Gaither Committee, back in 1957, that first attempted a realistic look at the weapons of mass destruction problem. The report issued by the super-secret committee, which included leading military officers and scientists, is known as the *Gaither Report* (even though Rowen Gaither had little to do with it, owing to ill health).

The *Gaither Report* was 29 pages long. Its official title was "Deterrence and Survival in the Nuclear Age." The report was given to President Dwight Eisenhower on 7 November 1957. The authors of the report saw serious long-term dangers to the United States and offered a number of solutions, of which only a few on the military side were adopted (like keeping SAC bombers in the air and putting long range missiles in underground silos).

Because we were then entering an era of hydrogen bombs and long range missiles, the *Gaither Report* said America needed a massive shelter system to protect the civilian population. A crash program costing over $20 billion (in 1957 dollars) would be necessary. If memory serves, the report also recommended diverting concrete from freeway construction to meet the demands of the shelter program. In addition, the civilian population needed to be schooled in anti-communism (as communism was the ideology of our adversary).

Unhappy with the report, Eisenhower rejected its key points. He was seconded by Secretary of State John Foster Dulles. They both envisioned a bloodless victory against Soviet communism. This victory would be achieved by the construction of shopping malls and freeways. Our nuclear deterrent would protect us by threatening the Soviet Union with massive retaliation. Meanwhile, the American people would live carefree and happy lives, unencumbered by civil defense or anticommunist education programs in the secondary schools. According to Eisenhower's vision, we would triumph over communism by living better than the Russians. We would show them how to live the good life. We would shop our way to victory.

No sacrifices, no hard decisions, no tragic confrontations. The formula of Eisenhower was irresistible in its appeal. It was a formula that quickly became institutionalized and intellectualized within the policy-making elite. We lived that policy, and we lived good. At the end of his term, Eisenhower indirectly warned against the authors of the *Gaither Report*, calling for Americans to "stand guard against the acquisition of unwarranted influence … by the military-industrial complex."

The left seized upon Eisenhower's words. A stereotype came into existence — of cigar-chomping militarists who had learned "to stop worrying and love the bomb." We were also taught to despise weapons contractors whose greed allegedly fueled the Cold War. "The potential for the disastrous rise of misplaced power exists and will persist," Eisenhower warned. The military and its industrial backers posed a threat.

> We must never let the weight of this combination endanger our liberties.... Only an alert and knowledgeable citizenry can compel the proper meshing of the huge industrial and military machinery of defense with our peaceful methods and goals, so that security and liberty may prosper together.

These are the words of a president — and a five star general — who feared anti-communism more than communism. Unlike George Washington's *Farewell Address*, which warned of the dangers of foreign entanglements and civil war, Eisenhower's Farewell Address warned of an internal danger from the institutions charged with defending America from the nuclear and biological weaponry of the communist bloc.

On one hand, Eisenhower's concern was sensible. On the other hand, the communist bloc was laying siege to America and the West. They were primed to infiltrate our institutions. They had already influenced the policies of two presidents, Roosevelt and Truman; and there would be others. Communism was a real threat to America — internally and externally. Afraid that a form of anticommunism akin to fascism would take hold, Eisenhower did not want to face the communist threat head-on. Therefore, Eisenhower's speech effectively established a psychological evasion at the core of American policy. Living the good life would come before security. Eventually, socialism would piggy-back on this hedonistic formula, until the demand for social spending would begin to crowd-out military spending.

This is how we came to live in the fool's paradise of today — unready to deal with our enemy's nuclear, biological and economic methods of waging war. Instead of a philosophy of preparedness, ours became a policy propelled by hedonism — *on the left and the right.* Trading with China and Russia will not transform these nations into friendly democracies. Trade will only guarantee that our military-industrial complex — so long maligned by the left — will be undermined and weakened.

We had our chance in 1957. We might have built defenses. But now we are addicted to the shopping mall regime. Serious solutions are now beyond our psychological reach. We haven't the political will or intellectual integrity to cut through our long-held delusion of supremacy. Something vital in us has rotted away. In order to fix the situation we must first have a diagnosis, a deep sociological analysis, followed by public understanding of the problem. *But this will never happen.*

If you presented the *Gaither Report* today, people would shake their heads as if you were a lunatic. Fallout shelters? National self sacrifice? Patriotic education for our high school students? The mere suggestion would cause the left to mobilize. There would be blood in the streets.

Of course, I know what most people will say. In a nuclear war we all die and there's no point. So eat, drink and be merry. Enjoy the moment. Forget about all that military stuff. Trade with China. Fund the Kremlin. Shop until THEY drop!

Here is your modern American solution. And most people think it worked perfectly. We won the Cold War by living high off the hog. Isn't that the real story here? We beat the Russians by talk and retreat, by growing softer and softer under a shopping ethic. We let our kids smoke pot, our schools descend into political correctness, while counter-intelligence collapsed — if it was ever there at all. But then, we didn't really win the Cold War.

Any academic or literary person who dared suggest that we lost the Cold War, that we built a regime of self-indulgence and self-delusion, would find his work — if published at all — completely ignored. He would be barred from a respectable career and denied a hearing by those in authority. In church and in town they would whisper, "There goes that kook."

Realistic solutions to realistic problems are not always *realistic*. This is the Catch-22 of our politics. And so, let us take one thing at a time. Let's not discuss solutions until we have a consensus on the problem. And the left, with all its culture-power, will never allow that.

Such was my reply twenty years ago — a few months before the September 11 attack on the Twin Towers. We have been at war against "terrorism" since that time. There was even an anthrax scare; but the country went back to shopping, on President Bush's advice. It is convenient that our enemy in that war had no national border, no recognized religion (since Islam is the religion of peace), and no visible support from any nation state. We have bombed and invaded a number of countries in this strange conflict, wasting trillions of defense dollars, which Viktor Suvorov predicted, in 1987, as a Soviet diversionary operation known as "grey terror."

If Suvorov is any guide, we are presently experiencing "the overture," described in his book, titled *Spetsnaz*. As everything edges closer to "red terror," a viral pandemic from communist China takes down the stock market. Hotels, restaurants, and airlines are bound to fail. Real estate is going to crash. A banking holiday is inevitable. The shopping mall regime is about to fail the test of history.

The dream of prosperity without vigilance, without appropriate defensive measures, without the proper identification of enemies, was doomed from the start. It is a sweet dream indeed; but it was a dream — used against us by the Chinese Communist Party, the Kremlin, and their allies. Our vulnerability to subversion and infiltration was something we never owned up to. As America faces its greatest crisis in many decades, we will now suffer the consequences of our chronic unreadiness. A Chinese bioweapon, probably intended for the purpose of eliminating global capitalism, has been accidentally unleashed. The pandemic is at the gate. Can a politically divided and subverted society meet the challenge?

Let us pray.

Marxism and Mass Destruction

03/24/2020

> We have already said … that the theory of Marx and Engels of the inevitability of a violent revolution refers to the bourgeois state. The latter cannot be superseded by the proletarian state … through the process of 'withering away,' but, as a general rule, only through a violent revolution.
>
> — V. I. LENIN

According to the founding fathers of communism, the final overthrow of capitalism will be *violent*. Friedrich Engels said future revolutionary wars will result in the extermination of whole classes and races of people.

As Lenin explained, "The panegyric Engels sang in honor of [revolutionary violence], and which fully corresponds to Marx's repeated statements … is by no means a mere 'impulse,' a mere declamation or polemical sally." The founders of modern communism relished the idea of exterminating the world bourgeoisie.

"Revolution alone can 'abolish' the bourgeois state," said Lenin, who did not believe in the peaceful politics of a democratic republic. "A democratic republic is the best possible political shell for capitalism," he noted. And capitalism must be eradicated. This is the underlying impetus of the Marxist revolutionary dogma. Democracy is a fraud because — Lenin argued — it establishes the power of the capitalists "so securely, so firmly, that no change of persons, institutions or parties in the bourgeois-democratic republic can shake it."

Lenin therefore believed in smashing democracy and capitalism at the same time. But he did not stop there. Lenin believed in leveling all institutions — the family, the church, private property, etc. This campaign of eradication would bring mankind to communism; that is, a modern technocratic form of communism.

Lenin's creed, of course, is a creed of destruction; for the Promised Land of peace and plenty will never be found. In the end, Marxism's revolutionary violence can achieve no positive results. In practice, communism always delivers war and poverty. Communism is a system of the psychopaths, for the psychopaths, and by the psychopaths. The form of state which they have perfected — in Russia, China, North Korea, Iran, Cuba, etc. — is geared toward the favored weapons of the psychopath; that is, the weapons of mass destruction.

The criminal rulers of the "socialist bloc" are always building nuclear and biological weapons. They are always dreaming of the day when these weapons will be unleashed on an unsuspecting world. A philosophy of revolutionary violence and extermination animates communist leaders.

The communist ruler wants to be God. He wants to flip creation on its head. His revolutionary theory begins with the grandiose premise that the bottom should be on top, that the creature should usurp the Creator, that destruction somehow deifies the destroyer.

"The necessity of systematically imbuing the masses with ... this view of violent revolution lies at the root of the entire theory of Marx and Engels," wrote Lenin in *The State and Revolution.* To imagine a peaceful or "democratic" transition to socialism is, according to Lenin, "opportunism"; that is, the sin of selling out the revolution for a piece of capitalist pie.

The emphasis on violence, mass murder and plunder, is intrinsic to Marxism. Please note: Marx, Engels and Lenin taught that the state is an *instrument of violence.* It consists of police and soldiers and prisons, said Lenin. These are always used by one class against another. Thus, in Lenin's view, the bourgeois state exists to oppress the workers and the workers' state exists to oppress — then finally destroy — the bourgeoisie.

Given this destructive impulse, a biological war should be an irresistible temptation. Capitalism accords with all the norms of social cooperation, economic optimism and free association. A deadly communicable disease derails the market system as it pulverizes economic optimism. Fear drives investment away. Terror strengthens the socialist state and the socialist revolution *at the same time.* Global Health Governance becomes the subversive slogan of the hour.

Given the communist thirst for power and inclination to destroy, a nuclear war is not altogether unattractive. This kind of war makes a nation dependent on top-down authority. And what could be more intoxicating than the power to incinerate cities, fleets and armies with hydrogen bombs. The planet will tremble. The human race will submit. The gods of socialism will be exalted.

There is also the logic of numeric progression: Stalin killed 30 million, Mao killed 60 million — why shouldn't Xi Jinping kill 120 million? The ambition is all; for the World Revolution has many agents, and many useful idiots. Behind them are the missiles of the new communist bloc.

When the virus has done its work, and America's financial power bleeds away, Lenin's disciples will begin their destructive war. If they succeed, they will dictate peace terms to other countries. Beijing will decide the demography of Asia, the Pacific ring, and the lower 48 states. Russia will rule Europe, Alaska, and parts of Canada.

The victory of Moscow and Beijing, if they achieve it, will signal the socialist eschaton — the "end of history" as envisioned by Marx, Engels and Lenin. About this Eschaton Eric Voegelin wrote:

> The eschatological interpretation of history results in a false picture of reality; and errors with regard to the structure of reality have practical consequences when the false conception is made the basis of political action.

The dictator states cannot build a new world on violence and lies. Any victory they achieve will be temporary. Their revolution "is a tale told by an idiot, full of sound and fury, signifying nothing." Marxism, as a whole, — in all its politically correct manifestations — is a doctrine of counter-principles which are opposed to the principles of existence. It facilitates a time of dying. Nothing more.

> To every thing there is a season, And a time to every purpose under heaven; A time to be born and a time to die.

The present self-defeating cycle of politics will bring about new conditions and a new beginning. Whatever happens, spring will come again.

The Sino-Soviet Long-Range Strategy: From Sputnik to World War III

03/26/2020

> Mankind is entering a period of the greatest scientific and technological revolution, resulting from mastery of nuclear energy and the conquest of space.... These developments will largely determine the nature of a future war....
>
> — *SOVIET MILITARY STRATEGY*[14]

In the two decades following the Second World War a revolution in military affairs occurred. In that period, Russia and America developed the H-bomb, and Russia launched the first man-made satellite, named "Sputnik." These advances prefigured the coming deployment of thousands of intercontinental rockets armed with thermonuclear warheads.

Recognizing the need for a strategic overhaul, Soviet dictator Nikita S. Khrushchev set up a committee of top Soviet strategists under Leonid Brezhnev. The role of Brezhnev was crucial, because of Brezhnev's interest in strategy, and his friendships with key strategic thinkers, leading to his political rise after Khrushchev"s mysterious "retirement" — announced, perhaps prophylactically, within a year of President John Kennedy's death, and 20 days after the Warren Commission final report omitted mention of Soviet involvement.

According to information provided by Czech defector Jan Sejna, the Brezhnev committee had four subcommittees under it, each headed by a Soviet strategist: Marshal V.D. Sokolovskiy (military); Dmitry Ustinov (military industry); Boris Ponomarev (foreign affairs); and KGB General Nikolai Mironov (intelligence).

The Brezhnev committee developed the following strategic "directions": (1) The Soviet military would prepare to fight and win an all-arms nuclear-biological war against the "imperialist powers"; (2) all economic and scientific means would be rallied to build weapons of mass destruction, a national blast

14 A Translation from the Russian of V. D. Sokolovskii with Analysis and Annotation by H. Dinerstein, L. Gouré and T. Wolfe: https://www.rand.org/pubs/reports/R416.html

and fallout shelter system, including underground mines, factories and scientific "cities" in the Ural's industrial region; (3) the foreign policy of the country would be flexible and pragmatic, focused on pushing arms control treaties that would limit American strategic defenses, biological weaponry, and offensive nuclear capabilities; (4) the communist bloc's military, industrial and diplomatic efforts would meet with success only if the West could be persuaded that communism had "collapsed" in the Soviet sphere. This part of the "long-range strategy" required a reorganization of the KGB into an "outer" shell of personnel, having no knowledge of the strategy or its directing principles, and an highly secretive "inner" KGB responsible for organizing serial deceptions.

KGB General Mironov's subcommittee recommended the following long-range deception operations, requiring the accomplishment of several tasks: (1) Penetrate the intelligence services of the West with "moles"; Convince Western intelligence services of the authenticity of fake intelligence offered by "dangles" and thereby gain promotions for "purveyors of a false disarming narrative" by penetration agents who will inevitably become the leading figures in Western intelligence; (3) while taking control of the intelligence game on the ground, promote the idea that "ideology is dead" in the communist bloc; (4) promote the idea of an "ideological" split between Moscow and Beijing so that the West will "play the China card"; that is, blindly rush in and build China into an industrial and technological giant to counter the USSR; (5) promote fake dissident groups and dissident celebrities in the Soviet Union and its satellites; (6) establish controlled opposition movements in bloc countries; (7) prepare to organize, through agents in the dissident movements, anti-communist revolutions throughout bloc; (8) promote the idea that a future Soviet leader is, in fact, a "liberal reformer"; (9) break up the Warsaw Pact and collapse the Soviet Union in a "controlled" fashion; (10) groom stealth communists as candidates for high office in America and Western Europe. These would present themselves as "moderates," but would operate as "penetration" agents dedicated to facilitating critical aspects of the strategy; namely, economic sabotage and reduction or *diversion* of U.S. military resources.

The complexity of the intelligence strategy is impossible to overstate. Yet it's overarching concept is simple and consistent with past communist practices. Those who carry out the "final phase" of the strategy were instructed not to worry about losses in the course of a "grand maneuver." The *modus operandi* was to follow the example of Dzerzhinsky's Trust operation, which facilitated Lenin's New Economic Policy and opened the Soviet Union to Western investment in the 1920s.

Because the West is blind with regard to Soviet plans, the economic optimism of the free market would naturally compel all shades of political opinion to accept the "collapse of communism" as genuine. A mad rush for markets would follow, though most of the invested monies would be lost.

The capitalists, under this dynamic, could not act with prudence. They would swallow the bait and find themselves on the sharp end of a hook — seduced by their Bolshevik enemy into arrangements that would compromise them and their commercial system. (A similar deception game was already unfolding vis-a-vis China.) Meanwhile, conservative pundits would be loathe to admit they'd been duped about winning the Cold War. Protecting their reputations, America's leading conservatives would be first in line to keep the deception going — despite an ever-growing body of unexplained facts (for example, the continuing advance of communism in Africa and Latin America). Anyone who dared to question the triumphalist narrative would be ostracized as an alarmist.

There is much more to this picture, having to do with joint KGB and military intelligence operations, ideological subversion, terrorism, national liberation movements, organized crime and drug trafficking. Because these operations involve strategic directions of the Soviet military *and* the KGB, it is best to outline them separately.

The long-range strategy called for increased training for leaders of revolutionary movements — in civilian, military and intelligence areas of expertise. As noted by Joseph Douglass, "The founding of Patrice Lumumba University in Moscow is an example of one of the early measures taken to modernize Soviet revolutionary leadership training."

The Russians also decided to set up terrorist training camps. This training took place under the umbrella of supporting "national liberation" movements connected with the Comintern's previous decolonization policy.

As part of the sustained "liberation" offensive in Latin America (especially Colombia), the Soviets and their Czech allies became involved with international drug and narcotics trafficking. According to Douglass,

> Drugs were incorporated into the strategy for waging revolutionary warfare as a political and intelligence weapon for deployment against 'bourgeois societies' and as a mechanism for recruiting agents of influence around the world.

In advance of the drug trafficking offensive, Soviet intelligence infiltrated organized crime. The KGB also established "Soviet Bloc sponsored and controlled organized crime syndicates throughout the world," Douglass explained.[15]

Organized crime, drug trafficking and the attendant money laundering proved to be the most profitable strategic direction of all. Here was an irresistible combination for infiltrating the banks, for acquiring intelligence on political corruption, for control of dirty cops, dishonest intelligence operators, and businessmen. This was a factor in the rise of the Clintons, a major factor in the Afghan wars, the Contra War in Nicaragua, and the wars of Pablo Escobar and the FARC. Terrorists could be funded by such operations.

The related strategic directions of sabotage, diversionary operations, and terrorist "armies" could now be fed with supplies of illicit cash (laundered by banks and protected by dirty politicians). According to Jan Sejna, "The network for this activity was to be in place by 1972." The Soviet decision to enter organized crime occurred in 1955, and became part of the long-range strategy in subsequent years.

As the "world bourgeoisie" accepted the liberalization of the Soviet Union and the collapse of communism as genuine, the Russian and Chinese strategists organized a diversionary terrorist operation. The Soviet GRU defector, Victor Suvorov described it as follows:

> [Widespread terrorist and sabotage operations in advance of World War III] are known officially in the GRU as the "preparatory period," and unofficially as the "overture." The overture is a series of large and small operations the purpose of which is, before actual military operations begin, to weaken the enemy's morale,

15 Joseph D. Douglass, Jr., *Red Cocaine: The Drugging of America and the West,* p. 47 e pp. 17-18: https://portalconservador.com/livros/Joseph-Douglass-Red-Cocaine-The-Drugging-of-America-and-the-West.pdf

> create an atmosphere of suspicion, fear and uncertainty, and divert the attention of the enemy's armies and police forces to a huge number of different targets, each of which may be the object of the next attack.
>
> The overture is carried out by agents of the secret services ... and by mercenaries recruited by intermediaries. The principal method employed at this stage is "gray terror," that is, a kind of terror which is not conducted in the name of the Soviet Union. The Soviet secret services do not at this stage leave their visiting cards, or leave other people's cards. The terror is carried out in the name of already existing extremist groups not connected in any way with the Soviet Union, or in the name of fictitious organizations.[16]

We should not be surprised to learn that KGB/FSB defector Alexander Litvinenko pointed to Putin as the true sponsor of al Qaeda in an interview with a Polish newspaper (which will be posted tomorrow on this site).[17] The following year Litvinenko was fatally poisoned with radioactive polonium 210 by agents of the Russian special services.[18]

This overview touches on the broad sweep of events leading up to the COVID-19 biological attack. If anyone doubts the existence of a long-range Sino-Soviet strategy to defeat the West, and if anyone doubts that COVID-19 is part of that strategy, they have only to reference Russia's support for China at this time. This support comes in the form of a disinformation campaign against the West.[19] Why would elements of the Russian state-controlled media,

16 Viktor Suvorov, *Spetsnaz*: https://books.google.com/books/about/Spetsnaz.html?id=L-VI2AAAACAAJ&source=kp_book_description

17 See "*On Global Terrorism: FAKT interview with A. Litvinenko*", 31 mar. 2020: https://jrnyquist.blog/2020/03/31/on-global-terrorism-fakt-interview-with-a-litvinenko/

18 "Anatoliy Golitsyn: The Key to Understanding Today's World Situation": https://thecontemplativeobserver.wordpress.com/tag/new-lies-for-old/

19 Kremlin disinformation: https://www.theguardian.com/world/2020/mar/18/russian-media-spreading-covid-19-disinformation

Kremlin disinformation narrative: https://euvsdisinfo.eu/report/the-coronavirus-is-part-of-a-us-war-against-russia-and-china/

Iran and China *all* suggest that COVID-19 is an American biological weapon? No telltale could tell us more.

Russia, Iran and China are led by persons who want to destroy the United States of America. You can deny it all you want, but the evidence is staring you in the face. The timing of the COVID-19 outbreak is more than suspicious. Too many details suggest that an attack has begun. But the West continues to sleep. It is said we are "fighting a virus."

Oh no. Something else is coming for us; something that is much larger and more deadly.

China and Russia vs. America

04/03/2020

> The fact that I will visit Russia, our friendly neighbor, shortly after assuming the presidency, is testimony to the great importance China places on its relations with Russia.
>
> — XI JINPING

The President of the United States mobilized a million servicemen on 27 March. The "essential staff" of the Pentagon was placed 2,000 feet underground in a Colorado bunker. Our two aircraft carriers in the Western Pacific, the USS Roosevelt and USS Ronald Reagan are stuck in port because of COVID-19. There are US military moves in the Caribbean which could be masking preparations against Cuba, Venezuela and Nicaragua.

What is the U.S. Government seeing? What are they thinking? Mobilization precedes war the way cooking precedes eating. Is President Trump signaling the Chinese? Is he warning them by way of non-verbal cues? Across the world a dividing line is being drawn. On one side, countries are lining up behind China. On the other side, countries are lining up with the USA.

An interesting event in all this: China and Russia have both closed their borders from the outside — so nothing can get in. This suggests more serious moves to come. Economically, the sealing of a border signifies economic autarchy. It suggests a pre-planned stockpiling of imports in advance of the crisis. It suggests, in fact, that Moscow and Beijing have been preparing for this exact moment — *that they planned it.*

Are you shocked?

The closing of the Russian and Chinese borders to incoming traffic has an additional meaning. It not only suggests the possible deployment of a more deadly COVID-19 strain, but presents a barrier to viral retaliation from the West. Here is a strange admixture of fear and military forethought. Of the 195 countries on earth, China and Russia are the only ones isolating themselves from all others. They are also using propaganda outlets to accuse the United States of starting a biological war. This in itself is a prewar operational measure. It's a justification for making war on America.

Why would such a justification be deployed by Russia, China and Iran?

As it happens, China has spent many years preparing for war. And so has Russia. Not only have the two "former" communist bloc partners been stockpiling gold — a classic war prep — but they have been building and modernizing their nuclear forces.

The recent congressional testimony of Admiral Charles A. Richard, commander of the United States Strategic Command, presented the following dire picture on 27 February of this year:

> ...the Nation is at a critical juncture regarding the future of our nuclear forces. Since the end of the Cold War, we led the world in reducing our nuclear stockpile while increasing transparency. While we reduced the number and types of nuclear weapons in our arsenal, our adversaries went in the other direction and continued to modernize and expand their strategic capabilities. We now find ourselves fielding a reduced Cold War era arsenal against a larger, more modern, and more varied Russian force and a continually improving and growing Chinese force.

Need I remind the reader that KGB Major Anatoliy Golitsyn predicted his exact situation? In Golitsyn's 1984 book, *New Lies for Old*, we learn about a Soviet long-range strategy predicated on a "deceptive liberalization." We learn about a plan where the Communist Party gives up power in the Soviet Union. We learn about the planned collapse of the Warsaw Pact Alliance. According to Golitsyn, if the West accepted these changes as genuine, the Chinese and Russians would fully exploit America's naïveté. America would stop building nuclear weapons while Russia and China would build and modernize. Then would come the moment of "one clenched fist" — when Russia and China would unite to overpower America.

Can it be a coincidence that Golitsyn's prediction came true? — that nearly all his predictions have come true?

Considering Admiral Richard's 27 February testimony to Congress, I think we are nearing the moment of "one clenched fist." The enemy's plan is coming into full view.

It is shameful that almost nobody knows the real history of the last thirty years. And now we must endure this pathetic admission from America's STRATCOM commander — as he begs a bankrupt U.S. government for the money to rebuild a rotting nuclear deterrent. Will there be any money left in the treasury after China's biological attack has crashed the federal government's tax revenues? Given the many warnings of defectors and dissidents, it is clear that nobody in our intelligence, government, think tanks or universities did their homework. None saw the dire consequences in store after swallowing Moscow's baited hook — along with the promise of cheap labor from China.

What must we do now? What can we do?

There are grim political tasks in store. We have to set our own house in order. In terms of our business community and their political hirelings, there must be a day of reckoning. All businessmen and politicians who made money from the Chinese communists, who facilitated Beijing's policies of subversion and war, should be driven out of business, or forced from office, and ostracized. There need be no law, no government edict. Let it be the personal, spontaneous act of every American to shun the CCP's American "partners in crime."

It is vital that we cultivate proper feelings in this regard. As a start, watch the profound and emotional declaration of this brave Chinese woman (below). A few weeks ago she stood up against the Chinese Communist Party (CCP). She has no one on her side, no hope but arrest, no future but execution. Yet she tells the truth. Watch her shining example. Stand with her. *The enemy she decries is your enemy.*[20]

20 NOTES AND LINKS:
https://www.youtube.com/watch?v=VfN_jtYmqG4

The Triumph of Inversion

04/10/2020

> Socialism will usher in a new era in this country. The great wealth of the United States will for the first time be for the benefit of all the people.
>
> — PROGRAM OF THE COMMUNIST PARTY USA

Twenty-one years ago I was having coffee in Washington, DC, with former British MP John Browne, Newsmax chief editor Missy Kelly, and Col. Stanislav Lunev, a GRU defector to the United States. John was waxing eloquent on the idea that Margaret Thatcher and Ronald Reagan had saved the West from socialism. As Missy showed interest in John's thesis, Lunev leaned over and whispered in my ear, "I don't understand this." Lunev then added, "America is the Marxist paradise. Russia is dog-eat-dog capitalism."

Along the same lines, Clare Berlinski recently made the point that the USSR "could be" defined as a "far-right, authoritarian regime." But that's going too far. In my *Origins of the Fourth World War,* I suggested there is no political right whatsoever; that everyone is now on the left.

How can I justify this?

The leading ideal of our time, embraced from east to west, is leftist. It doesn't matter if this ideal finds expression in an authoritarian government or a democracy. America is on the left because everything here is done in the name of "the people."

Who are "the people," in this context? They are those who are portrayed as "less than equal," who must be given a leg up, who must be *made equal.* And why must they be *made equal*? Because socialism is the coming religion — a secular religion — where man's salvation is accomplished by political leveling.

Look at what children are being taught in school. Egalitarian indoctrination is everywhere. Socialism has hijacked the education system. As a result, you cannot talk about the weather without risking an earful on climate change from a college student.

Our taxes cannot begin to cover the expenses resulting from socialism's growing list of demands. We are gradually going broke, and with the economic panic resulting from the COVID-19 pandemic, financial collapse is now inevitable.

The free market is only free for the moment. Once the markets flatline, the usual suspects will blame capitalism for "failing." It takes very little imagination to envision what follows. Disastrous government intervention, followed by shortages, followed by rationing, followed by worse shortages. The United States military won't be funded after our leftists take power. Once America is disarmed, everyone will see the nuclear missiles in Russia and China as supporting the socialist agenda. Given the irresistible power of those missiles, how could Socialism be repealed? How could the United States regain its sovereignty?

As a side note: Perhaps it is an exaggeration to say "everyone" is on the left. I'm not on the left. I assume that my readers aren't on the left. But practically speaking, what can we do? We are stuck with a society where the leading institutions are dominated by leftists.

Socialism is a religion. It is not a pretense because people do believe in it. Even if all leftist regimes turn out, in practice, to create an authoritarian order, it does not make leftists into "right wingers." They are still worshippers of a leftist ideal: Namely, that all men should be brothers; that the world should be as one; that there is no heaven, so we must try and build a perfect world here on earth. These are the ideals that make the left dangerous, that lead to "the immanentizing of the gnostic eschaton."

Socialism is a dangerous creed because the socialists are obliged to fill God's office. They must rescue man from the destitution of his condition in the capitalist "state of nature." It is a grandiose mission that requires *real* power. And the greatest power available to man is state power. Thus, the socialists have amended their egalitarianism in principle — preferring the formula, "From each according to his ability, to each according to his need." This ideological refinement avoids the paradox of a left-wing hierarchy. Inequality may be allowed for the greater good.

It is a mistake to say that authoritarianism is strictly a right-wing phenomenon. Clare Berlinski is confusing herself when she suggests that the USSR was a right wing polity. The Soviet ideal was leftist. Whatever hierarchy they built, in practice, turned out to be an inversion of aristocracy — with the worst criminals and psychopaths in the highest offices. This is Russia's ruling principle to this day.

In fact, some theorists have claimed that fascism is also a phenomenon of the left. It is collectivist in the same sense as communism. It is revolutionary, guaranteeing that envious mediocrities — like Himmler or Goebbels — will govern in the shadow of a Hitler. Look how closely this follows the Soviet model, where Stalin, with his freakish retinue of dwarves and misfits, carried on a paranoid campaign against society itself. In contrast to this, Aristocracy is an ideal — in principle — where the very best people ought to hold rank, where the good and the noble are asked to lead, protect and defend the community. However poorly this ideal has been practiced, it never sank to the level of Lenin's dictatorship of the lumpen proletariat, or the gangland police state of Kang Sheng.

The noble man allows freedom to others because he is noble. The ignoble man lives in fear that others, discovering his wicked intentions, will denounce him — because he is, indeed, a villain.

Freedom is also about checks and balances, which the left and the fascists abhor. The inferior man can govern only by criminal means. He could not survive in a proper constitutional setting. He who is sinister by nature opposes checks and balances out of paranoia. He opposes the aristocratic veto on envy, on the mob, on the lower instincts. He suspects a plot against himself and will not stand for it.

We find many related lessons in the history of the ancient Roman Republic, with plebeians vying against patricians. Only we find the plebeians had more sense than today's "Democrats." What evolved in Rome was a relatively balanced constitution, generally thought to be one of the most effective and unique forms of government in all history. By no means was it utopian, or something above reproach. It was something far more significant. It was durable and sensible, and produced a competent collective leadership — in the conscript fathers of the Roman Senate. This was a governing body that united Italy and conquered the Mediterranean. Harking back to the Rape of Lucretia, it's ideal was liberty (that is, aristocratic liberty, not proletarian liberty).

One might similarly praise the British system of government after the Glorious Revolution — despite its corruption and venality and all the wickedness of its imperialism. But again, there was an aristocracy back then. It allowed for the steady moral improvement of society. It also evolved toward liberty.

There was never a perfect time — an ideal yesterday. But there were centuries of improvement and growth. Now we've had a century of decadence and decline. You ask when this began? One should give a different date for Britain than for America. Would 1911 suffice for Britain? (If my memory can be trusted, in 1911 the House of Lords lost its veto power).

When we get to the theory that "all men are created equal," we are removing the mainspring of constitutional government. The door is open to leveling. How can you have a real system of checks and balances when you have eliminated the classical Aristocratic basis for it? If all men belong to one order of society, what happens to our concept of rank? — of conscript fathers? — of motherhood and fatherhood? — of family? — of authority itself? One is left with a bureaucrat — a nobody invested with absolute power, enviously disposed toward his superiors.

The leveling wind of egalitarianism leads to other pathologies as well. It not only takes away class. It attempts to do away with tribe. It attempts to do away with sexual differences. This may be suitable to individualists — who freakishly persevere in developing their unique individuality outside the limitations of tribe. But most people cannot exist as atoms — that is, as solitary individuals. They find it to be an unbearable burden. Alas, *thinking* is the most dreadful drudgery!

And then, under the egalitarian flag, you have the problem of parties competing to give "the people" more and more "things," basing their power on an unchecked welfare state consumerism. Bankruptcy is only a matter of a war, a market collapse, or a pandemic.

When I say the *political right* no longer exists, that everyone is on the left, I am saying that the representative class of the right — the iron spine of every organic constitution — is gone. The very idea of a proper ruling class has been delegitimized. The political right is now an ersatz right. It is a self-misunderstood collective whose conservatism is underlaid with leftist presuppositions. That is why they inevitably give in to the far left. If you share the premises of the left, you will not be able to hold out against the left's arguments. And this is what we are routinely treated to. This is what we have all witnessed.

It's important to add that a system of checks and balances, within a constitution, entirely depends on real class distinctions. Once you do away with aristocracy as a construct, you will be stuck with an egalitarian oligarchy — the most degenerate form of oligarchy. It is a regime where "all men are created equal," with no social standpoint from which to check the licentious urges of the people — with no argument for stopping the people from devouring their own seed corn.

To make this case to an educated person is not so difficult. Given a materialist plebeianism, with all its misunderstandings, a clever person keeps quiet. As H.L. Mencken once wrote, "Democracy is the system where the people get what they want, and get it good and hard."

What we call the "right" (today) is merely a mix of nationalist/traditionalist/Christian sentiments standing on principles of plebeian supremacy. What we call the left is also built on plebeian supremacy, but opposed to tribal and religious folkways. One might say our traditional folkways are in an advanced state of decay and/or disintegration.

After this long explanation many readers will disagree, clinging to the idea that there really is a political right, because common usage acknowledges there is. But I would offer one more argument, if I may. Language is important, and we must always fight to preserve it from the machinations of political subversives. As an example of such corruption, the word "marriage" was recently redefined by the Supreme Court; whereas through all history heretofore marriage meant the union of man and woman, it now has no such meaning. If a supposedly conservative Supreme Court can redefine marriage, and nobody hangs them as traitors to God and country, then the right has no real existence at all. The scandal is laid bare, though almost no one is scandalized.

When language is politically debauched, especially by the left, it makes the rotting carcass of the body politic smell ever riper. What then, if the so-called *political right*, does exactly the same thing as the left? — Debauching language by accepting the redefinition an essential word, without a peep!

The communist party has a saying: "Today's left is tomorrow's center, today's center is tomorrow's right, etc." And this goes to the heart of it. The political spectrum has been steadily moving to the left for a hundred years. This was aptly demonstrated by Tim Groseclose in a book titled *Left Turn*. He proves — with remarkable dexterity — that the majority Democrat congress in 1980 was considerably to the right of the Republican Congress of 1999. He uses objective criteria, so there can be no arguing the point.

Of course, rank order has not entirely disappeared. It fades by inches, more senile and decrepit, decade after decade. The leveling is steady and continuous. Socialism holds us in a death-grip. It can be slowed but never stopped. Trump is not to the right of Ronald Reagan. He is to the left of Reagan. The same is true of all Tory PMs after Thatcher. Leftward, leftward, always leftward. All enemies to the right. The outstanding individual who appears, against all odds, to slow the march leftward, is an exception to the rule. One person can momentarily stop the process, but one person does not an aristocracy make.

Psychological Warfare in the Midst of a Biological Attack

04/15/2020

> ...we'll never use the damn germs, so what good is biological warfare as a deterrent? If somebody uses germs on us, we'll nuke 'em.
>
> RICHARD NIXON

Professor Yanzhong Huang is a political scientist and "expert" in pandemics. He is an exemplar of the mainstream media's approach to the COVID-19 bio-weapon question. It might be more appropriate to list him as an expert in "polemics." Professor Huang clearly dislikes the idea the virus was weaponized in a Chinese lab. One might even say he is sensitive on the question.

He has written an article in *Foreign Affairs*, titled "U.S.-Chinese Distrust Is Inviting Dangerous Coronavirus Conspiracy Theories, And Undermining Efforts to Contain the Epidemic."[21] The very title of Professor Huang's article reads like an indictment of anyone who says the virus is an engineered bio-weapon. He alludes to the *Zero Hedge* article which quoted my *Epoch Times* piece on the subject. Professor Huang says, in essence, that such views (as mine) endanger world peace and "Sino-American cooperation."

But today's "Sino-American cooperation" has never signified real peace. It has always been a form of low-intensity warfare, practiced by China, while America sleeps — unaware that its position is gradually eroding away.

To obfuscate the question of the virus's weaponization, the best defense is (evidently) a strong offense. Huang denies the virus came out of a bio-weapon program. He smears anyone who says otherwise as a "dangerous ... conspiracy theorist." He blames *Zero Hedge* for quoting me. He says they are contributing to the severity of the pandemic. To say that Professor Huang's article is honest, in this regard, is to miss the underlying political purpose behind his statements.

21 https://www.google.com/amp/s/www.foreignaffairs.com/articles/united-states/2020-03-05/us-chinese-distrust-inviting-dangerous-coronavirus-conspiracy%3famp

What is more important: Professor Huang is not alone in what he says. Marxist academics and media leftists have tilted favorably toward communist regimes in the past, and will continue to do so. This kind of thing is not entirely unexpected from the magazine of the Council on Foreign Relations (CFR), where Professor Huang is a fellow. Some of us suspect the CFR is a hub for communist infiltrators, piggy-backing on the naive internationalism of the capitalist elite. In effect, Professor Huang uses the CFR as a platform for attacking anti-communists as "dangerous conspiracy theorists." Those of us who write about the communist threat are, at best, ignored by the mainstream media. In this instance, we are singled out for ostracism; — *that is to say, Establishment ostracism*. We have no voice. But the Chinese Communist professor, promoting Chinese Communist disinformation, has a voice. The Establishment gives him a platform to attack those who warn the West about Beijing's intentions.

Professor Huang and his kind are readily published in all the mainstream newspapers and magazines. From his privileged position, this foreigner from mainland China guides American opinion. *Who is he? What does he represent?*

It was interesting to read the many positive student reviews he received as a professor at Seton Hall University.[22] But among these are some negative evaluations: "I don't like him. Bad attitude toward some students…." — and even more specific: "This man is ignorant, stubborn, disrespectful, and very difficult to comprehend. *A hidden Chinese communist*." [Italics added.]

There seems to have been animosity between this professor from Red China and a subset of his American students. Was this animosity ideological? Is Professor Huang beholden to the government in Beijing? Why did *Foreign Affairs* magazine invite him to write a propaganda piece?

Or is it propaganda?

Professor Huang argues for good relations between communist China and the United States. Naturally, none of us want a war; but the Chinese communists are not trustworthy friends. They have committed many crimes, they have damaged America's economy using trade as a weapon — stealing technology, corrupting our political system with cash, making us dependent on supply chains that are now used as weapons of economic and medical coercion.

22 https://www.ratemyprofessors.com/ShowRatings.jsp?tid=336548

We see, in this prestigious magazine, the magazine of the Council on Foreign Relations, a readiness to blacken the name of anyone who suspects the People's Republic of China of a serious treaty violation in connection with the COVID-19 virus. The article is a clear warning to every writer in America. Get in line behind China's power. Praise China's good intentions. Berate those who warn of a Chinese communist threat.

If you want to know what a biological war looks like, consider our empty town squares and the overloaded morgues of New York City. If you want to know what psychological warfare looks like, read Professor Huang's article in *Foreign Affairs*.[23]

23 NOTES AND LINKS:

https://www.google.com/amp/s/www.nytimes.com/2020/01/01/opinion/china-swine-fever.amp.html

https://www.ncbi.nlm.nih.gov/m/pubmed/26552008/

https://apnews.com/PR%20Newswire/ff548c99a03afb0d69bb7871f7cd4fc0

What President Trump Must Do to Stop China's Invasion

04/17/2020

An appeaser is one who feeds a crocodile – hoping it will eat him last.

WINSTON CHURCHILL

The President of the United States must publicly change his position on China. In the past, President Trump has described China's President, Xi Jinping, as his "friend." It is necessary, at this pivotal moment, for President Trump to say that President Xi is *not* his friend. He must admit, instead, that Xi is America's enemy. To do otherwise is to paper over President Xi's many hostile actions, his preparations for war, and his policy of blaming America for the pandemic.

It is time for the President of the United States to face the truth — and tell the truth — about Xi Jinping and the Chinese Communist Party. It is time to return enmity for enmity, to reciprocate communist China's hostility, and prepare to repel their aggression. For they have used our openness and generosity against us. They have taken our kindness for weakness. They have practiced treachery on our good faith, and they have made war on our economy. We can no longer refer to communists as "friends." *They are enemies.*

We must *hear the truth* from our president about communist China's fifth column in the United States. This truth must not be softened, or watered down with the usual stupidities about free trade and peace; domestic concord or racial tolerance. We are in a life-or-death situation now. Enemy propaganda and enemy propagandists should be identified and ostracized. We cannot allow communist agents of influence to turn the tables, blame America, condemn patriotism, and open the country to enemy attack.

Regarding those who wish to return the country to economic dependence on China: *Communist regimes will always use trade as weapon.* They will corrupt everyone and everything they touch — businessmen and politicians, sports stars and Hollywood producers. To negotiate with communist China is a fool's errand. A treaty, for them, is like a pie crust — meant to be broken.

The history of communism is long, and the criminal nature of all communist regimes cannot be denied. There is no excuse for having relations with them. To make partners of them is to become *their partner in crime.*

President Xi made a conscious decision to allow the CCP virus to incubate in Wuhan until the Chinese New Year — the biggest calendar day of outgoing travel from China. Reports about the outbreak in China are not ambiguous in this regard.

What happened in Wuhan was directed — every step of the way — from the office of President Xi. Party officials were forced to allow crowds to congregate during the New Year holiday in Wuhan. They were compelled by Beijing to host 40,000 people at the city potluck, even though an infectious form of viral pneumonia was spreading through the city. Xi's intentions can be read through dozens of news reports and official edicts. Xi only allowed Wuhan to fight the pandemic after the city's holiday visitors had returned abroad — carrying the infection to Europe, Australia and North America.

The decisions made by the Chines leaders, in this regard, were not improvised. Chinese strategic decisions are carefully thought out in advance. Years of study had already gone into bat viruses at the Wuhan BSL-4 virology lab. In fact, the placement of the BSL-4 facility in Wuhan defies logic — unless we recognize Beijing's remarkable foresight.

In order to launch a biological attack, China would need an alibi to avoid retaliation. The alibi would have two sides: one alibi would focus blame on America, the other would mask Xi's malevolent intentions.

The two-sided alibi would, by necessity, have the following features: (1) To forestall retaliation against China, evidence would be planted regarding safety issues and a leak at a Chinese virology lab; (2) to silence criticism from the Chinese public, Communist Party officials would claim the CIA or U.S. military planted the virus as part of an attack on the Chinese people.

To make these parallel alibis deployable at the same time, Chinese planners would first have considered which Chinese city an enemy would target in a biological war. As the central hub of China's rail and waterway communications, Wuhan would be the logical choice. Therefore the Chinese planners would have built their strategy around a Wuhan infection scenario. To make this scenario compatible with the "leaky lab" alibi, China's strategist would also have to place their BSL-4 facility in Wuhan, instead of a more remote location in the Gobi Desert.

It is impractical to carry on a biological war without giving the first iteration of the virus to your own people. Because an alibi is paramount, Wuhan had to become the center of the pandemic. Chinese people would be the first to suffer. Therefore, the initial iteration of the weapon would be designed according to the principles of asymmetric warfare, with the following stipulation: First, the weapon would strategically benefit China; second, it would harm the West.

Consider the virus's effects. It typically kills the elderly and infirm. From a Darwinian standpoint, the virus favors survival of the fittest. For An overpopulated country like China, such a viral outbreak is useful for thinning the herd. Given a half century under China's "one child policy," that herd is not only too large, but too old. Meanwhile, America and the West are irrevocably committed to protecting the weakest and least fit members of society. The West could be counted on to expend untold trillions to stop the virus. China would suffer a brief shock, of course, and economic losses, but these losses would be made up in the end. China would be ordered back to work — with countless elderly citizens sealed alive in body bags for cremation.

Do you think such a plan is too monstrous for someone like Xi Jinping?

Xi Jinping is a Communist. His heroes are Mao, Hitler and Stalin — the three greatest mass murderers in history. Do you see a connecting theme here? Come now! Such a person is easily capable of euthanizing the elderly! Why would he hesitate under the circumstances?

Xi Jinping is not a normal person. He belongs to the ancient Machiavellian traditions of Chinese philosophy. He is steeped in the writings of Sun Tzu and Han Fei-Tzu. These thinkers believed in the ruthless use of force and fraud. They opposed the idea that rulers could be friends. Such an idea, in the Chinese legalist tradition, is criticized as dangerous. Therefore, Xi is not President Trump's friend.

In 1999 I interviewed a famous Chinese dissident, Harry Wu. He spent 19 years in the Lao Gai camp system. When I asked Wu to describe China's leaders, he said, "They are murderers."

How can President Trump be friends with a murderer? Xi Jinping imprisons and executes honest Chinese citizens for telling the truth. And like all murderers, Xi Jinping lies — if only to hide his many crimes.

Xi Jinping's intelligence services have been using international commerce and corporate deals to infiltrate our political system, steal our technology and undermine our economy. His agents have used money as a carrot and a stick. They have bought politicians. They have corrupted our media. They have entered our research institutes.

President Xi's agents infest Washington. Some of us think these agents should be driven out. Give us one good reason they should be permitted to stay in our capital? — and give us a reason that is *not* tainted with cowardice or greed.

Think, now, what is coming. Ask yourself where our relationship with communist China is taking us. Xi Jinping is a follower of Mao Zedong. In 1958 Mao gave his generals a strategic directive. He said: Prepare the People's Liberation Army for the day when Chinese troops will land in Manila and San Francisco.

This directive is still in effect. How do we know? Because China has built an amphibious fleet with a six thousand mile range.[24] This is exactly the range needed to land Chinese troops on the U.S. West coast — in San Francisco. Two divisions have been prepared for an immediate landing (to secure port facilities). Does anyone think Xi needed amphibious transports with a six thousand mile range to invade Taiwan? Defeating Taiwan gets him nowhere. Taiwan is not his primary objective. He must defeat the United States. If America loses a war, Taiwan will surrender without a fight. What, then, is the point of invading Taiwan?

Bypass it!

When a country develops military capabilities, like an amphibious fleet with a six thousand mile range, you have to sit up and take notice if you are six

24 https://www.globalsecurity.org/military/world/china/yuzhao-capabilities.htm

Note: the range of the type 071 transport is "several thousand nautical miles" for a transport that can carry 1,000 troops, plus armored vehicles and (in later versions) helicopters. Ten were built according to one source. There may be 15 presently, but some of the articles appear confused. Add to this existing assault carriers with similar range and China can deliver two divisions of 18 battalions to the U.S. West Coast. the actual lift capacity may be higher, given other ships and conversions not listed.

thousand miles away. Strategic thought guides China's force development. The attack range of these troops was not haphazardly assigned.

Consider the grand strategy behind Xi's war preparations: Biological weapons soften, then cripple the target country. Nuclear weapons and cruise missiles, launched from hidden locations, can destroy America's naval, air and strategic assets. China's amphibious fleet then lands on the West coast and secures port facilities for follow-up merchant ships loaded with men, tanks and artillery.

Is the invasion of the United States by China possible? Yes — *it is more than possible*. The Chinese have been preparing to invade us for decades. They have been secretly stockpiling supplies in Mexico, as Journalist Scott Gulbransen learned many years ago. He published his findings in a book, *The Silent Invasion*.

There is an old Chinese saying attributed to Lao Tzu: "A journey of a thousand miles begins with a single step."

Years ago Gen. Chi Haotian, China's defense minister, made a speech to high-level party officials. He spoke of a future biological attack "to clean up America." He said that Beijing's threat to Taiwan was diversionary. The real plan, he said, was to invade and occupy the United States.

Eighteen years ago a British journalist contacted me. She had been with a documentary film crew, interviewing Chinese sailors during amphibious exercises off the coast of China. She asked how they felt about practicing an invasion of Taiwan. The sailors were baffled. "We're not practicing to invade Taiwan," they told her. "We're practicing to invade America."

When Chinese military officials realized what the British crew had uncovered, they confiscated the cameras and the recordings. She told her experiences to colleagues in the UK — but she was ostracized for being "anti-Chinese." She heard of my work through a reader and contacted me. "Listen," she said. "I damaged my career. But I have to tell someone in America. You must promise not to use my name in telling this story. I have to make a living. I have to get my career back."

Xi Jinping is not President Trump's friend. He is America's enemy. The Chinese have been preparing for war. Their Russian, Iranian, Cuban, and North Korean allies have also been preparing.

I represent a growing number of Americans who don't want to hear President Trump refer to Xi Jinping as his "friend." Xi is a murderous dictator, and he is our enemy. We need President Trump to acknowledge this.

There isn't a moment to lose.

The Lies We Believe

04/23/2020

> The people who brought Vladimir Putin from St. Petersburg to Moscow never cared about his credentials as a specialist in developing business. For them he was an expert in controlling business. All the time Putin worked in St. Petersburg, he played an official role as deputy mayor and chairman of the Committee [for Foreign Liaison], but, behind the scenes Mr. Putin operated in his most important identity — the Case Officer. In St. Petersburg, Vladimir Putin was an 'operative.' Businessmen were not partners but targets.
>
> — FIONA HILL AND CLIFFORD GADDY
> MR. PUTIN: OPERATIVE
> *IN THE KREMLIN*, P. 166

Most people, including journalists and political leaders have the wrong idea about the "fall of the Soviet Union" and the changes in Russia. They also have the wrong idea about China.

Between outright nonsense repeated on television, and the subtle misreading of experts, the threat from Russia, and from China, has largely escaped notice. These two countries have cultivated a deceptive image of themselves. They have masked their hostile intentions; and despite Moscow and Beijing's bad behavior during the viral pandemic, we are still not learning.

In the quote above, Fiona Hill and Clifford Gaddy accurately describe Putin's function and usefulness to Russia's "post-Soviet" structures. They point to Putin's ongoing secret police activities, suggesting that economic liberalization in Russia was under control of state security. Putin, as an officer of State Security, was one of the controllers.

Russia's heralded transition to democracy and capitalism was fraudulent. It simply did not happen. We were misled by the false front of deputy mayors like Putin, and Russian big-shot "liberals" like Anatoliy Sobchak and Boris Yeltsin. The economy of the Soviet Union, which was largely a black market economy, was managed by the communists the same as before. Only the appearances changed.

In Karen Dawisha's excellent book, *Putin's Kleptocracy*, she quotes from a Spanish prosecutor's report on Russian involvement in narcotics trafficking and money laundering during the Yeltsin years. Dawisha quotes the prosecutor as follows: "[In Russia] one cannot differentiate between the activities of the government and OC [organized crime] groups." Furthermore, the KGB/FSB "control organized crime in Russia.... The FSB is 'absorbing' the Russia mafia" and — Dawisha adds, "using them for black operations on Russian territory." (Loc 263-269, Kindle Ed.)

It would not be safe to assume that organized crime took over Russia after 1991. It would be more accurate to say that the KGB and the old party structures took over (or activated) the various Russian mafias — turning them into instruments of state. As Arkady Vaksberg pointed out in his 1991 book on the Russian mafia, the regional factions of the Communist Party Soviet Union generated indigenous mafia clans. These were useful to the communists for a variety of reasons.

By way of explanation, Vaksberg received a letter as the Soviet Union was "collapsing." It was from a "devoted reader ... in close proximity to the organs of power," pseudonymously signing himself, V.N. Voloshin. According to Voloshin the liberalization of the Russian economy was set up to fail.

> Our leaders are deliberately destabilizing the country.... everything is being done to provoke the people into crying, as one: 'Let us have strong government back.'
>
> *THE SOVIET MAFIA*, P. 266.

Voloshin further explained how criminals were recruited by the politicians: "We 'hook' these people by letting them off petty crimes ... after which they conscientiously carry out our bidding."

> We [communists] operate as we always have, except that we have adopted a lower profile and changed our tactics. We have stopped taking protective measures ... but just gather information ...

> which will enable us … when the right moment comes. Everybody here curses the reforms and expects the fall of democracy, and it will happen sooner than you think. And the army is behind us too.
>
> IBID, P. 266-67.

Voloshin added, "The only thing which might save us is a complete disbanding if the KGB…." Of course, getting rid of the KGB was never part of the plan. In fact, the KGB became more powerful than ever, being critical to the capitalist facade of Russia's false liberalization. Here was a reform process that Polish scholar Wisla Suraska characterized as a "police-sponsored civil society" working toward "a police-sponsored revolution." (*How the Soviet Union Disappeared*, p. 49.)

Without subjecting the reader to an avalanche of books and analysis, here is but a flavoring of intelligent writings on the process we idiotically heralded as "the collapse of communism," or the "end of the Cold War." As noted by one Soviet official, Georgi Arbatov, in December 1988, Gorbachev's plan was to "take away the image of your enemy." The substance of that enemy would remain, preparing for war as the West relaxed its vigilance.

It is shameful that we have been fooled by the Russians and their Chinese allies. Conservative pundits like Sean Hannity and Patrick Buchanan, who would not deign to read Hill and Gaddy, would squirm to hear of Putin's deceptive gamesmanship. The truth would not only confuse such pundits, but draw them afield from their favorite narrative — namely, how Ronald Reagan won the Cold War.

To begin with an error at the beginning of your analysis, is to build an edifice of error, until the truth disappears from sight. And how do our lost conservatives go back? How do they retrace their steps? Who has the humility to walk back the last thirty years?

If you take all the specialized writings on the subject of China, on the subject of Russia, on the subject of nuclear war, you will find an undiscovered country. Today's ruling opinions, built on foundations of error and misunderstanding, are larded with untruth. The first and greatest of these untruths? —

THE COLLAPSE OF COMMUNISM

Conservatives have congratulated themselves, over and over, for defeating communism. But they have done no such thing. It is a classic case of conceit. To show how deluded this conceit is, recall the cancellation of the Rose Parade in Portland Oregon during 2017. It was cancelled because communists threatened violence against Republicans slated to participate.[25]

Communists have always been a small group. But they have always exercised power and influence beyond what their actual numbers would suggest. Why? Because they possess a missionary zeal. Because they are ruthless. Because they are better organized, better at strategy, better at infiltrating, sabotaging, and taking control.

Stopping a rose parade in Oregon, the communists flexed their muscles in an important city. But elsewhere in North America, the communists have become masters of an entire country. Consider Evan McGuire's 2018 piece in the *American Spectator*: "A Cold War Communist is Still Killing People in Nicaragua." Oh yes. Reagan won the Cold War, but the Sandinistas are ruling Nicaragua as before.[26]

Consider what happened in Venezuela. According to Luis Henrique Ball, writing in the *Pan American Post* of 17 December 2017, the oil-rich prize of Latin America was converted into a communist stronghold through a strategy of socialist incrementalism. What made this possible? Our conservatives made it possible, because they were no longer concerned with the spread of Marxism-Leninism. Why? Because they were swindled to believe that communism collapsed.

It is a disastrous situation. The "domino theory" has been overtaken by "domino history," where one country after another succumbs to communism. Sadly, the so-called "fall of the Soviet Union" did not herald the end of communist expansion, but opened a new phase — in which communism advanced from victory to victory, unrecognized and unhindered.

South Africa was the first great prize to be taken by the "defunct" communists after 1991. While the West celebrated an unearned victory over

25 https://www.google.com/amp/s/amp.theatlantic.com/amp/article/524334/

26 https://spectator.org/daniel-ortega-a-cold-war-communist-is-still-killing-people-in-nicaragua/

Leninism, the Leninists had a great laugh. The progress of communism in South Africa is a long story. In the 1950s the South African Communist Party ordered its members to join the African National Congress (ANC). As Richard Monroe pointed out in his *Lessons of the 1950s*, "Whatever the Communists did was done through the Congress movement.... Apart from one or two minor instances, nothing was done by the CP [Communist Party] which was in conflict with Congress policy."[27]

As history records, the National Party surrendered its monopoly of power to the African National Congress (ANC) in 1994. For the past 26 years South Africa has been a one-party state ruled by ANC communists who have followed the same gradualist strategy used by Hugo Chavez in Venezuela. Once again, a strategic country was conquered.

How strategic?

South Africa sits astride the Cape sea route used by Europe's oil tankers returning from the Persian Gulf. South Africa is also the "mineral storehouse" of Africa. Control of this country by the communist bloc, during the Cold War, would have frightened Western strategists. In military/economic terms, the bloc now enjoys a metals monopoly — with crippling implications for American aerospace. But no alarm has been raised. The conservatives do not care who governs South Africa — as long as the flow of precious metals continues. The West will soon discover its error when the communist bloc's economic offensive accelerates. Essentially, South Africa is now a communist bloc country ruled by the African Nation Congress — a false front behind which lurks the Russians and Chinese.

Like Zimbabwe and Namibia, Angola and Congo, South Africa has gone communist. In each country we are deceived about the rulers, who pretend to be democrats. But they are not Democrats. Once again, our own conceit gets the better of us. These countries are on China's side. They are on Russia's side. And this is no minor matter.

The myth of "the collapse of communism" could be turned into a very fat book. But who would buy such a book? The preference of the market is clear. People crave lies. They want myths. The communists have fostered these myths. As Lenin said at the advent of his New Economic Policy in 1921, "Tell the capitalists what they want to hear."

27 https://www.sahistory.org.za/archive/chapter-4-role-communist-party-anc-richard-monroe

NUCLEAR WAR CANNOT HAPPEN

People love nonsense, especially about war and peace. It's very soothing to imagine nobody will launch a nuclear war. It's also naive. There are people in this world who enjoy killing, who enjoy wrecking things, and find a self-affirming joy in annihilation for the sake of annihilation.

The normal world — the civilized world — never really explored the abyss of communism (as a psychological phenomenon). They did not see that a spirit of destruction for destruction's sake had appeared alongside Marxism. They failed to understand the fate in store when this spirit got hold of nuclear and biological weapons. They failed to understand that these weapons would be used — with reasonable explanations deployed in favor of usage. Here, the task of reason, deep down, would operate in accordance with a spirit of destruction.

Once the totalitarian powers got the bomb, a catastrophic war would only be a matter of time. It is only the optical illusion of the moment, when normal people project their own thinking onto totalitarian rulers, that we imagine a successful and perpetual regime of global restraint.

The illusion of perpetual peace is plutocratically endorsed, in theory and practice, by market hedonism. Here self-indulgence carries over to national policy — to the ever-poorer maintenance of our nuclear deterrent. We simply do not believe in nuclear war. We do not believe in bomb shelters or ballistic missile defense. There is something inherently mad, or dangerous, in thinking about it. But if we cannot think about it, how are we to defend against it? And that's the point. We long ago stopped taking it seriously. But Russia and China continue to make bombs and missiles. Meanwhile, ours rot in their silos.

And so we tell ourselves that a nuclear war cannot be won. We believe that these weapons can "destroy the planet" many times over. We imagine there is a "balance of terror." But these are stories you tell to children. The reality is very different. Readers are directed to consult Peter Vincent Pry's book, *Nuclear Wars: Exchanges and Outcomes* — which is Volume II of his larger work, *The Nuclear Balance.* Readers should also consult William Lee's *The ABM Treat Charade*, Sokolovskiy's classic *Soviet Military Strategy* and Sidorenko's *The Offensive.*

Or read up on Ted Bundy, the serial killer. He is a good model for this subject. He presents himself as a benign, friendly and rational human being. But he is actually murderous, malicious, and irrational. Put this type of person together with weapons of mass destruction and you have the perfect marriage. In this case, of course, the bridegroom has already found his bride.

It is, once again, the West's conceit — and the conceit of all "normal" people — that such a marriage can never happen. And so, year by year, our vigilance attenuates. We have bought into the deceptive talk of the totalitarians. We want to believe them. In time they will nuke us. What will stop them?

AMERICA IS INVINCIBLE

A flattering myth is always believed — to the ruin of the believer. Life is full of hard lessons, hard knocks, and hard heads. Many people born after World War II act as though America were indestructible. This goes a long way to explaining their readiness for destructive policies, destructive behaviors, and destructive thinking.

When the survival of a society or country is taken for granted, and every kind of social experimentation is indulged on the back of this conceit, you can be sure that a massive pile of rubble is going to be the legacy.

Look at the "baby boomer" generation: they grew up in a country that beat the Nazis and Imperial Japan. It was so rich, so powerful, that nothing could harm it. *So a great deal of harm was done*. The fabric of the society was not treated with gentleness or respect. Everything was subjected to ruthless criticism. Motherhood, patriotism, spanking, honesty, sobriety, chastity, common sense, anti-communism. It became fashionable to mock or discount these items. The more they were associated with the past, the more they were mocked.

In the 1980s Ronald Reagan's "morning in America" came to the fore, as if the Republic was not already staggering from internal wounds. The true situation was papered over, and insincerity was given wider latitude. This was the context in which we embraced Gorbachev and built China into a colossus. We did it with a Reagan Happy Face.

Invincible? *No*. Stupid and self-deceiving? *Yes*. Nothing here is intrinsic to invincibility. Everything conspires to strip the whole, preparing the way for a destructive nihilism. What we have, in America, is a series of illnesses — and COVID-19 is the least of them.

Aside from these points, *there are no invincible countries — especially in an age like ours.* Biological and nuclear weapons can destroy any country at any time. Especially, they can destroy a country that refuses to deal realistically with them; a country that wants to live as if such weapons do not require more from us.

CONCLUDING REMARKS

Everything written here is inadequate. But there is nonetheless value in what is written, if only as a point of departure. We cannot go forward at all unless we dispense with the corrupting myths listed above. But how do we overcome these myths?

A mountain of misunderstanding is not removed by a single sentence, a paragraph or an essay. No words suffice to remove such a mountain. But the words must be pronounced, nonetheless. And they must be pronounced in the face of those who violently disagree.

Perhaps the most disconcerting thing about writing these essays is the poor quality of the critics. It's tiresome to be criticized for things never said — for things that other people imagined; for example, that I advocate war with China or Iran or Russia; or that I want America to occupy the Middle East — or dominate the world.

I was treated, this week, to several emails from a libertarian writer who bragged that he reads this site — despite holding opinions "the opposite" of mine. He congratulated himself on his open-mindedness, reminding me that "patriotism is the last refuge of a scoundrel." He pointed to the Pentagon's wasteful spending, taking me to task for being a "warmonger" who seeks to convert others to "warmongering." He said, in essence, that I should not be concerned with the crimes of communist China when America has murdered hundreds of thousands of innocent people in the Middle East.

Forsooth, he implied I was a propagandist for baby-killers. He asked how I could say America is good while China is evil? China didn't bomb Iraq, he noted. China didn't invade Afghanistan. If I were a moral person I would be concerned with the immorality of Americans, not the immorality of Chinese communists. He said that China was no threat at all because our nuclear arsenal protects us. My concerns, he said, were therefore "silly."

He complained that my subsequent reply was "condescending." But how else should I answer a Jackass? A respectful reply would have sounded sarcastic. Accused of being a scoundrel and a warmonger, a friendly reply would have sounded obsequious, unmanly, perhaps even sniveling.

Patriotism is the last refuge of a scoundrel? Defending the country against China or Russia is "warmongering"?

My critic misunderstands the meaning of the word "patriotism" The word refers to fatherly love and concern for one's country. It does not signify inordinate praise for one's country, or bragging about the flag. It has nothing to do with making America "great again." What I express, in my writings, is real concern for the *survival* of my country. It is the only genuine expression of patriotism I know. Now let us consider what it signifies to list this genuine expression as "the last refuge of a scoundrel."

Who lives without concern for his country? Who takes his country for granted? Who glibly runs down his country on account of his ideology? Who mocks expressions of genuine patriotic concern as "silly"? Is that a patriot? No. What does such a writer love? The truth? His country? Or the sound of his own, empty words?

If I am wrong, it is NOT because I am a scoundrel. If war erupts it will NOT be on account of my "warmongering." It seems that there are two approaches to this subject. Only one is motivated by genuine concern for the country. The other is completely unserious.

Economic Crisis and Political Unrest

04/29/2020

You are waging economic warfare on Texas!

— SEN. TED CRUZ
TO THE SAUDI AMBASSADOR

KGB defector Anatoliy Golitsyn, who successfully predicted all the stages of the long-range communist bloc strategy in 1984, warned us about "the economic weapons of the bloc," grain and oil. We can readily see that precious metals are also part of this game. As events unfold, it is increasingly obvious that America is under intensive economic attack.

China, Russia, Iran and associated countries are applying pressure across the board to flip America's allies to their camp; most recently, Saudi Arabia is believed by some observers to have turned against Washington. In response to collapsing oil demand the Saudis did not reduce their oil production. Instead, they increased it — devastating America's oil industry.

Of course, the Saudis resent America's energy independence. They resented our past abandonment of their friend, President Hosni Mubarak of Egypt. They also resent our support for Shiite majority rule in neighboring Iraq. From their point of view, we are not the reliable ally of decades past. We are bungling, erratic, and exasperating.

Resentment is the mother of all treachery. And as we have — for so many years — believed the lies of Russia and China, why wouldn't we believe Saudi lies? So the Saudis raise their oil production in the midst of a glut, crash the price of oil to less than zero, and pretend they are doing it to hurt Russia when the whole thing is almost certainly Russia's idea. Who is the big winner in this game? The People's Republic of China gets to amass millions of barrels of cheap oil. Russia and Saudi Arabia drive American oil producers out of business. The U.S. economy takes a massive hit when it can least afford it.

Here is a strategic victory of incalculable significance. It appears that Moscow and Beijing have persuaded Saudi Arabia to align itself with *them*; for how can the relationship between Riyadh and Washington be restored after the U.S. energy market has been so devastated? An inevitable break — though officially denied — must come. And there will be a financial hit, as well, when the dollar comes under attack in the next round of battle. Here is Riyadh's Rubicon. There is no going back. And we must not forget an old rule of Bedouin politics: Treachery leads the betrayer to become more paranoid than his victim; for the betrayer must expect payback, and must thereafter distance himself from his victim.

If this is so, we are at the beginning of a very desperate sequence of events in which economic warfare becomes the heart and soul of the Great Game. It is easy to predict that the economic war against America will intensify. China and Russia will use all their economic weapons — and it is clear that they have been preparing for a long time.

The idea here is to cripple the U.S. economy, prevent effective U.S. war preparations, distract the political authorities with internal unrest, force currency devaluation, collapse tax revenues and incite domestic violence between various political camps, and divide America from its allies.

If Saudi Arabia has flipped to the Moscow-Beijing bloc, pressure will build for other countries to change sides. The unfolding economic reality will be grim, indeed, for any nation that stands with America; for America — as the defender of the West — is the primary target. Any nation that turns against the United States will be given a pass. Any nation that opposes the Moscow-Beijing bloc, will suffer accordingly.

Serious economic and financial pressure will be applied against Japan, the EU, Australia, India, Brazil, etc. If these powers give way to Russia and China, America's economic isolation will be assured. America would then suffer slow strangulation, economic collapse and domestic political turmoil. Even if the West holds firm, the economic weapons of the bloc will be deployed, one by one. The softening of allied resistance will be encouraged every step of the way. We will read and hear that China is the economic leader of the world. Who dares break their economic ties to China? Small countries and backward countries will tremble.

The threat against Japan and Europe will involve the denial of strategic resources coming from the Middle East and Africa. Moscow and Beijing are sure to make a series of devastating moves — long in preparation. The attack on America's oil industry, by collapsing oil prices, is only the beginning. China and Russia have been stockpiling gold and strategic resources for decades. They are laying siege to us, having already set aside the necessary supplies for a prolonged struggle. Their military units have been modernized, their nuclear arsenals upgraded — all in readiness prior to economic disruptions calculated to prevent America from ever catching up.

Are the people in Russia and China economically suffering? Yes. They suffer as subjects of autocratic regimes are destined to suffer — in every age, for all time. In China the ranks of the People's Armed Police have swollen. Revolution against the regime is impossible. Its organization is geared entirely toward security and the smashing of dissent. Disobedience is punishable by death. Who dares stand against the Chinese Communist Party? Its might is measured in millions of armed troops, missiles, nuclear weapons, and a blue water navy with its sights set on control of the Pacific Ocean.

The Russian and Chinese preparation for the present phase of economic warfare has been long and arduous. All American presidents, from Reagan to Obama, wittingly or unwittingly helped the Russians and Chinese achieve the advantages they now wield against us. Washington made a conscious decision to build up China. The United States is presently vulnerable to Moscow and Beijing's economic warfare. This is also due to years of fiscal irresponsibility and bad national habits. During decades of prosperity we encouraged indebtedness — at all levels of government, and in the private sector. Congress gave money to various interest groups. Welfare payments ballooned. Pensions ballooned. Obama Care was instituted and nobody had the courage to overturn it. Politicians have even suggested the concept of "guaranteed income." It was all madness. We could afford none of it, neither could we afford the military adventures that followed the 9/11 provocation. Meanwhile, our enemies watched from afar, encouraged by our lack of foresight.

An unprecedented economic crisis is now underway. This crisis will have political effects unlike anything we have seen. It is not an exaggeration to say that the shocks already administered will require great patience and discipline from the American people, and great statesmanship. Imagine millions of desperate Americans without work, facing food shortages. Imagine a bankrupt federal government — and bankrupt states, counties, municipalities. *All bankrupt together.*

The divide between right and left will be exacerbated. The left will say that capitalism has failed. A downward spiral will begin, propelled by the voting public. We will be driven by the left to destroy our economic wherewithal because of a flaw in our ruling political ideology.

The Great British historian, Lord Macaulay, predicted the future unraveling of America's economy in a letter written in May 1857. Macaulay's prediction was based on his analysis of American institutions. Discussing the life of Thomas Jefferson with an American author, Macaulay wrote, "You are surprised to learn that I have not a high opinion of Mr. Jefferson, and I am surprised at your surprise. I am certain that I never wrote a line, and … uttered a word indicating an opinion that the supreme authority in a state ought to be entrusted to the majority of citizens [counted] by the head; in other words, to the poorest and most ignorant part of society."

According to Macaulay the United States was becoming increasingly democratic throughout the nineteenth century. And this tendency, he argued, was dangerous to liberty and to the country's economic well-being. As Macaulay explained, "I have long been convinced that institutions purely democratic must, sooner or later, destroy liberty or civilization, or both."

Macaulay pointed to the French Revolution and to the tendency of democratic movements to despoil the rich. "You may think that your country enjoys an exemption from these evils," Macaulay wrote to his American correspondent. "I will frankly own to you that I am of a very different opinion. Your fate I believe to be certain, though it is deferred by a physical cause. As long as you have a boundless extent of fertile and unoccupied land, your laboring population will be far more at ease than the laboring population of the Old World, and, while that is the case, the Jefferson politics may continue to exist without causing any fatal calamity."

Eventually, of course, the United States must fill up with people. It must lose its economic advantages. "[T]he time will come, noted Macaulay, "when New England will be as thickly peopled as old England. Wages will be as low, and will fluctuate as much with you as with us." America will then be urbanized, with a large population of "artisans." Then it will happen that large numbers of these artisans will sometimes find themselves out of work. "Then your institutions will be fairly brought to the test," wrote Macaulay. "Distress everywhere makes the laborer mutinous and discontented, and inclines him to listen with eagerness to agitators who tell him that it is a monstrous iniquity that one man should have a million, while another cannot get a full meal."

With the supreme power in the hands of a discontented multitude, what kind of government are they likely to elect? Would it be a government committed to "the security of property and the maintenance of order"? Or would it be a government that gets through hard times by robbing the rich "to relieve the indigent"? Eventually, wrote Macaulay, the Jeffersonian bent of the United States will result in the destruction of property, the plundering of the wealthy. "It is quite plain that your government will never be able to restrain a distressed and discontented majority. For with you the majority is the government, and the rich, who are always a minority, absolutely at its mercy."

As we see today, all levels of government in America are involved in relieving the distress of the poor and unemployed, and we also see that this is presently accomplished by taxing the rich as well as by taking on debt. Presently the United States has the most progressive income tax system in the industrialized world. The problem here, in respect of the future, is the role played by the rich in investment and general economic progress. Without the rich, there is no future economic opportunity for the poor.

The process Macaulay wrote about, as anyone with eyes can see, is now on the point of playing out. The COVID-19 crisis has brought things to a head. Macaulay explained to his American correspondent, "I seriously apprehend that you will, in some such season of adversity as I have described, do things which will prevent prosperity from returning, that you will act like people who should in a year of scarcity devour all the seed-corn, and thus make the next a year not of scarcity, but of absolute famine. There will be, I fear, spoliation. The spoliation will increase the distress. The distress will produce fresh spoliation. There is nothing to stop you. Your Constitution is all sail and no anchor." As the process of unraveling continues, he added, "Either some Caesar or Napoleon will seize the reins of government with a strong hand, or your republic will be as fearfully plundered and laid waste by barbarians … as the Roman Empire…."

The "barbarians" who lay in wait are the Russians and Chinese. The communist demagoguery they have supported in Africa and Latin America, especially in their control of Venezuela and South Africa, is predicated on the dynamic Macaulay outlined in 1857. When people are struggling in poverty, why not encourage them to despoil the rich and thereby empower the militant left (which works closely with Beijing and Moscow)? Here is the dynamic of a popular socialist revolution. The way things are playing out now, this destructive process falls directly in line with the Chinese Communist Party's strategy of asymmetric warfare.

Economic warfare is imbedded in Moscow's long-range strategy. This strategy was described in detail by Czech defector Jan Sejna, in a 1982 book titled *We Will Bury You*. Starting on page 100, he described a plan to hobble the U.S. economy and foster domestic unrest. There is no question that the communists have long intended to bring down the U.S. economy through a series of strategic moves. We can now see these moves taking place. It is a process that will continue as military pressures intensify.[28]

28 NOTES AND LINKS

https://www.breitbart.com/politics/2020/04/27/producers-warn-america-is-facing-protein-shortage-in-coronavirus-era/

https://www.google.com/amp/s/oilprice.com/Energy/Crude-Oil/Saudi-Arabia-Claims-The-US-Was-Not-Their-Target-In-The-Oil-War.amp.html

https://www.haaretz.com/amp/middle-east-news/saudi-russia-oil-war-continues-despite-official-truce-1.8784180

https://www.youtube.com/watch?v=BfVTu3JEYmo

https://www.realclearpolitics.com/articles/2020/04/09/the_case_for_getting_back_to_work_142896.html

https://romancatholicworld.wordpress.com/2013/02/15/it-is-bad-feng-shui-to-ignore-the-truth-so-im-keeping-my-eyes-on-china/amp/

THE PREPARATORY PERIOD

05/01/2020

> Nuclear war ... should not be thought of as a gigantic technical enterprise alone — as a launching of an enormous number of missiles with nuclear warheads.... Nuclear war is a ... many-sided process, which ... will involve economic, diplomatic and ideological forms of struggle. They will all serve the political aims of the war...
>
> — *MARXISM-LENINISM ON WAR AND ARMY*, P. 12

The generals in Moscow and Beijing were educated under war-fighting principles antithetical to ours. Marxism-Leninism borrowed its military theory from Clausewitz; especially believing that "war is simply the continuation of politics by other means." (*Ibid*, p.2) Though Americans will refuse to believe this, Russia's strategists have long held that nuclear war is no exception to Clausewitz's rule.

In *The Philosophical Heritage of V.I. Lenin and Problems of Contemporary War*, edited by Gen. Maj. A.S. Milovidov, we read on page 37 that American strategists are mistaken in their beliefs about nuclear war. The "overwhelming majority" of those who discount nuclear war as a continuation of policy are making a purely "subjective judgment." This judgment, says Milovidov's text, "expresses mere protest against nuclear war."

Moscow's generals, and Beijing's generals, have long understood that nuclear weapons are asymmetric. Totalitarian society is adaptable to conditions of nuclear war. Bourgeois society is not. To the American mind, nuclear war makes no sense. Therefore, Americans do not take Russian strategists seriously when they write, "preparation and waging ... [of nuclear war] must be regarded as the main task of the theory of military strategy and strategic leadership." (See the Harriet Fast Scott trans. of *Soviet Military Strategy*, p. 195.) Denying that Russian and Chinese strategists are serious, American strategists think in terms of deterrence. Once deterrence fails, America has no strategy. Being uniquely vulnerable, our thinking devolves into denial; that is, the denial of nuclear war, the denial that the enemy means what he says, and that adjustments must be made.

Naturally, the Russian and Chinese strategists agree it would be best to avoid a nuclear war. But the avoidance of war, for the communist bloc, has a completely different meaning than it does for the free world. For the communist, the only alternative to nuclear war is political and social convergence on communist terms. Such may be disguised under the auspices of "sustainable development," by way of "climate change" treaties, or through trade. There is also the possibility of convergence by way of pandemic — through "global health governance" and the "managed" depopulation of entire regions (i.e., the United States). The present Chinese communist pandemic may be exactly such a device — to accelerate "convergence." It may also be a nuclear war precursor, deployed to divert and disrupt target societies in advance of the mass use of nuclear rockets. Of course, a pandemic may serve both functions. If the free world does not embrace China's plan for global health governance, Moscow and Beijing lose nothing. In that event, the turn to war could be seamless, the *maskirovka* undetected.

Given the central role the Chinese have given to biological attack (as described by Defense Minister Chi Haotian), the communist bloc would have long ago targeted, for infiltration and subversion, the National Institutes of Health and the Centers for Disease Control. America's engagement with China would provide an even more powerful opening for attack; namely, the American pharmaceutical industry — current bedfellows of China's military-industrial-medical complex, providing medical ingredients and vaccine-related "precursor" elements (opening a path for binary biological/chemical attack, combining medicines and/or vaccines with a viral weapon, enhancing the lethality of each vector by combination.)

If the West should balk convergence, drawing back from mandatory vaccinations and medical martial law, full-on nuclear war may follow. Sabotage, in this context, is not an imaginary activity of the Chinese and Russian special services. It is one of their specialities, designed for the "preparatory period" in advance of nuclear strikes. The presence of Russian and Chinese agents in our government pose a special danger during this period. The enemy's operations in Washington, evident in the recent impeachment fracas, are as yet unchecked. In all probability, their attack on the country's institutions will intensify. Perhaps the most devastating sign of impending attack will be news that hundreds of officials, generals and legislators are in the pay of the enemy. According to GRU defector Vladimir Rezun, the Russian special services will betray all their high-level agents on the eve of the war — to sow a maximum of distrust and confusion. They will also prepare false allegations against innocent persons — a prewar tactic underway since 2016.

What inclines to the suspicion we are now in the "preparatory period," is the disappearance of various communist leaders. Vladimir Putin fired his government in January, immediately before the pandemic hit China. Yet the fired Russian prime minister, Dmitri Medvedev, retained his position on the Russian security council. The Russian cabinet vanished (with sparkly nobodies in their place). And now Putin has disappeared as well.

The communist leaders of Nicaragua and Venezuela have also vanished from view. If this is not a strange coincidence, consider the case of Kim Jong-un of the Democratic People's Republic of Korea — missing for more than two weeks. Meanwhile, intelligence sources in Asia report that top Chinese leaders are bunkered somewhere in northwest China.

I quote from an Asian source as follows: In Vietnam, Laos and Cambodia, "our intelligence organs can confirm: … key leaders … [party and military] have been hiding alternately." The Asian source adds that China and Russia are studying the West's reaction to the virus, preparing for "their next moves in more aggressive coordination towards the final phase of thunderous war…." The timing, says the source, will be sudden.

According to Marshal of the Soviet Union K. Moskalenko, writing in *Voyennaya mysl'* (January 1969), "The employment of qualitatively new weapons … will create conditions in a future war for the achievement of results in its beginning period which cannot compare with the results of … the past war. The first nuclear strike can immediately lead to the disorganization of the government, military control, and the whole rear area of a country and to stopping the systematic deployment of the armed forces and all measures being conducted for mobilization. All of this will have a telling effect…."

The present situation is not one of peace. When countries of the East Bloc maintain strict secrecy, prohibiting investigations and inquiries, hiding their leaders in remote locations, we ought to set all naive assumptions aside.

We have been under intensive ideological attack for many years. Advanced methods of psychological warfare have been deployed against our institutions. Our media has been subverted and used against us. But we elected Donald Trump anyway, and Trump defied the mechanisms of convergence. He balked the communist plan.

So here we are.

On the Shortness of Insight

05/13/2020

> Most human beings ... complain about the meanness of nature, because we are born for a brief span of life, and because this spell of time ... rushes by so swiftly and rapidly that with very few exceptions life ceases ... just when we are getting ready for it.
>
> — SENECA

Seneca complained that ancient Rome's degradation stemmed from people's preoccupations. To rush around, without careful thought, was a waste of one's life. To live, he said, is to be alive to the truth — to take account of reality. The problem with preoccupation, with ambition and career, is the way ambitious and preoccupied people disregard truth. After many years, instead of growing wiser, the ambitious man resembles a fool. He has not stopped to take account of his surroundings, or his associations, or his country, or the truth about himself.

Socrates famously said "the unexamined life is not worth living." Playing off this idea, Seneca penned his book *On the Shortness of Life*,[29] saying the unexamined life is not only worthless, but painfully short. Those who live hurriedly, without stopping to think, succumb to the hamster wheels of greed, lust, ambition and envy. Life, under these imperatives, becomes a blind rushing to and fro.

The preoccupied man moves very quickly. He grasps every opportunity, without thinking. He does not see. He does not read. He does not think. His excuse is always the same. "I have no time." Being empty, being thoughtless, the shallow ideas of such people are not even their own. When they try to reason, their immaturity is glaring. There is only the immediate reward of acting promptly, of seizing an opportunity. But since they haven't thought things through, their opportunities lead nowhere.

"Old age overtakes them while they are still mentally childish," says Seneca. This describes the result of the fast-paced Roman life of the first century

29 https://www.amazon.com/dp/1941129420/ref=cm_sw_r_cp_api_i_6DiVEb2GXDMCX

— and the fast-paced American life of the twenty-first century. We are, at this time, confronted with a mass of fellow-citizens who do not reason well, and leaders who have led the country into the blind alley of dependency on enemies. The situation of the country is desperate — growing worse by the day. One hears foolish things from both sides of the political aisle. Everyone reverts to a knee-jerk series of reactions. Why? Because they were never very thoughtful in the first place. They never developed their curiosity, never asked the right questions, and never understood where they were headed.

If, as Seneca says, "the preoccupied find life very short" — one might add that the life of society may also be shortened when such people are in charge. Our politicians and pundits misjudged all the big events of the last 31 years. The West is now under attack from a Chinese virus. Did any of them see this coming?

I look to the left, and I see slogans. I look to the right, and I see slogans. Ours is an age in which thinking has been replaced with political nonsense. Such comes naturally to preoccupied people — as Seneca argued. How much do these people understand? Not much.

And now, more than ever, the masses are disoriented. There is nothing but confusion, nothing but the noise of contrary opinions. Our leaders' focus is "economic," not philosophic. We have set aside all the most important questions, being preoccupied with entertainment and prosperity.

"Oh what darkness," noted Seneca, does great prosperity cast over our minds." — Such has been America's prosperity, which now undoes itself. Everything here is not merely idiotic. Seneca tells us that bad men take pride in not knowing what they do. "Indeed," he wrote, "the state of all who are preoccupied is wretched … as they rob and are robbed, as they disturb each other's peace, as they make each other miserable, their lives pass without satisfaction, without pleasure, without mental improvement."

The Meaning of Enmity

05/25/2020

> Social and political revolt erupted in the European and world periphery in the decade prior to World War I, beginning with the First Russian Revolution in 1905, followed by the Iranian revolution of 1906, the great Rumanian peasant revolt of 1907, the Young Turk rebellion of 1908, the Greek military revolt of 1909, the overthrow of the Portuguese monarchy and the beginning of the Mexican revolution in 1910, and the Chinese revolution in 1911.
>
> — STANLEY G. PAYNE
> *THE SPANISH CIVIL WAR*

What triggered the revolutions and civil wars of the last century? What triggered the first and second world wars? One thing triggered them: **ENMITY**.

What is enmity?

Enmity is ill will, hostility, antipathy, animosity, rancor — and, above all, it is hatred — not passive, but active. It is a hatred that fuels the cruelty of war. It is the meaning of war. It is the reason for war. It is the all-in-all of war.

Recently the best-selling author, Graham Hancock, passionately decried the stupidity of America's Pentagon budget to Joe Rogan. Money wasted on armaments, he said, could be used to end poverty or cure diseases. Hancock spoke as if enmity toward America was a kind of convenient fiction of the "powers-that-be." He did not properly consider those who actively hate America, who want to see America burn.

It may be that Mr. Hancock's intuition about a lost prehistorical civilization is worth considering, but his intuition about our present civilization is without merit. If America disarmed as he recommends, not only would a dismal poverty inflict the whole planet, but America's collapse into military insignificance would signal a dark age of Sino-Russian global dominance — an age of slavery and persecution; an age in which dissenters would be imprisoned, tortured and executed by the tens of millions. One only has to look at the bloody oppressions of the police state in China, at the assassination of journalists in Russia, to know the fate that would be in store for us all.

To hear Mr. Hancock speak against my country's weapons of defense, as if my country was the problem, is more than a little perplexing; especially as Mr. Hancock has no declared expertise in world affairs, no military knowledge, or degrees in political science. I cannot help wondering, as well, that he might be be speaking German if not for my country's armament. Yet he damns my country's defense establishment as if it alone stood in the way of mankind's progress.

Hancock, who is by no means an enemy of America, has adopted the talking points of America's enemy. If everyone believed in such talking points, who would benefit? It is, indeed, a case of *cui bono*; for nonsense of this kind has a purpose. Those who hate America want to see her defenseless. They have worked incessantly toward this end for decades.

Recently a reader sent me a picture of a mob of protestors burning an American flag in Los Angeles. Apparently I was supposed to express shock or surprise. If anyone is shocked, it is not me. Los Angeles is, in many respects, the territory of a foreign power. Many places in America are no longer American. They are opposed to the country, opposed to its defense, and want it to burn.

When I was in graduate school more than thirty years ago, many professors and graduate students were working to undo the country. I heard expressions of snarling hatred and contempt for America. It seemed, in fact, that this hatred was gradually becoming academically obligatory. It was, in those very days, that flag burning was judicially approved as "free speech" by the Supreme Court." Many libertarians and conservatives approved of this decision. But then, given that dragon's eggs were incubating inside the universities, the Supreme Court decision was more on the order of a landmark — halfway between the censuring of Joseph McCarthy and total destruction by fire.

Seriously. This is a country governed by very special fools. It has been governed by these fools for fifty to sixty years or more. Nearly all men, in all times, are foolish. But to live without a shred of instinct, without a sense of self-preservation, and to arrogantly regard one's stupor as a superior state of consciousness, *is damnable*. God does not smile on it.

Enmity is hatred. It is the kind of hatred that burns flags. It is the kind of hatred that burns police precincts and suburbs. It is the kind of hatred that launches ballistic missiles with nuclear warheads. It is the kind of hatred that organized the terror famine in Ukraine 90 years ago. It is the kind of hatred that gassed millions of Jews in the Second World War — that firebombed Dresden and put mushroom clouds over Hiroshima and Nagasaki.

Do you think enmity is a fairytale? Do you think it is a myth advanced by the "military-industrial complex"? Think again. If we did not have a single rifle to defend ourselves, would the flag burners in Los Angeles suddenly salute our flag? No. They would proceed to burn down the whole country. Why? Because the flag signifies the country. They burn the flag now because they cannot burn the country.

When somebody burns your country's flag what do you think they intend? Do you think burning a flag is a fun pastime? Do you think burning a police precinct is protected speech? Do you think burning the suburbs is an understandable form of protest?

And now Minneapolis burns. What other cities will burn? Let us consider, once more, that curious Latin phrase — *cui bono*. Let us consider the connection between the flag burning (by communists) in Los Angeles, and the burning of a police precinct in Minneapolis. They are, in fact, intimately connected.

One might ask, rhetorically, why the flags of America's enemies aren't burning? It is simple. They are the ones doing the burning — of flags and police precincts. They have incited the frenzy of the mob. They have used race and class and sex to divide America into hostile, warring camps. Their game is "divide and conquer." And we — suckers that we are — play along with this game.

Does anyone see what is happening? Does anyone see who is behind it? Does anyone realize who stands to gain by it? — Not blacks, not whites, not Americans of any color.

Oh yes. We are very, very, special fools.

Myth and Apocalypse

06/02/2020

From ancient Chaldean and Hebrew sources (Gen. iv and part of x), we learn of a mythic age of giants and heroes — before the *deluge*. Today we eschew this prehistory. We do not believe in a lost Golden Age or the deluge that swept it away. We do not believe in Plato's Timaeus and Critias, or in Polybius' fragment on cosmic catastrophes that periodically annihilate civilization. We do not believe the Chaldean and Hebrew accounts of a great flood.

We moderns prefer to believe that the past was entirely primitive, that progress has been gradual and "evolutionary." We prefer to believe there was no Golden Age, no giants or heroes, no deluge, no antideluvian world. We believe that time runs in a straight line. The further back you go, the more backward the men. The further forward, the more knowledgeable and advanced. (A self-flattering conceit if there ever was one.)

The ancient Chaldeans, Egyptians, Hebrews and Greeks would be shocked at our disregard of oral and written traditions. They would have disliked our view of history as "one damn thing after another." Surely, history has meaning. Surely, there is a pattern — the hint of something larger and grander at work.

Ask yourself: Why did prehistory last so long, with so little accomplished? Our Stone Age ancestors had brains as big as ours, and supposedly failed to discover anything — to build anything — for 180,000 years.

More than a hundred years ago, the orientalist William Saint Chad Boscawen referred to the deluge as "a dividing line between the mythic age of gods and the beginnings of history…." Being mythic, however, did not mean it wasn't real. If we find metaphor, parable and symbol in our myths — all the better.

Giorgio de Santillana and Hertha von Dechend attempted to elucidate the profundity of ancient myth in their little book, "Hamlet's Mill". They denied that myths were a garbled kind of history. Instead, they suggested that mythology contains coded messages for posterity. Here is something to baffle the literal-minded scientist, to confound our latter-day plunderers of the unconscious (i.e., psychologists). Santillana and Dechend suggest that myth represents something higher than history and more profound than science. It is even suggested that myth represents something that makes these latter outcroppings possible; for myth doesn't tell us what happened in as much as it tells us why. Here is the ground of meaning which has been drained out of our science, out of our history, drop by drop.

Could it be, all along, that the edges of our world have advanced or receded, not by the explorations of Columbus and Magellan, but by the beneficial or deleterious effects of mythological understandings — or the lack thereof? Could it be that dragons and sea serpents are not only depicted on the margins of ancient maps, but are also depicted at the margins of time as well?

The Greek-Chaldean, Berosus, wrote:

> A great multitude of men of various tribes inhabited Chaldea, but they lived without any order, like the animals.... Then there appeared to them from the sea, on the shore of Babylonia, a fearful animal of the name of Oan. Its body was that of a fish, but under the fish's head another head was attached, and on the fins were feet like those of a man, and it had a man's voice. Its image is still preserved. The animal came at morning and passed the day with men; but it took no nourishment, and at sunset went again into the sea, and remained there for the night. This animal taught men language and science, the harvesting of seeds and fruits, the rules for the boundaries of land, the mode of building cities and temples, arts and writing, and all that relates to the civilization of human life.

The intrinsic absurdity of the text should be no objection. It is a story which is found, in altered form, among the Dogon people of Mali, thousands of miles from Mesopotamia. The Dogon people have retained their oral traditions up to modern times. They tell of the Nummo, an amphibian creature comparable to a lizard or chameleon. This creature was also described as a fish who stood upright — and also as a serpent!

Curiously, it was a serpent that talked to Eve in the Garden of Eden; and so talking, talked the first man and woman out of Eden — into the rigors of civilized toil. A reptile, a snake, a "dragon" — with feet! And this reptile appears again, in the **Book of Revelation**, Chapter 12.

> A great sign appeared in Heaven: a woman clothed with the sun, with the moon under her feet and a crown of twelve stars on her head. She was pregnant and cried out in pain as she was about to give birth. Then another sign appeared in heaven: an enormous red dragon with seven heads and ten horns and seven crowns on its heads. Its tail swept a third of the stars out of the sky and flung them to the earth. The dragon stood in front of the women who was about to give birth, so that it might devour her child the moment he was born.

Is this woman Eve, the mother of mankind? Is our aversion to reptiles, in this event, reciprocated? And here is the most terrible reptile of all, gathering a third of the stars as a means of bombardment — to kill mankind in its cradle. If the snake lured us out of Eden with the forbidden fruit (containing the knowledge of good and evil), promising that we would be "as gods" — then that snake was an enemy whose strategy was to destroy us with a dangerous conceit.

Could the latter-day re-invigoration of this conceit be a coincidence?

The thing about mythologies — from all over the world — is the subtle ways in which they connect (even if they do not fully agree). There is the palpable absurdity of a walking fish, or a serpent that talks to women, or a chameleon that teaches the arts of civilization, or a dragon bombarding the earth with a third of the stars of heaven to "devour" a newborn. But the witnesses are everywhere in agreement. The fish, the serpent and the dragon are integral to our story. And however metaphoric, or symbolic, or even cryptic, these archaic creatures are, as Santillana and Dechend maintain, "cosmological from first to last."

> It was understood only by a very few, it appealed to many, and it is forever intractable to those who approach it through 'mathematics for the million' or by speculation on the unconscious. In other words, this is a selective and difficult approach, employing the means at hand and much thought, limited surely, but resistant to falsification.

This latter point deserves our attention. While we laugh at our ancestors' ignorance of science, their mythology yet resonates. While we falsify reality with our "facts" — while we are lost in "facts" — we imagine that "scientific" discoveries speak for themselves. This is more absurd than a talking and walking amphibian; for the empty "scientistic" notions of modernity must prove to be inherently falsifying. We talk about facts all the time, and pretend to respect them. But we use facts as a puppeteer uses his puppets. We make them say, in the depths of our corruption, what we wish them to say.

Whereas a myth esoterically relates what is forbidden to captives and hostages, "facts" taken out of context can be used to ensure continued captivity. Likewise, to descend into triviality is the fate of those imprisoned in a false reality, absorbing the light of an ersatz sun, fighting for an ersatz liberty, adhering to an ersatz science.

The question may be: What has captured us? What is the evil thing that yet holds us hostage? — with a serpent's promise still ringing in our ears?

To the Americans Who Are on Their Knees

06/04/2020

> The king orders the Swiss to lay down their arms at once, and retire to their barracks.
>
> — LOUIS XVI
> TO HIS SWISS GUARD
> 10 AUGUST 1792

We are near the end of the Republic. A revolution has begun and no decisive counter-revolutionary actions have been ordered. Why has this happened? Because we have been psychologically and linguistically disarmed.

For example: — The oath of allegiance of federal officials is to defend the Constitution against all *enemies*, foreign and domestic; but if we refuse to acknowledge the existence of enemies, *if we cannot name our enemies*, no defense will be possible. And this is the one thing, above all, that has been forbidden: *We are not allowed to name our enemies.*

This is the raw essence of linguistic and psychological disarmament. Add to this a process in which America's enemies have flooded into the government itself. And now, when mob violence has been deployed on a massive scale, the country finds itself unprepared, disoriented, and defenseless.

How did we get here?

Leftists have gradually taken control over the curriculum of our schools. This curriculum was copied from designs made in the USSR for our express use.[30] This curriculum destroys the mind's ability to work competently with abstractions. It leads our children away from patriotism. It leads women to turn against men, blacks to turn against whites, and Americans to turn against their own country. It is a very simple process of indoctrination that nobody has seriously challenged. We have supported this treason ourselves, with lucrative funding. In consequence, we have been gradually Losing control of our own institutions, decade after decade. And that is how we have come to this tragic moment in time.

30 See Robin Eubanks, *Credentialed to Destroy: How and Why Education Became a Weapon*: https://www.amazon.com/dp/1492122831/ref=cm_sw_r_cp_api_i_JdM2Eb4HBATWR

The phrase that best describes this overall process is, "psychological and linguistic disarmament." We have been intellectually disarmed and now the process has advanced from the realm of ideas to street violence. If the process is allowed to continue, Americans of all races and beliefs will be slaughtered when the foreign enemy moves his missiles, armies and fleets into action. At present, our economy is under attack on a number of fronts. Law and order is being stripped from us. First, the police will be defunded; second, the Revolution will defund the U.S. military; third, the Chinese and Russians will bomb and invade the country.

Consider the following occurrences; Around the country police officers are kneeling before "protestors," begging forgiveness. Whites in the suburbs are also kneeling before blacks. An appeasing and obsequious spirit has taken hold of a neutered middle class. It is a portent of impending mass expropriation. It is a portent of atrocities, killings, massacres, arbitrary arrests, rampaging mobs, foreign invasion and military dictatorship.

In blue states, Marxist revolutionaries are using black anger to cover an attack on the country's economy — to take over the streets, to burn and loot businesses, to intimidate the government and subdue the populace. As of this moment, their strategy is working. If the government does not take back the streets and stop the destruction of property, the revolutionaries will begin to dictate terms. In that event, every negotiation will go against the government until the revolutionaries ARE the government.

Presently, the revolutionaries demand that the prisons be emptied and police disbanded. This will assure their control of the streets indefinitely. It will allow them to use force at will, to confiscate property and commit "extra-judicial" killings. The revolutionaries will form their own government, modeled after Robespierre's Committee of Public Safety.

There are many who will say, in answer to the above paragraphs, that I am exaggerating the present troubles. They will say that my anticommunist prejudice has led me to a distorted view of events. They will argue that these protests are "peaceful," and not about Marxism at all, but have to do with "white privilege" and "systemic racism." While many protestors are genuinely worried about police brutality and systemic racism, they are but pawns — and a screen for the revolutionary left to conduct its violent attacks.

Many good and generous people believe in a leftist utopia of love and peace. But their's is an upside-down world in which all facts are seen through the ever-inverting eyeglass of ideology. Sadly, they are ignorant of the actual forces manipulating them. Their knowledge of history and politics is too limited for safe involvement in controversies they do not fully understand. Vladimír Lenin had a name for these good people. He called them "useful idiots."

The present riots have little to do with white racism and everything to do with Chinese and Russian war preparations against the United States. The left in this country — wittingly or not — is the catspaw of foreign powers. To not realize this is to be a political child. It signifies ignorance.

The battlecry of "systemic white racism" is a theme fronted by our enemies. This theme has always been supported by Beijing and Moscow. *It is supported for strategic purposes that are now coming into focus.* Whatever our domestic problems may be, kneeling before a protest that is used as a screen by communists and foreign enemies, *is suicide.*

If we bend the knee to this, nothing will go back to normal. There is a video of vandals breaking into a business; the people inside are shouting, "We are on your side! We are on your side!" But the vandals do not stop. They proceed to smash everything in sight.

Many of our politicians and military leaders are sympathetic to the "protesters." They are afraid to use force against rampaging looters and incendiaries. And so the looting, the burning and the violence, will continue. The revolutionaries are emboldened, primarily by a weak response — a response reminiscent of the French monarchy of 1792.

It is a dangerous task to defend weak governments. Such governments are never steadfast. They are ready to appease or even capitulate. The police are sworn to protect society with their lives, but they will not be supported (in turn) by weak politicians. They will be hung out to dry. Their every action will be second-guessed. They are, even now, collectively slandered as racists.

The Minneapolis city council is — at this very moment — deliberating on whether to disband the police. In Los Angeles, a measure to partly defund the police and divert the money to black radicals has been approved.

Consider what happened in the French Revolution: King Louis XVI, seeing an insurrection being prepared, and wishing to spare the lives of his subjects, put himself into the hands of the revolutionaries, saying, "Gentlemen, I come here to avoid a great crime; I think I cannot be safer than with you." He abandoned his palace and gave up the protection of his Swiss guard.

The Revolutionaries, having the king in their custody, ordered the Swiss guard to lay down their weapons and surrender. "We should think ourselves dishonored," replied the guard. "We are Swiss, and the Swiss do not part with their arms but with their lives."

Heavy fighting began in and around the palace. The Swiss defended themselves. The revolutionaries were infuriated by the resistance. Louis XVI heard of the fighting and ordered his guard to lay down their arms at once. They attempted to obey and were slaughtered. Of the 900 Swiss guards, 600 were killed immediately. Another 200 died of wounds or were murdered later on.

Here is a summary of the whole process: — To avoid bloodshed the King gave himself up. His guard was slaughtered. The king was later beheaded by the revolutionaries (who had previously promised his safety). His wife, the queen, was beheaded. His children were imprisoned. Thousands of innocent persons were beheaded in turn. The Paris mob dominated the politics of those years, until a young artillery officer, named Napoleon Bonaparte, fired grape-shot point blank into the Paris mob and dispersed it. No more mob. Guess who the country's next ruler was?

Do we have any bold, capable, leaders in the U.S. military? Presently, the Army leadership is terrified that racial division within the armed forces will break the Army into mutually hostile camps. It is impolitic, they say, to use the military to stop the burning and pillaging of the leftist revolutionaries.

And so, even the Army generals have bent the knee. The Chinese troops, when they arrive, will tell them to get off their knees. The Chinese will give them shovels, and order them to dig. And when the holes are sufficiently deep, shots will ring out; then body after body will fall into the holes. And the People's Liberation Army will, with soft dirt, cover the holes into which the corpses have dropped.

To our politically correct jackasses: You ought to be ashamed — because you are a pack of unmanned, sniveling, disgusting, senseless, dead-men-walking. You have earned the fate that is in store for you. You die on your knees because of your foul, weak-minded, moral cowardice. Tomorrow they will burn the suburbs and decimate you. And while you are digging your grave for the "nice" Chinese soldiers, I want these words to be burned into your mind: **You betrayed your country for thirty years of peace and prosperity. When your enemy took over the schools, you didn't care. When everything at the store was made by your enemy, you liked the low prices. When your enemy ran for Congress and the White House you voted for him. And you congratulated yourself on being virtuous. But you aren't virtuous. You are cowards.**

You went along with the communist lies. You flattered yourself about winning the Cold War. You pretended that China was a country we could do business with. But now the time has come for *you* to suffer.

The Tarantulas

06/09/2020

> Lo, this is the tarantula's den! Would'st thou see the tarantula itself? Here hangeth it's web: touch this, so that it may tremble.
>
> — FRIEDRICH NIETZSCHE
> *THUS SPAKE ZARATHUSTRA*, 29

Nietzsche wrote to the tarantulas: "Revenge is in thy soul; wherever thou bitest, there ariseth black scab...." The tarantulas of Nietzsche's parable preach equality. But their preaching is not honest.

Nietzsche wanted to expose the motives of the tarantulas, rebuking their vengefulness with laughter. "Therefore," wrote Nietzsche, "I tear at your web, that your rage may lure you out of your den of lies, and that your revenge may leap forth from behind your word 'justice.'"

Nietzsche warned that the tarantulas want to fill the world "with the storms of their justice." Their "Will to Equality" has become the basis for a false system of valuation. Today's tarantulas are better known as "social justice warriors." They are, in Nietzsche's words: "against all that hath power." But this outcry against power masks the tarantulas' very own lust for power.

Many years ago I confronted a political activist whose inordinate desire for power was suddenly exposed. Instead of covering up and denying, he said to me: "I do not want to be an insect, like my father." This shocking admission is something that Nietzsche, as the psychologist of the "will to power," addressed with the following lines:

> What the father has hid comes out in the son; and oft have I found in the son the father's revealed secret.
>
> Inspired ones they resemble; but it is not the heart that inspires them — but vengeance. And when they become subtle and cold, it is not spirit, but envy, that makes them so.
>
> Their jealously leads them also into thinker's paths; and this is the sign of their jealousy — they always go too far: so that their fatigue has at last to go to sleep on the snow.

> In all their lamentations sounds vengeance, in all their eulogies is maleficence; and being judge seems to them bliss.

Nietzsche warned his readers to distrust all "in whom the impulse to punish is powerful." Out of such countenances "peer the hangman and the sleuth-hound." They are, in reality, preachers of death. Nietzsche said, "they themselves were formerly the best world-maligners and heretic-burners."

The world is never going to be a paradise in which everyone has everything in equal measure. Universal peace is *not* in prospect. The design of this life, of this world, is one in which the soul advances to maturity through difficulties of every kind. The path intended for man is not socialist utopia. The path of man is an upward path, made for climbing. Each individual climbs at his own pace. It is not a world in which the foremost climbers should be forced to retrace their steps for the sake of those who remain below. According to Nietzsche, the world requires elevation and, therefore, it requires steps, and "a variance of steps." Life strives to rise and, in doing so, to surpass itself.

In quoting Nietzsche I am not endorsing his philosophy. Yet, when a man has good insights to offer, it is best to acknowledge them. The social justice warriors of the present day are not liberators. They are jailers. They are not helping women and minorities, they are destroying the country.

As the psychologist of "the will to power," Nietzsche saw that something incredibly dangerous was destined to congeal inside the Western mind, and inside Germany. To clarify his actual positions, Nietzsche was not a racist or antisemite. He despised German chauvinism. He despised socialism and nationalism and communism. It is one of those ironies of history that Hitler used Nietzsche as a prop for his demagogy, meeting with the dead philosopher's sister, giving Nietzsche's collected works as a gift to Mussolini. In fact, Hitler perverted what he found in Nietzsche — if only to mask his own career as the ultimate tarantula, *eager for revenge and lusting for power*.

What we find, when examining Nietzsche's writings, is someone who feared for the future of Europe, who warned of the advent of "European nihilism." This nihilism offers free play to the tarantulas, because few are able to stand firm. Nihilism fills men with doubt. This doubt quickly turns to despair. Despair turns to self-pity. Self-pity devolves into the politics of the victim. Here we approach to absolute cynicism — to the point at which faith crumbles. And there stands the tarantula with his "new faith." He is offering you "equality" and "justice." But as Nietzsche warned, the tarantula is motivated by envy. He is fixated on revenge as he thirsts for power.

Are you ready to join the tarantulas? They are asking you, now, to bend your knee. Many are going to do it, and they have no idea what they are about to unleash. The people they are empowering are not psychologically normal. The process is disintegrative. What we have failed to appreciate, after so many years of stability and prosperity, is that all institutions are fragile; that life itself is fragile.

The power of the tarantulas is growing. Many local and state governments are in their hands. The mainstream media is in their hands, along with many publications. One example should suffice.

If you open the pages of *The Atlantic* (which was my favorite magazine two decades ago), you will find a concentration of such venom, of such spite and hatred, that to read the whole thing is to be poisoned with a hatred of America so violent, and so profound, that you either become a tarantula yourself, or turn against them for all time.

When every single article is oriented against America's national interest, against American feelings, against the Founding Fathers, against the president, against the maintenance of a national border — as if all these things were manifestations of "fascism" — you must conclude that tarantulas are behind the work; for it is advanced under the banner of "justice" and "equality." It is as condemnatory as a hangman, as implacable as its pose of reason is false, and as seditious in spirit as the communist insurrection it complements.

It's Communism, Stupid

06/14/2020

> The ideological erosion of the bourgeois order at every level — economic, political, cultural, social — would proceed the initiation of direct frontal assaults on the state.
>
> — CARL BOGGS
> *GRAMSCI'S MARXISM*, P. 52[31]

Professor Carl Boggs admires Antonio Gramsci. As a socialist, Boggs understands that Gramsci's idea of the communist revolutionary "process" depends on "the continuous and organic development of the ... oppressed classes...." This development is driven by "novel forms of social participation" which gradually extend "the domain of egalitarianism, [and] non-bureaucratic [forms of] social authority...."

At present, Black Lives Matter functions as the "novel form of participation" for extending "the domain of egalitarianism." The United States is now destabilized. The Communist game of divide-and-conquer has reached its mature stage. There is an ongoing breakdown of authority, an unserious attitude toward law and order, and a lapse of patriotism.

The death of George Floyd has been used as a catalyst. It was the kind of "event" for which the aforesaid revolutionary formation (Black Lives Matter) was created. Now, Black Lives Matter has become a power in its own right.

It is only the ignorance of the many, and the "fog of war," that makes the casual observer dubious as to authorship of the present insurrection. For those who have not studied communist tactics, further shocks are in store. The existing political system failed to support the thin blue line, and that line is crumbling. The communists are winning.

To make matters worse, the generals of the U.S. military have signaled their neutrality. General Mark Milley, Chairman of the Joint Chiefs of Staff, referred to the rioting and vandalism as "domestic politics." Misrepresenting

31 Gramsci's Marxism: https://www.amazon.com/dp/0904383032/ref=cm_sw_r_cp_api_i_aWL6EbTEDEPX1

the Officer's Oath as a commitment to egalitarian values, Milley ignored his duty to defend the Constitution against "all enemies, foreign and domestic." As long as the nation's enemies give lip service to egalitarianism, General Milley will not list them as enemies. Therefore, a green light has been given. The revolutionaries are free to commit any number of outrages.

Consider the 1,500 buildings damaged or destroyed in the Twin Cities area of Minnesota. America's generals say this is a police matter — though the police in Minneapolis may soon be disbanded in favor of armed revolutionary gangs (i.e., community policing).

When Senator Tom Cotton wrote his Op-Ed in *The New York Times* on 3 June, he wrote, "The nation must restore order. The military stands ready." But our military leaders were not ready. And the editors of *The New York Times*, criticized for publishing Cotton's piece, begged pardon for indulging the Senator's "harsh tone." The editors objected to Cotton's claim that "cadres of left-wing radicals" were behind the riots, the violence, the looting and burning of buildings. In fact, said *The Times* editors, "those allegations have not been substantiated and have been widely questioned."

According to the paper's editors, "The Op-Ed [of Senator Cotton] should have been subjected to further substantial revisions … or rejected." It is a difficult job, indeed, to be an editor of *The New York Times*. Such an editor is able to substantiate that the sun is warm, that water is wet — but he is *unable* to substantiate the presence of left-wing incendiaries and vandals behind left-wing political rhetoric and slogans. Was it laziness or incompetence that *Times* reporters hadn't by then participated in left-activist group-phone calls about bolt cutters, gasoline cans and matches? (I know a conservative journalist who listened in on such calls.) And what is the theory of these journalistic geniuses? — That mobs of looters, in city after city, were summoned out of the night by political apathy?

The *The New York Times*'s denial of communist involvement in today's revolutionary actions, is yet another dimension of the revolution. Here America's "paper of record" is teaching the country how to be skeptical of capitalism — not communism. We are not allowed to blame the left. All blame is directed at *systemic white racism*; that is, the supposed racism of the capitalist system.

We are not allowed to say that a communist revolution has begun. We are not allowed to say that Marxist groups are engaged in a power grab; that they are using racial issues as camouflage, "extending the domain of egalitarianism"; that looting stores, beating white citizens and police officers has everything to do with communist supremacy (and nothing to do with good race relations).

For those who have studied communism, who have sat in communist meetings, the situation is perfectly obvious. Yet the mainstream media pretends there are no communists. They pretend the left is blameless. Our generals wink at the rioters. The President is opposed or mocked by governors and mayors. The communists are immune to counterattack because *they have seized the egalitarian high ground of American politics*. They have followed Gramsci's method.

Communism's overthrow of our culture was accelerated by the feminists, by the abortionists, by the mainstreaming of "illegal aliens," by gay marriage, by sympathy for the transgendered. And now it advances as the enemy of the police and the champion of the African American. Each of these "causes," one after the other, has been used to turn civilization's extended flank. It is exactly as Boggs said: The Revolution is driven by "novel forms of social participation" which gradually extend "the domain of egalitarianism, [and] non-bureaucratic [forms of] social authority…."

Gramsci's first priority," wrote Boggs, "was the multidimensional transformation of civil society, which he considered the ultimate key to the 'war of movement,' since there … must be political hegemony even before the attainment of power." And here we see how political hegemony prior to the seizure of power works in practice.

Yesterday I interviewed the famous talk radio caller, Jimmy from Brooklyn, who is an expert in communism. Explaining the meaning of Boggs's book on Gramsci, Jimmy said, "Basically, the communists have to get large numbers of people on their side before they can seize power."

According to Jimmy, a small Marxist cadre, lacking the support of numbers, would have to reeducate and also exterminate millions of people *after* taking power. It is therefore better to make unwitting Marxists out of nearly everyone in advance. If people from every walk of life have accepted leftist ideas, if they no longer understand or uphold the ideas of their forefathers, the Revolution advances without serious resistance.

The communists made a strategic decision, long ago, to champion the "cause" of women, blacks and other minorities. The whole idea is to carve out a majority in opposition to the "white patriarchy." According to Jimmy, "It's similar to how a pimp recruits a young girl. He sympathizes with her. He offers her help. He listens to her complaints about her father. Once she sees that his guidance is necessary, she begins to obey him. Soon enough she becomes a prostitute."

"This is the real nature of community organizing," said Jimmy. "They offer genuine help to people at the local level. But that help comes with a price." Now they are offering an alternative order, without police. "In this process the communists are winning," said Jimmy, "and the conservatives are too stupid to see it."

To save the country we must begin to call things by their proper names. We cannot be afraid of the enemy's egalitarian rhetoric. We must not allow them to intimidate us. We must take charge of our own language. We must name our enemy. We must identify the communists and expose their activity. If we fail to do this, we are lost.[32]

32 NOTES AND LINKS:
https://www.google.com/amp/s/www.marketplace.org/2014/11/26/lingering-cost-rioting/amp
https://www.google.com/amp/s/www.forbes.com/sites/jackkelly/2020/06/02/cities-will-see-citizens-flee-fearing-continued-riots-and-the-reemergence-of-covid-19/amp/

Chinese Strategy and the Solar Minimum

06/20/2020

> Global warming has always been followed by deep cooling within regular two-century cycles.
>
> — KHABIBULLO ABDUSSAMATOV
> ASTRONOMER, PULKOVO OBSERVATORY
> RUSSIAN ACADEMY OF SCIENCES

What they didn't tell you, what they won't tell you, what their active measures were designed to conceal from you, is the significance of the coming solar minimum.[33] If we want to understand China's strategic timing, in terms of destabilizing actions and military preparations, the coming solar minimum needs to be taken into account.

What *is* the solar minimum?

It involves a cyclical weakening of the Sun's electromagnetic field, resulting in a more intense bombardment of the oceans by cosmic rays, increasing the formation of low-level clouds that can reflect up to 60 percent of the Sun's heat. The effects on weather would include more frequent spring flooding and a shortened growing season in northern latitudes. There would follow, from these and other effects, a significant decrease in world food production.

The Russian government knows all about this. The Chinese government also knows. And both these governments have been preparing, in secret. Already the weather has caused crop losses in China (masked by talk of COVID-19-related losses). Meanwhile, the West has been swindled with an active measure called "anthropogenic global warming science." In fact, "anthropogenic global warming theory" is pseudo-science. Some who promoted this pseudo-science were agents of Moscow. Others were "useful idiots."

Contrary to the prevailing narrative, global warming is a cyclical phenomenon — as Dr. Abdussamatov explained in his 2009 paper. Anthropogenic global warming dogmatists have slandered Dr. Abdussamatov, calling him

33 https://www.amazon.com/s?k=grand+solar+minimum&hvadid=78271608348644&hvbmt=be&hvdev=c&hvqmt=e&tag=mh0b-20&ref=pd_sl_8wkgkb0eqs_e

a "hack." Yet his credit runs high in Kremlin circles. A few years ago, when asked about global warming, Russian President Putin said, "I believe in global cooling." Putin supports the Uzbek-born astronomer's assertions, in which the following facts are underscored:

> ...the eleven-year and two-century cycles of identical and synchronized variations of luminosity, sunspot activity and diameter of the Sun, is one of the most reliably ascertained facts in solar physics.
> The climate of the Earth has always been periodically changing and our planet has already experienced several global warmings, similar to the one we [now] observe. Global warming has always been followed by deep cooling....

In 2015 Abdussamatov published a paper in *Thermal Science*, titled "Earth is now entering its 19th little ice age." The Russian government put Abdussamatov in charge of all solar experiments conducted on the International Space Station. Russian scientists and government officials know the Sun is the number one causal factor when it comes to climate. And they know the Sun, like the solar system itself, operates cyclically. They also know we are about to enter the 25th solar cycle, which they believe will bring a decade of colder temperatures.

Are the Russians right?

Australian researcher David Archibald agrees with the Russians. His book is titled *Twilight of Abundance: Why Life in the 21st Century Will Be Nasty, Brutish, and Short.* Archibald cites scientific evidence that a solar minimum is upon us. We are just now reaching the end of a warm period. *But this was no ordinary warm period.* "From 1930 to 2010," writes Archibald, "the world's population increased by 250 percent while world grain production increased 392 percent." In other words, we have lived through the greatest period of prosperity in man's history; but now, due to changes in the Sun, our luck is going to run out.

As it happens, 1816 was the worst year of the previous solar minimum (also known as the Dalton Minimum).[34] Archibald warns: "A repeat of the

34 https://en.wikipedia.org/wiki/Dalton_Minimum

climate experience of 1816 in the world's temperate-region grain belts would most likely result in almost all of the grain-exporting countries ceasing exports in order to conserve grain for domestic consumption." He then lists various countries that must import grain to avoid mass starvation. What countries are in greatest danger? Saudi Arabia, Syria, Iraq, Iran, Egypt, Israel, Afghanistan, Tunisia, etc. These, he says, are "populations on the verge of collapse." Archibald's chapter on China is titled, "China Wants a War." It is only natural that an overpopulated country, unable to feed itself, would consider a path of conquest.

Let us consider a few historical parallels. Mankind has faced famine and cold many times in history. This is almost certainly what compelled Germanic tribes to cross the Rhine in the early fifth century, resulting in the fall of the western Roman Empire. It is even suspected that global cooling caused the collapse of the Sumerian and Hittite empires in the second millennium BC. Though unrelated to global cooling, a more recent calamity is even more illustrative of the danger: Germany experienced starvation during World War I, resulting in military aggression to acquire "*lebensraum*." The Germans needed more land, said Hitler, to avoid a repeat of the starvation which resulted from the Allied blockade of 1914-1919. (Please note: the blockade was maintained after the war, during the Paris Peace Conference that convened in January 1919. In consequence, several hundred thousand German children died of starvation and disease.)

If global cooling threatens major powers with effects *more* catastrophic than those suffered by Germany in 1914-19, what policies of aggression are likely to emerge? Furthermore, with the global population at a precarious 7.7 billion, the question of who starves and who eats, becomes a political question, a nationalities question, and — as the example of Hitler suggests — *a race question*. In this context we might ask why China, as a communist regime, has recently adopted "great Han chauvinism." The founder of communist China, Mao Zedong, denounced Han chauvinism. Yet Mao's disciples are adopting this racial ideology. Regarding this ideological shift, we ought to ask a question: Was this shift prompted by the approach of the solar minimum?

Think of it this way: Great tribal migrations, involving masses of human beings, under threat of famine, have been known to inflict war and rapine on weak and unprepared nations. Americans see their wealth and technological prowess as advantages. But these "advantages" invariably soften those who enjoy them most. Today this softening is called "white privilege" — a term designating those who are about to be expropriated, plundered, or even starved. If Stalin took the food from the Ukrainian "kulaks," starving them by the millions to feed the Bolsheviks in the cities, how will the rising leftist movement of today distribute food during a global famine? We listen to the rhetoric of the revolutionaries in our streets. If three billion people have to starve, who will they single out as a "kulak," deserving of starvation? Touching on this matter, Lawrence Pierce, author of *A New Little Ice Age*, wrote:

> Food will become the ultimate weapon, and the best way to defeat your enemies without being the bad guy is just to find a way to not ship food to them.

The United States would be, under these circumstances, one of the few food exporting countries in prospect. The strategic significance of North America, in an overpopulated world, cannot be underrated from the perspective of a country, like China, which contains 1.4 billion people — unable to feed themselves from their own land. The sheer scope of America's arable land, and the defective character of American statesmen and generals, makes the country a tempting target on the eve of the solar minimum. The present activation of a communist fifth column on American soil, and the use of Chinese economic (and other) blackmail on America's elite, promises to divide (and conquer) the United States at the outset of the 25th solar cycle. Is this a coincidence or is it policy? Is it an attempt to grab America's food supply?

In this context, we should reevaluate one of the most significant active measures advanced by the communists over the last three decades. The intimate connection between former Vice President (and global warming activist) Al Gore, Jr., and a prominent KGB agent named Armand Hammer (see Edward Jay Epstein's dossier on Hammer, linked below),[35] is more than suggestive. Together with assorted dupes and communist allies in the West, the Russian special services promoted the theory of "anthropogenic global warming" from the outset. It was, without doubt, a strategic deception of the highest order.

35 Edward Jay Epstein, *The Hammer File*: https://www.amazon.com/-/de/Dossier-Secret-History-Epstein-1996-10-01/dp/B01FKUZHIE/ref=cm_cr_arp_d_product_top?ie=UTF8

Our great centers of learning have not only succumbed to the dictates of Gramsci's Marxism (discussed in my previous essay), but to the nonsense of "anthropogenic global warming science." If we look closer, it appears that our great centers of learning are largely composed of political stooges, dupes and brilliant mediocrities, whose words and stock phrases are plagiarized from the pages of "liberal" magazines. There yet exists a handful of sensible people who have been blackballed out of the academy — who are unwelcome in government and big corporations. These have been excluded by a subtle process of peer ostracism. These desperately needed people must be redeemed to the nation. Rather than defunding the police, we must defund our "great" centers of learning and create new institutions dedicated to the nation's survival, free from enemy interference and subversion. But first, we must have clarity. We must understand the enemy's strategy and the rationale behind the timing of that strategy.

Readers are encouraged to study the links below and draw their own conclusions.[36]

36 NOTES AND LINKS:

The Chilling Stars: A New Theory of Climate Change: https://www.amazon.com/dp/1840468157/ref=cm_sw_r_cp_api_i_hAQ6Eb12XR3WC

https://www.whatsorb.com/news/global-warming-by-co2-or-cooling-by-a-grand-solar-minimum

Cold Sun:

https://www.amazon.com/dp/1426967918/ref=cm_sw_r_cp_api_i_hxQ6Eb3MN313X

NASA officially denies little Ice Age Theory, clinging to its obsession with CO2: https://climate.nasa.gov/blog/2953/there-is-no-impending-mini-ice-age/

Faction, Subversion and Insurrection

07/08/2020

> WE put first as a general maxim that factions and parties are dangerous... They must therefore be prevented wherever possible by wise counsel... and every means should be taken to cure them...
>
> — *JEAN BODIN*
> *ON SOVEREIGNTY*[37]

The sixteenth century political theorist, Jean Bodin, warned that, if factional differences cannot be resolved by a process of law, then the sovereign "ought to resort to force to extinguish them altogether, by punishment of the manifest leaders before they become so strong that there is no prevailing against them."

As of this writing, the United States of America is beset by factional differences that cannot be resolved by a process of law; for the law itself has been subverted. And presently, however we might hope otherwise, there is no princely sovereign that can "resort to force to extinguish them ... by punishment of the manifest leaders" because under our political system "the people" enjoy sovereignty, and the people themselves are divided into two hostile camps, each opposed to the other.

By way of example, President Donald Trump made a July 4 speech at Mount Rushmore. He honored presidents Washington, Jefferson, Lincoln and Roosevelt, vowing to defend this and other monuments against vandalism. In response, CNN said, "Trump doubles down on divisive messaging" while CNBC claimed that Trump was stoking "national divisions."[38]

In America today there are two sovereign powers — two distinct notions of "we the people" — laying claim to words like "justice" and "freedom," and "good government." But each of these powers understands words differently;

37 Bodin: *On Sovereignty: Six Books Of The Commonwealth:* https://www.amazon.com/dp/1438288700/ref=cm_sw_r_cp_api_i_oEobFb3GEHK8E

38 https://www.google.com/amp/s/www.cnbc.com/amp/2020/07/05/trump-stokes-national-divisions-in-fourth-of-july-speech.html

https://edition.cnn.com/2020/07/04/politics/trump-july-fourth-remarks/index.html

and their differences are not negotiable, neither can there be a compromise between them.

Bodin warned that "it is easier to prevent an invasion than to expel the enemy once he has effected entry" and likewise "it is better to prevent sedition than to try and cure it." And then he added, as if for our benefit: "This is even more difficult in a popular state than any other."

The problem of sovereignty in a divided popular state (such as our own) is one which we now confront; for the Constitution of the United States is something alien to *most of the persons who occupy the actual government* formed under it, even as the government's interests and ideas are at variance with "the people," or what remains after various "victim" groups have seceded to form a "new people."

For several decades a subversive minority has attempted to make itself into an unassailable sovereign majority — more recently by importing millions of non-white illegal aliens, smuggled across a border that is decried as "racist." This would-be sovereign majority wishes to do away with the country's national traditions, its national symbols, and even its national ideals.

Here is an attempt to overthrow "the people of the United States" in favor of a piracy and brigandage rooted in "socialism," or "Marxism," or "communism," but for tactical reasons prefers to camouflage itself as "anti-racism." In attempting to build a new sovereign majority, various Marxist groups have cobbled together a coalition of angry women, brainwashed youth, "disenfranchised" minorities and aliens. Referring to themselves as "progressives," this faction claims to represent "the people." Those who were previously signified by the constitutional phrase "we the people," are now denounced as "racists." America's political institutions, the free market and the police are said to be "systemically racist." Consequently, the statues of America's heroes and Founders are to be torn down, the national flag burned, and national monuments desecrated.

This campaign to destroy American symbols and slander its Founders should surprise no one. During the past half century a "faction of subversion" began to dominate American universities, government and the media. Barack Obama's presidency further raised their hopes. In fact, their consolidation of power was nearly complete by 2016. The "faction of subversion" merely needed one more "stealth socialist" president before victory would be final and irreversible. Hillary Clinton was nominated to complete the process, her election being "guaranteed"; yet she failed to defeat a dark horse candidate — Donald J. Trump.

Trump won the election with slogans like "lock her up" and "drain the swamp." But the "faction of subversion," now dominant within the Justice Department and FBI, had established an "insurance policy" in the Trump/Russia collusion hoax, which was used to dispute the legitimacy of the new president. Thus began a coordinated campaign of lies, prosecutions and insubordinations, erupting across the government, supported by a media campaign of unprecedented viciousness.

After repeated calls for impeachment, there followed an actual impeachment — with a circus of bureaucratic tattletales, and a narrative of alleged crimes too niggling for serious consideration. Then, in the midst of a Chinese-originated pandemic, an insurrection began, coinciding with an electoral challenge to Trump from an overtly senile, meritless, corrupt, nonentity.

This brief overview of our situation does not lend itself to an optimistic forecast. Too many of our fellow citizens, year after year, have hidden themselves in the "riskless private sphere," resting on the safe possession of their "private property," staying out of political controversies, yielding political ground to increasingly pathological narratives and persons. At long last this "riskless private sphere" is no longer safe. The exits have been blocked. A confrontation is now unavoidable.

There is a silver lining to all this, according to Jean Bodin. If an insurrection fails, its poison is purged from the body politic. A deluded mob can be cured once its ringleaders are apprehended. And who are these ringleaders, in truth? At beginning of Bodin's book, *On Sovereignty*, there is a listing of principles necessary to a well-ordered commonwealth. The cornerstone of these principles might surprise you. In the first place, wrote Bodin, right ordering involves distinguishing "a commonwealth from a band of thieves or pirates. With them one should have neither intercourse, commerce, nor alliance."

The dangerous faction which presently divides the country is rooted in an ideology of brigandage and piracy. Make no mistake. Such is also the ideology of Beijing, Havana and other hostile powers. It was the gravest mistake imaginable that we entered into "intercourse" and "commerce" with the Chinese communists. It was also a grave error that their ideology of universal spoliation was allowed to take root in our own schools and universities. From thence the poison has spread, and revolutionary violence now threatens us.[39]

39 Some people see more clearly than others: https://townhall.com/tipsheet/elliebufkin/2020/06/03/nobody-takes-america-philly-woman-shuts-down-protestors-outside-city-hall-n2570000

NOTES ON A KGB OFFICER'S INSIGHTS

07/16/2020

> Pressure could well grow for a solution of the German problem in which some form of confederation between East and West Germany would be combined with neutralization of the whole....
>
> — ANATOLIY GOLITSYN
> *NEW LIES FOR OLD*, 1984 [40]

I had a long conversation with a retired KGB officer in January 2011. He outlined the untold story of the Soviet Union's collapse. KGB Lt. Col. Victor Kalashnikov was a KGB analyst who worked in Austria during the events of 1989-1991. The fall of the Soviet Union, he says, was an event that has been widely misrepresented and misunderstood. "We are going to mark the 20th anniversary of that event this year," he noted. "I happened to be a witness, and I will comment, from memory, what I experienced; how the authorities acted, and how they reacted."

According to Kalashnikov, "There is a widespread opinion that economic problems were the main cause of the USSR breakdown, that economic problems led to Gorbachev's reforms. My counter-arguments are: (1) the USSR was a society run by people with particular interests and motives; (2) these people were perfectly happy with the economic arrangement of the Soviet Union."

Kalashnikov pointed to the southern Russian city of Tagonrog, where his uncle Alexei was the head of the city's KGB. "I have visited him and his family various times in the sixties and seventies," said Kalashnikov. "My uncle, who was a KGB general, occupied the best flat in this nice southern city. He had two Volga cars, and one from the KGB with a driver, for traveling. I remember at the time how people brought huge quantities of delicacies into my uncle's flat. He had a huge villa on the Black Sea shore. Moreoever, he together with his Party colleagues, had an airplane at their disposal, an old lend-lease plane, so they could fly to Moscow for shopping. They also made European tours

40 *New Lies for Old:* https://www.amazon.com/dp/0945001088/ref=cm_sw_r_cp_api_i_T8oeFbM31J29Y

through the Mediterranean. Summarizing all that, my uncle had no economic problem in the old Soviet Union. Most sections of the Soviet nomenklatura [ruling class], lived an upper middle class average existence. Today many of them live much higher, of course. But in the 1980s they were not motivated to change anything radically at all. That is my point."

While the ruling elite lived comfortably, the people of the Soviet Union lived miserably. This was the way things were, during the entire Soviet period. According to Kalashnikov, "Marina and myself made very expensive trips through the USSR as researchers, together with other researchers and students from our university. In 1980 or 81 we visited the Urals. Let me tell you, frankly, I visited hundreds of industrial enterprises and farms, city governments and hotels, and villages, and there was practically no food in the stores because everything was distributed through a sophisticated system by the population. The shelves in the stores were empty. There was one type of canned beans, a few staples, and nothing else. Now, in summer time, the water was hardly drinkable at all. The smell was horrible. The living condition of the vast majority of people was absolutely miserable. The nomenklatura lived well, but up to 90 percent of the people lived in squalor. The housing for normal citizens was desperate to catastrophic. Yes, indeed, the Russian people were facing very severe problems, it is true. But so what? The economic situation of the people had no impact on the stability of the regime. Was there any danger of a revolt? Absolutely not. After Stalin's terror, the rulers knew how to block dissent, how to put people in jail. They had the gulag [prison camp system]. There was, of course, no labor movement. It was absolutely quiet, and this was normal. There was a sort of joke told at the time: 'What is the Polish Solidarity [union]? When there is no food in Sverdlovsk they go on strike in Gdansk.' The situation was absolutely horrible in Russia, but they strike in Poland. This is the Russian sarcastic form of humor. To evaluate this development in point of view of general economic problems, if you look at social groups, we easily may discover that there was *no* political or social unrest from the population. In the Urals, for example, everything was okay. Gorbachev could have governed in the same way for another 20 years. So why did everything change? I do not believe the economic problems were the major cause of the Gorbachev changes."

Kalashnikov makes an important point, which few in the West have considered. In addition, we know from the writings of Soviet Bloc defectors (like

Jan Sejna[41] and Anatoliy Golitsyn) that a change in the Communist system was contemplated long before the 1980s. This change was envisioned as part of a long-range strategy. The immediate occasion for reverting to this strategy, according to Kalashnikov, was Ronald Reagan. "Not only him personally," explained Kalashnikov, "but his administration, his policy, his strategy and that of NATO. In the early and mid 80s I was in the Analytic Department of the KGB, and there was concern about military-political pressure from the West, from the Americans especially. There was competition in space, the oceans and in the military area. To assess all this properly, you have to look at events in the early 70s. What I mean is, of course, the war in Vietnam. Moscow drew a simple conclusion from that war. The conclusion of the Soviet General Staff was that the Americans could be defeated on the battlefield without recourse to nuclear arms. For that we only needed a Third World country, armed and trained by ourselves, and a good proletarian party with a strong leader. To gain such countries, the Soviet Union embarked on a worldwide expansion under the policy of détente [or разрядка]. The Soviets intervened in Africa, taking over Angola and Mozambique, and they involved themselves in Nicaragua. There was a successful global offensive, with some setbacks. This occurred at a time of general American weakness, due to the support we had from leftists and pacifists. I had access to General Staff reports from 1984, with operational military assessments. These included the effects of mass demonstrations on American military and rocket bases. The Soviets continued in this way until something changed quite unexpectedly for us."

As Kalashnikov explained, President Ronald Reagan had begun putting military pressure on the Soviet Union during his first term. Reagan proposed the construction of anti-ballistic missile defenses for America (the Strategic Defense Initiative). He oversaw an increase in the size of the U.S. Army and Navy. There were qualitative and technological improvements to American forces as well. Were the Americans bluffing? Was the period of U.S. weakness at an end? Then, in 1986, Arab terrorists struck a discotheque in Germany. "This was carried out by Libyans with help from the East German Stasi," said Kalashnikov. "Three people were killed, including American servicemen, and 200 wounded. Some days after that, American aircraft bombed Libya. It was

41 *We Will Bury You,* de Jan Sejna (1985-08-03): https://www.amazon.com/dp/B01FEONCKG/ref=cm_sw_r_cp_api_i_K-oeFb6W08FMG

a massive military response, which was serious. My superiors evaluated the situation carefully, and I was at several meetings. Just one attack on a disco, and the Americans sent in bombers. There would be no joking with Ronald Reagan or his people. This episode showed that the Soviet strategy of applying pressure on the West had reached its limit. We must now think things over. My bosses were upset and concerned about the American behavior. It was one of those crucial events, along with other indications of growing will on the Western side to contain the Soviet offensive, and to launch strategic counter-attacks wherever possible, with no serious compromises."

Since the Soviet Union had begun pushing into Africa, into Afghanistan, and into Central America, the Americans felt obliged to firm up their defenses. From the Soviet strategic vantage-point, there was nothing further to be gotten from direct expansion. A reversion to another strategic model, long held in reserve, was to begin. The new strategy would employ diplomacy. "It's about the idea of launching the common European house," said Kalashnikov, "allowing the Germans to unify so that they would ask the Americans to go home, and they would pay off Moscow and transfer technologies to the USSR, etc. I know that the German unification was a scheme to produce a favorable outcome for the Kremlin, because pro-Soviet forces would come to power in Germany, mainly from the Left. We were confident of this. The main goal was to drive the Americans from Europe. If we succeeded, in that case, with destabilizing NATO, we would have more options from our fellow Europeans. In the first stage of this so-called German-Soviet condominium, the fate of Czechoslovakia and Poland was unimportant because the framework was ours. We were working with the Germans directly. It was all in the spirit of the Rapallo Treaty [1922], or the Ribbentrop-Molotov Pact. The slogan was, 'The Americans out, the Soviets in, the Germans up.' What happened next, however, was not expected. The unification of Germany was carried out very rapidly, in a few months. Nobody expected this. In the course of 1990 the Soviet armed forces, which were intended to occupy Western Europe, found themselves sitting on NATO territory. There was no option for keeping this force in Germany. So the Moscow was placed in an impossible situation. The Soviet forces had to leave. The process of that massive retreat had a huge impact on the Soviet Union. The Soviet machine was a massive military industrial monster. So the withdrawal of Soviet armies from Europe meant that the system was largely destabilized. It meant that a ripple effect was felt throughout the Urals [i.e., military industry]. The entire enforcement apparatus went out of balance. The situation dictated an abrupt change of domestic policy. In August 91 conservative forces supposedly took over in a coup. Gorbachev arranged this himself because he felt cheated in Europe. At the same time they engaged Saddam Hussein to occupy Kuwait, and Saddam started to threaten Saudi Arabia. Bush senior was clever enough not to engage too deep in Iraq at that time, while Moscow became an indispensible partner for the West in the United Nations Security Council. Later, the 9/11 catastrophe was necessary to lure America's military might into Afghanistan and Iraq. That made Washington even more dependent on Moscow, and that is the strategic situation of today. What happened in 1991, with the collapse of the USSR, was due to the escalation of a political crisis in Ukraine. This was a huge and important part of the Soviet Union, and the Ukrainians continued to offer resistance, leading to serious discontent and opposition. And I know from Ukrainian KGB people that they worried all the time that something was going on; and if they lost control, there would be serious trouble for Moscow itself. That's why the Ukrainian KGB was even more cruel and stubborn than it was in Russia. In our conversations, when they came to Lubyanka to various meetings, we expressed our criticism of their harshness, and their various scandals. They would reply, 'You have no idea how dangerous and difficult the situation is in Ukraine.' So when the Soviet military and Soviet forces suffered the shock of withdrawal from Europe, the activists in Ukraine organized a revolt. The Ukrainians were ready for armed resistance. They also had units within the Soviet armed forces. We were warned of this, that it was serious and reality-based. The leadership in Kiev kept calling Moscow for help, for any kind of support. But Moscow was unable to help, because it was engaged with Germany and NATO. So it was absolutely impossible to mobilize units to suppress the Ukrainian resistance. That was the real problem. As Ukraine got its independence, the national democrats came to power there, and the Soviet Union was done. This was clear to everyone. Without Ukraine, the USSR was a fiction. The political influence of Ukraine spread in all directions. It spread to Russia, infected the Russian democrats. Ukraine became a major stumbling block for the Soviet elite."

But all was not lost for the KGB or the Communist elite. Decades earlier, Soviet planners had looked ahead to a time when a reform of the Soviet system would be necessary. In a book published in 1984, KGB defector Anatoliy Golitsyn wrote about a secret Soviet plan to do away with Communist Party dominance. This, he said, would be a deception. The Communist Party would still exist underneath the surface. It would merely go underground, or break into various new parties that would control the Russian political process according to a script. In facing the crisis, Kalashnikov noted the Kremlin's agility: "Moscow managed to regroup itself, to recuperate, by launching Islamist forces. In this way they kept Soviet legitimacy. This is extremely important to understand. In diplomatic terms, the Russian Federation is the Soviet Union of today. It has all the prerequisites, with the Security Council, central structures, etc. And it retains the status of nuclear superpower. Back in 1991 we were told, 'Listen comrade, it is a defeat for us. But it is a temporary setback.' *The Soviet Union never accepted defeat in the Cold War, not for a minute. There was not even a temporary break in the policy from Gorbachev to Yeltsin to Putin.* We have been reorganizing and will be back on track. You may remember the removal of the Dzerzhinsky monument from in front of KGB headquarters. Now let me describe the reaction in our ranks, in our residencies. When we saw what happened in Moscow, there was a general sigh of relief. We knew that someone had masterfully distracted the crowd in front of our headquarters so that poor Dzerzhinsky monument on our premises remained untouched. That was a huge difference from what happened in East Berlin. We immediately realized that the leaders and organizers of that crowd were KGB assets, our agents. The fall of Dzerzhinsky's statue was arranged by the KGB. It was ultimately a fake event."

And what was the attitude of the KGB's top leadership at the time? "In October of 91 I went to Moscow to meet with Gen. Victor Ivanenko, who was the person commanding the security of the KGB. He wanted to see me to discuss the situation of the money of the Communist Party and KGB. Austria, where I worked for the KGB, was central to the international business of the Soviet Communist Party. In Austria we had several banks under our control, and the general directors were KGB officers; that is, in capitalist Austria. The Russian presence in Austria was overwhelming. My point in telling about my visit with Gen. Ivanenko was that the KGB elite showed no nervousness or bad feelings about what happened. They were just rearranging their business according to a new situation. In Vienna itself, the Communist Party boss changed his suit and became a capitalist."

The turn to capitalism in Russia was not an honest turn to freedom. The privatization of the Soviet Union merely signified the transfer of state property into the hands of the nomenklatura. According to Kalashnikov, "In plain words, they started a process of transferring national wealth, factories, resources, etc., for nothing, into the hands of the Soviet elite, and trusted persons. In Russia, the nomenklatura took everything for themselves. They were not preoccupied with limiting themselves with laws, norms, or institutions of any kind."

This was the formula for controlled capitalism in Russia. In this manner, explained Kalashnikov, the Russian Communists used the process of "privatization" to make themselves into a business class that could make deals with the West. "The Russians," he said, "needed to gain legal status for their companies in the West. So again, the Russians are putting the West in a dire strategic position, because of al Qaeda, because of a new dependence on Russian gas and oil, because sections of the Western business community are collaborating with Russia in commercial ventures; and this will allow Moscow to expand its military-political endeavors across the globe. Russia today has resources it could only dream of during the Cold War. They need not spy on British Petroleum, since they are helping British Petroleum. The same is true of the Western media, finance, etc., etc. The field of intelligence has changed, and different tactics are being used. So the nature of spying has changed. It is not less than before, but even more intense."

So ended a remarkable monologue by a retired KGB official on how and why the Cold War never came to an end. It is not something you will find in academic journals. This story will not be told by television news outlets, or by prominent politicians. However, it better explains what we see today.

I think he was telling me the truth.[42]

42 If you know how to read the following book, all the facts verifying Kalashnikov's claims are here — *Putin's Kleptocracy: Who Owns Russia?*: https://www.amazon.com/dp/1476795207/ref=cm_sw_r_cp_api_i_H.oeFb07VCGGS

Hamlet's Truth

07/25/2020

> Give me that man that is not passion's slave, and I will wear him in my heart's core, ay, in my heart of heart.
>
> — *HAMLET*, ACT 3, SCENE 2

On 10 June 1859, at the Royal Princess's Theatre in London, Charles Kean played the lead role in Shakespeare's *Hamlet, Prince of Denmark*. He wrote a laudatory preface for the play, characterizing it as "the most stupendous monument of Shakespeare's genius, standing as a beacon to command the wonder and admiration of the world...." It constituted, according to Kean, "the perfection of tragic art — the grand, the pitiful, and the terrible." Kean interpreted the play as "a history of mind — a tragedy of thought" containing "the deepest philosophy, the most profound wisdom; yet speaks the language of the heart...."

Adding to what Kean says, Shakespeare's brilliance lies in the dramatic presentation of life's recurring dilemmas: the calamity of wicked government, the treachery of the envious, the primacy of virtue and the blindness of fools. Whatever story Shakespeare tells, it is always *our* story.

Today it may be argued that Shakespeare's *Hamlet* has special significance; for it poetically grapples with the tragedy of a country subverted by intrigue, overthrown by secret conspiracy, seduced by false appearances, and corrupted by a desire *not to see.*

Hamlet's backstory goes like this: The young Danish prince was away, studying at the University of Wittenberg, when his uncle Claudius murders his father, marries his mother and usurps the crown. On returning home, Hamlet is deeply troubled by his father's death and his mother's fast-track marriage to his uncle. In the desperate intrigues that follow, Hamlet searches for the truth. He encounters false friends, useful idiots and unwitting pawns. He has reason to be disillusioned by what he finds, and that disillusionment becomes a problem all its own.

Many of the best lines in this play might be used to describe the present day. The corruption of American political life finds its expression in Shakespeare's character, Marcellus, who famously says, "Something is rotten in the state of Denmark."

Consider the parallel story of a retired CIA official I recently spoke with. She did not notice the slide into corruption until, like Hamlet, she returned from abroad. At first she was "shocked" by what she discovered. Then she was disillusioned, and then depressed.

"I spent four dreadful years in Texas," she told me, "but didn't really know what I was up against there." The intelligence officials she encountered — especially those in authority — were not impressive. "They all had impressive degrees, of course, which they liked to throw around, but … it was difficult to get anything done." As she further recounted:

> Nobody was prepared to listen to me, or the other few conservatives I knew there. Arrogant, dismissive, and childish are the descriptions that most come to mind. Gone [were] the days when people were truly interested in honing analytic skills. It's all political now.

A latter-day Hamlet, who wanted to survive in the intelligence community of today, would have to feign madness — would have to hide behind an impenetrable mask. Failing that, a CIA prince of Hamlet's sensitivity and worth, would be rudely dealt with — pushed to resign, or forced to sit at a small corner desk with a meaningless assignment.

"I discovered the true and increasingly political nature of the IC (Intelligence Community)," she explained. The obstacles placed in her way were far from trivial. The rot, she noted, has spread beyond the intelligence community into the military, which "has been corrupted, too —

> mainly because the Colonels (and many generals) of today have been indoctrinated by the left since they were in kindergarten. I've seen a dramatic shift from right to left (sense to nonsense) since I [had contact with the military side].

If Hamlet was unable to solve the problem of a corrupt Danish state, could he have done any better with the rottenness at Langley and the Pentagon? Is there a cure for the ideological cancer eating away at our security state?

"I do not think our intelligence services can be fixed," she replied. Years earlier she thought the problems could be addressed, "but I sincerely doubt it now. It would take someone like Trump, only with more power to dissolve the entire system, to do anything constructive." She further explained:

> Unfortunately, the Intelligence Community has become so ensconced within the larger system that even if it were dissolved and resurrected, it would only come back with the same people....

She thought President Trump might dismantle "the bureaucracies one-by-one ... rebuilding them without the partisan bias." But how was this ever practicable? Perhaps the answer was to build the successor organizations concurrently, before the full dissolution of existing agencies. "This, of course, is almost impossible," she admitted, "and a 'pie-in-the-sky' approach, regardless."

This situation, like that of Shakespeare's play, can only have a tragical end. The rotten something in the state of Denmark cannot be fixed. The plot is untangled only by the natural end toward which all wickedness and stupidity tends. Fending off one intrigue after another, Hamlet takes the approach we will inevitably take. He waits for his enemy's final act of aggression, knowing he is at a disadvantage, yet bravely resolved. "We defy augury," Hamlet tells Horatio:

> ...there's a special providence in the fall of a sparrow. If it be now, 'tis not to come; if it be not to come, it will be now; if it be not now, yet it will come: the readiness is all; since no man has aught of what he leaves, what is't to leave betimes?

It is true, perhaps, that we are "sicklied o'er with the pale cast of thought" — only because this characterizes our spiritual preparation for the enemy's final act of aggression. People write books about the evils of communism, about the left's takeover of the schools, the government, big business, entertainment and the media. What does anyone ever do to stop the communists? Decade after decade they advance. Everyone looks the other way. Those who saw this happening have always been alone in their knowledge, without support from the country or the government. Those who see and understand are carriers of Hamlet's truth.

At the end of Act 1, Scene 5, Hamlet says, "The time is out of joint. O cursèd spite, / That ever I was born to set it right!" Hamlet must depose a deceptive, cunning and murderous enemy — whose chief method is conspiracy, who jealously guards the power he has taken; a "damned villain" who has seduced Hamlet's mother, and has the loyalty of the bureaucrats (Lord Polonius). It is a seemingly hopeless predicament. Thus, disillusionment gives way to depression:

> To be, or not to be, that is the question: Whether 'tis nobler in the mind to suffer / The slings and arrows of outrageous fortune, / Or to take arms against a sea of troubles / And by opposing end them.

How does one "take up arms against a sea of troubles"? The decisive word here is "faith." Trust in Providence. Virtue prevails in the end not because the good always win and evil always loses. Virtue prevails because Truth is eternal. Think of that champion of the Republic, Marcus Cicero, whose severed head and hands were displayed by Marcus Antonius to terrorize the party of freedom. Yet think how, 18 centuries later, John Adams carried Cicero's words with him, every step of the way, through the American Revolution.

The eloquence of virtue, after 18 centuries, was not used up. It was not defeated. It was and is and is to come. Such was the final triumph of Hamlet the Dane — who found the truth and lived by it.[43]

43 Shakespeare's Tragedy of *Hamlet, Prince of Denmark*, arranged for representation at the Royal Princess's Theatre with Explanatory Notes, by Charles Kean, F.S.A., as performed on Monday, January 10, 1859: http://www.gutenberg.org/files/27761/27761-h/27761-h.htm

The Anthropogenic Global Warming Scam and the Grand Solar Minimum

08/03/2020

> "[The] Solar Minimum is becoming very deep indeed. Over the weekend, the sun set a Space Age record for spotlessness. So far in 2019, the sun has been without sunspots for more than 270 days, including the last 33 days in a row. Since the Space Age began, no other year has had this many blank suns.
>
> — SPACEWEATHER.COM
> *"SUNSPOTS SET A SPACE AGE RECORD"*
> 17 DECEMBER 2019

New Zealand solar physicist, Dr. John Maunder, in a 2012 essay titled "Reflections on a changing climate," reported on a UN-sponsored climate conference held in Villach, Austria in October 1985. According to Maunder, one of the principal findings of the conference was that "greenhouse gases are likely to be the most important cause of climate change over the next century."

Maunder is now embarrassed by this statement because he is one of many scientists who have come to strongly oppose so-called anthropogenic global warming theory. For the truly intelligent, non-ideological scientist, this theory has poisoned scientific discourse, replacing the spirit of free inquiry with career intimidation and outright bullying. If we want to be scientific, if we want to be honest, the world is not getting hotter. *It is getting cooler.* Watch the following video of a snowstorm that struck western China last June 29.

VIDEO: *Snowfall In China In Summer - Xinjiang*[44]

Yes. Seriously. And believe it or not, on July 26 it snowed in Beijing. Only for six minutes, of course, but seriously. But it snowed. Watch for yourself.

44 https://www.youtube.com/watch?v=dLRGoWYNIPM

VIDEO: *Beijing's snow in summer*[45]

And what does Greta Thunberg say? She says people are "suffering and dying," and ecosystems are collpasing as the planet is getting hotter and hotter. Therefore, we need socialist controls imposed on the world economy. So the child lectures adults, and shames them. "Change is coming," she says, "whether you like it or not." Let's pause for a moment to listen to the "Karen" of climate change:

VIDEO: *Greta Thunberg to world leaders: 'How dare you? You have stolen my dreams and my childhood'*[46]

Aside from the sinister perversity of a child scolding adults on matters she cannot possibly understand herself, the so-called "science" of anthropogenic global warming is a scandal. It is only comprehensible in light of a larger set of *philosophical* scandals; first, the scandal of our post modern epistemological nihilism, the scandal of our metaphysical nihilism, and last but not least, the scandal of our moral nihilism — as exemplified by the cynical exploitation of a child.

The following video may be a little dated, but listen carefully to the evidence and arguments of Peter Temple, who is a student of cycle theory. Whatever criticisms we might make of such theories, they have more data and logic behind them than poor little Greta.

VIDEO: *Global Cooling*[47]

Heavenly bodies and subatomic particles move in circles, orbiting other bodies or spinning on an axis. Therefore, many phenomena hold to cyclical patterns. This ought to make perfect sense. The female menstrual cycle famously follows the lunar cycle. The seasons track with the Earth's path around the Sun. Day and night derive from the "turning" of the Earth upon its axis.

45 https://www.youtube.com/watch?v=412PeskwnpY

46 https://youtu.be/TMrtLsQbaok

47 https://youtu.be/B1KYvz7FFrE

The idea that our world is going to get hotter and hotter, burning through a feedback loop, setting off irreversible chain reactions, is communist propaganda. It has been imposed on our scientific community by agents of influence who have grown in power, and whose ruthless bullying tactics have not been properly resisted — as they should have been.

Some years ago a researcher in Germany sent me an essay by Soviet academician Ivan Frolov, written in 1982. The essay refers to the greenhouse gas theory of anthropogenic global warming. It blames capitalism and is titled, "Global Problems and the Future of Mankind," Frolov remarked that the "pollution of the environment, the destruction of ecosystems, the destruction of many species ... have now reached threatening proportions." These "dangerous disharmonies in man's interactions with nature are associated with ... the capitalist socioeconomic formation...." Therefore, these disharmonies require a "fundamental social transformation" if they are to be resolved.

Let's make a connection, here. Fundamental social transformation is what Black Lives Matter is all about. Fundamental social transformation is what "climate change" is all about. Fundamental social change is also what communism is all about. Shouldn't we assume a relationship between these three celebrated causes?

Greta Thunberg and former vice president, Al Gore, Jr. are basically on the same page as Antifa and Black Lives Matter and the Communist Party Soviet Union! It's time for a revolution, comrades, because capitalism is "destroying the planet." It's time for a revolution, comrade, because "capitalism is racism." Listen to Greta promote the Black Lives Matter Revolution, using the same language she uses to promote "climate change" alarmism:

VIDEO: *Greta Thunberg says people are 'waking up' to racial injustice as they have with climate change*[48]

The source of both narratives is the Communist Party Soviet Union. Both the BLM/social justice warriors and the "climate change" alarmists are ideological subversives in a long war against our civilization.

48 https://youtu.be/AyRbfteCex8

To blame capitalism for all our problems, especially when these problems are either fake or exaggerated, is incredibly self-serving. We can see, in Frolov's essay, that everything is so designed. It follows the Cold War template, and is an aspect of communist strategy, as explained by KGB defector Anatoliy Golitsyn, on page 95 of his notorious book, *New Lies for Old*:

> ...due regard should be paid to the fact that [KGB Chairman] Shelepin, in his May 1959 report and articles for KGB staff ... called for the preparation of disinformation operations designed to confuse and disorient Western scientific ... programs; to bring about changes in Western priorities; and to involve the West in costly, wasteful, and ineffective lines of research...

I ought to remind readers that "disinformation" is a kind of information warfare in which poisonous ideas are spread through *Western outlets* — not Soviet or Russian outlets. These ideas must appear to originate in the West. Thus, Moscow and Beijing reap a twofold advantage. First, Western scientists and politicians are contaminated by false ideas; second, Russian and Chinese academics are not contaminated. They can quietly continue their work with the advantage of knowing their Western counterparts are barking madly up the wrong tree.

The anthropogenic greenhouse gas theory of runaway global warming was a *Soviet original.* But nobody in the mainstream media noticed. Here are the words of Soviet academician Frolov, in his 1982 essay:

> As a result of the formation of a layer of carbon dioxide around the Earth which encloses it like a glass cover, the threat of unfavorable changes in climate has arisen that may transform our blue planet into an enormous greenhouse ... with possible catastrophic effects.

Here is the inspiration of little Greta. In 1996 Frolov's old Politburo colleague, Mikhail Gorbachev, acknowledged that the "threat of environmental crisis will be the international disaster key to unlock the New World Order." As Frolov originally formulated the idea in 1982:

> The effect of such an approach could be enormous if it could also be applied on a wider international scale in situations in which the interests of mankind at large are harmed by the activities of individual persons or organizations pursuing private interests.

Anthropogenic global warming theory is a weapon of war — a weapon of ideological subversion, demoralization and sabotage. The fact that this weapon remains deployed, as it continues to damage the economies of various Western countries, should not go unnoticed. *We should not be so stupid as to imagine that the weapon's inventors are no longer in the game.*

Our defenses, as usual, are down. Society is not fighting back against its poisoners and saboteurs. We are intimidated by the bullying of the climate alarmists. We fear the label "racist," just we fear the label of "climate change denier." Many of our greatest scientists have been labeled as "deniers," including Freeman Dyson, Zbigniew Jaworowski, Antonio Zichichi, Christopher Landsea, Hendrik Tennekes, Paul Reiter, David Bromwich, Edward Wegman and Henrik Svensmark — to name only a few.

Those heroes who would contradict the false claims of "fake science," have sometimes been marginalized, defunded or threatened. The enemy's "change agents" dominate a culture that is *not defended* against its enemies. Conceptual weapons are deployed against us on every front, on a continual basis — in terms of race relations, immigration policy, the Islamic threat, gay marriage, environmentalism, poverty, economics, education and crime. These weapons continue to be used, day after day, year after year. Our civilization is reeling under repeated propaganda hammer-blows.

Most people either concede the enemy propaganda, nonchalantly evading responsibility, or they agree to it on the lazy assumption that the loudest bullies of the day are right. Consequenlty, the worst people in the country, with the worst of motives, are pushing us to the edge of an abyss in every area of policy. Our civilization and our thinking has been eroded, year after year, decade after decade, by narratives *designed* to destroy us.

As Joseph Peiper noted in his book, *Abuse of Language — Abuse of Power*, "All men are nurtured, first and foremost, by the truth, not only those who search for knowledge…." Everyone, indeed, depends on the truth for their continued existence. Peiper further explained,

> The natural habitat of truth is found in interpersonal communication. Truth lives in dialogue, in discussion, in conversation — it resides, therefore, in language, in the word. Consequently, the well-ordered human existence, including especially its social dimension, is essentially based on the well-ordered language employed.

If you think that our system of order has gone awry, you would be correct. It is the routine and dishonest use of words, first and foremost, that has allowed the enemies of civilization to impose their calamitous revolution on us. The anthropogenic global warming theory, as a distinct part of this revolution, was never really about the climate, any more than defunding the police is about systemic racism. The whole thing is about power. It is a pretext for seizing power.

Every issue taken up by the left today is a pretext for extending socialism, and socialism is nothing but a system for extending despotic power. The truth is, anthropogenic global warming theory was a politically inspired hoax that Soviet scientists have never believed in — and neither do Chinese scientists, though they are undoubtedly ordered by their communist masters to play along for the sake of appearances.

As an aside, we may not fully appreciate our enemy's reasons for aggressively promoting the "climate change" hoax. In the 1970s scientists feared an ice age. What, after all, is more dangerous to man's survival? A warmer climate means a longer growing season and larger harvests. A cooler climate means a serious constriction of the food supply. Now think about this from a grand strategic perspective. Wouldn't advanced knowledge of global cooling be the most important information of all,? Consider the strategic value of denying the West advanced knowledge of a cooling-induced global famine! Thus you might delude your enemy to sell his grain stockpiles and neglect his own. Wouldn't that preserve you from the effects of global cooling while his society disintegrates from hunger and mismanagement?

The importance of knowing and preparing for global cooling should not be understated; for such a preparation would necessitate a strict policy of with regard to food and water. Depending on where cold air masses form and at which latitudes, global cooling would signify flooding in some regions and drought in other regions. Historically, global cooling has coincided with decade-long droughts in China. Therefore the question should be asked: Is this why China has constructed 87,000 dams over the last seventy years? Have they been attempting to store water because they anticipate severe droughts, which have historically devastated their agriculture during grand solar minimums in the past? Consider this Indian report on China's dams. Is it a case of water war for its own sake, or is it about water storage on a dry and overpopulated continent?

There are many factors to consider, and the picture is not entirely clear. But one thing is certain: The "climate change" narrative of the left has been artful misdirection from the start.

In the last 35 years there is no *real* evidence that humanity caused the warm period of the previous three solar cycles. The data, even on a simple graph, shows that we are headed toward something very different; that is to say, a cooling period. By common sense, nearly all our warmth comes from the Sun. We certainly do not get it from the moon, and we do not get it from the Earth itself, or from our SUVs. The Sun is the ultimate driver of climate; not man, not greenhouse gases. *No! Carbon dioxide doesn't drive climate. The Sun drives climate.* The cause and effect relationship has here been misunderstood by those geniuses who believe what they are told by communist "change agents." Consider *real* science, for a moment, if you can stand it. Consider what has been happening to the Sun's electromagnetic field during the past four decades:

FIGURE: Graph – *Sunspot Area: 1985-2019.*[49]

Sunspot activity is in decline, and so has the Sun's electromagnetic field (which tracks with sunspots). To explain this chart: Approximately every eleven years the Sun's electromagnetic field collapses, reverses and recharges. The above chart, therefore, portends a steady weakening of the Sun's electromagnetic field.

With each successive collapse of the solar electromagnetic field, the field recharges at a weaker level. This is significant because the Sun's electromagnetic

49 https://i0.wp.com/jrnyquist.blog/wp-content/uploads/2020/07/clip_image012-2.jpg?w=606&ssl=1

field blocks cosmic rays which accelerate cloud formation. Clouds reflect heat from the sun back into space, cooling the planet. Presently we are at the dead bottom of the solar minimum, and all the evidence suggest the Sun's electro-magnetic field will not rebound to the previous high, leading to a decade of significantly colder temperatures; that is to say, we will have shorter growing seasons, erratic weather — including floods and droughts (like the flooding in China).

The Danish scientist, Henrik Svensmark, has demonstrated that cosmic rays, known as muons, or heavy subatomic particles from exploding stars, definitely accelerate rain-cloud formation over the oceans, cooling the earth while increasing global precipitation. At the low point of the 24-to-25 solar cycle, the weather will begin to turn oddly cold in places, and some regions will be flooded. Cold air masses will appear, the jet stream will change. Tropical air will be redirected. Arctic air will be pulled down to lower latitudes over continents. Freezing weather will occur at times and in places it should not. Crops will be ruined. Some regions will experience warming (due to the jet stream), while global temperatures will drop overall. (For example, some sources I have consulted say that during periods of global cooling, the western United States will experience warmer than average temperatures.)

If you think Svensmark is a clown, and you insist on believing the greenhouse gas theory, then you must also lump Chinese and Russian scientists in the clown department. These did not, of course, falsify their data to eliminate the medieval warming period of several centuries ago. They do not slavishly believe in a "scientific consensus" on "climate change." They quietly go about their work.

From the *South China Morning Post* of 11 August 2019, Stephen Chen's headline reads: "China scientists warn of global cooling trick up nature's sleeve."[50] According to Wu Jing of the Institute of Geology and Geophysics under the Chinese Academy of Sciences, the effect of man-made greenhouse gases has probably been "exaggerated." Indeed, China is not suffering from global warming, but from the effects of cooling, as the July snow in Beijing testifies. China is also suffering from major floods. The South China Morning

50 *"China scientists warn of global cooling trick up nature's sleeve"*, by Stephen Chen, *South China Morning Post*: https://www.scmp.com/news/china/science/article/3022136/china-scientists-warn-global-cooling-trick-natures-sleeve?onboard=true

Post blames "cold air" in the North Pacific, forcing moist tropical air into China. Thus, the flooding in China is caused by abnormal cold and not abnormal warmth.

Chinese scientists are worried that strident talk about "global warming" leaves the public with "misplaced confidence" that we can change the weather. The fact is, there's not much we can do. The real threat to mankind may not be global warming, but global cooling, which Chen's article says "might catch us totally unprepared — causing chaos, panic, famine and even wars...."

Now there's a point to consider. Given China's patient rise from backward status to superpower, why would they begin acting aggressively now? Looking at China's vulnerability to weather, especially at China's loss of crops to flooding and to the late spring freeze in the north, there appears a hint of desperation. Have the Chinese been expecting drought and famine? Are they preparing a war because of these expectations?

Is anyone in Washington asking the right questions here?[51]

51 VIDEOS, NOTES AND LINKS:

"Solar Minimum Approaching: A Mini Ice Age?", Bob Berman, 02/27/2019, *The Old Farmer's Almanac*: https://www.almanac.com/news/astronomy/astronomy/solar-minimum-approaching-mini-ice-age#

"Chinese scientists say region to get cooler", de KG Chan, *Asia Times*: https://asiatimes.com/2019/08/chinese-scientists-say-region-to-get-cooler/

"What Lengths Will China Go to Feed Its People as Ancient Cycles Repeat?", de David DuByne, 01/30/2019: https://medium.com/@globalcooling/what-lengths-will-china-go-to-feed-its-people-as-ancient-cycles-repeat-156f0b2c7052

Cultural Subversion and Socialist Dictatorship

08/18/2020

> It is the... building of a new collective consciousness by attacking, through ideological-cultural struggle and political action, all of the 'intellectual-moral' foundations of bourgeois society. This means... a thoroughgoing cultural revolution...
>
> — CARL BOGGS
>
> *GRAMSCI'S MARXISM*, PP. 121-123

According to a history of the Soviet State Security "organs," published in 1977, politically "unstable" Soviet citizens were kept track of and "managed" by the KGB. As it happened, such management required a special kind of "prophylactic" work. The key was to persuade the Soviet citizen in question to recognize the "political harm" of "indiscretions committed ... [so they could] get back on the right path." If this "persuasion" was successful, it would prevent criminal breaches of the Soviet security system and social structure.

A similar process of "prophylactic" correction has been set up today, in the United States. Only it has been done without reference to state security organs or the police. If you are a professional in almost any field, you have probably been compelled to accept politically correct dogmas or programs. For example, your employment or career might suffer if you were overheard saying marriage is the union of man and woman. Or your grades might suffer in a college course if you questioned the "settled science" of anthropogenic global warming. Worse yet, you could be attacked and beaten in the street for saying, "All lives matter."

Our emerging system of cultural control anticipates a future system of police control. Anti-socialist elements are routinely identified and demonized (as seen in the case of President Donald Trump or his followers). A vast indoctrination, utilizing peer group pressure and career incentives, has long been under construction in America. Citizens in all walks of life are judged as "responsible" or "irresponsible," based on their willingness to cooperate with the agitation-propaganda of the socialist camp. Those who oppose socialism are deemed "reactionary." Those who waver, and attempt to adopt independent thinking, are labeled "immature." It is not a matter of being arrested. The system works by propagating social and administrative consequences — enforced by managers, teachers and colleagues. It has progressed slowly, imperceptible, using code words that avoid direct socialist declarations. Always, in this process, the socialist camp advances under cover, using environmentalism, anti-racism and concern for the poor.

The whole thing is a cynical swindle. Those who see through it are targeted for ostracism. This is especially true for those attempting to expose the subversive activities of the socialist camp. Such people are denigrated. They are made to feel like kooks, driven from respectable society into the fringes; fired from their academic or government jobs, forced into retirement or worse.

This process has had many victims. Naturally, in a free society, those who are pushed out of jobs in teaching or government or the media can try a new profession. They can find employment as dishwashers, baristas or night janitors. They do not get thrown in prison or executed, as would happen in China, Cuba or North Korea; so one might ask why there should be any talk of victims at all. The soft tyranny of the American left thinks of itself as humane. Yet a society that believes a lie and muzzles truth-tellers will not stay humane for long.

What has been happening in America, for many years, is a cultural revolution which prepares the way for a more violent kind of uprising. As Carl Boggs explained in his book on Gramsci's Marxism, we are talking about "a thoroughgoing cultural revolution that sets out to transform all dimensions of everyday life and establish the social psychological underpinnings of socialism *before* the question of organized state power is resolved."

Here is an approach advocated by the Italian communist, Antonio Gramsci. It is an amendment to Lenin's revolutionary theory, offering the prospect of cultural changes that will facilitate the revolutionary seizure of power in an advanced capitalist country (like the United States).

To understand Gramsci's contribution to Leninist theory, it is worth examining the Leninist concept of the "dictatorship of the proletariat [i.e., the working class]." According to Marx the state is a machine of class oppression. Therefore, the present form of government in the United States is called by Marxists "the Dictatorship of the Bourgeoisie [i.e., the dictatorship of those who own businesses]." It is, according to the Marxists, a form of government in which the rich employ democracy and the free market to rob the poor. The objective of the Marxist-Leninist revolution is to overthrow the dictatorship of the bourgeoisie in favor of the dictatorship of the proletariat.

What, then, is the dictatorship of the proletariat? First, it is "the instrument of the proletariat revolution." Second, it signifies "rule over the bourgeoisie." As such, it is concerned with political power. But the seizure of power is *not* the final objective. According to J.V. Stalin, in his *Foundations of Leninism*, "The seizure of power is only the beginning." Why? Because the power of the bourgeoisie is not broken by taking over the government. In many cases, the bourgeoisie can take the government back. The question is how to prevent this. According to Stalin, "the whole point is to retain power, to consolidate it, to make it invincible."

The consolidation of power in a federal system, subjected to checks and balances, with state governments and a national government operating separately, is not easy. It requires decades of painstaking work. (Here is why Gramsci is so useful!) We see how the Marxists in the United States have always sought the centralization of power in a way that no mechanism of law — no checks and balances — could effectively oppose. Their control of the bureaucratic levers is the essence of the "deep state." It refuses to obey checks and balances, legal procedures and legal orders from elected magistrates. It will only obey when a president of the socialist camp enters the White House.

To attain invincibility in the consolidation of power, noted Stalin, three main tasks must be carried out. First, to break the resistance of landlords and capitalists, "to liquidate every attempt on their part to restore the power of capital." Second, to prepare the elimination of the middle and upper classes. Third, "to arm the revolution, to organize the army of the revolution...."

Resistance can be broken, for example, by defunding the police, by widespread looting, by collapsing the currency. At the same time, Marxist infiltration of big business can be used to stage provocations which underscore the wickedness of the capitalists. It is important, from the point of view of the revolution, that the capitalists are always blamed.

Psychologically, the expropriation of the rich needs to happen suddenly. It must be ruthless and thorough. It is facilitated by the fact that the rich are numerically insignificant and the government can be turned against them. If, at the same time, the masses are rioting and looting, the rich will find themselves in a hopeless position.

In terms of establishing a socialist society, the hardest thing to accomplish, in all of this, is the expropriation of the small business owners. These people are quite numerous. They are independent in their thinking. Wherever they exist, capitalism continues. To make the new dictatorship secure, according to Lenin, "the abolition of classes means not only driving out the landlords and capitalists" which is accomplished with comparative ease. It means "abolishing the small commodity producers…."

Yes, it means that all small businesses must go. They cannot be allowed to exist. Naturally, their resistance may become violent. Thus, Lenin explained, "The dictatorship of the proletariat is a … ruthless war waged … against a more powerful enemy, the bourgeoisie, whose resistance is increased tenfold by its overthrow."

Revolutionary theory anticipates a very violent bourgeois reaction. The counterrevolution which follows the establishment of "the dictatorship of the proletariat" will require the Marxists to use bloody and bloodless forms of struggle. It will involve violent and peaceful means of persuasion. It will rely on educational, economic and administrative weapons to smash "the forces and traditions of the old society," noted Lenin.

About this process, Karl Marx said to the workers: "You will have to go through fifteen, twenty, fifty years of civil wars and international conflicts … not only to change existing conditions, but also to change yourselves and to make yourselves capable of wielding political power…."

Lenin wrote: "It will be necessary under the dictatorship of the proletariat to re-educate millions of … small proprietors, hundreds of thousands of office employees, officials and bourgeois intellectuals, to subordinate them all to the proletarian state and to proletarian leadership, to overcome their bourgeois habits and traditions…."

Lenin joked that the workers would not easily give up their "bourgeois prejudices at one stroke, by a miracle, at the bidding of the Virgin Mary…." It would only happen, he said, "in the course of a long and difficult mass struggle against the mass petty-bourgeois influences" of tradition.

The struggle that Lenin described will involve slogans and stratagems; but it will also involve the violent breakup of the old order in all its particulars.

The dictatorship of the proletariat, as a new form of government, said Stalin, "is a revolutionary power based on the use of force against the bourgeoisie."

Perhaps the most important note that Stalin attaches to his summary of Leninist teachings on the dictatorship of the proletariat, is that this dictatorship "cannot arise as the result of the peaceful development of bourgeois society and of bourgeois democracy…." This dictatorship, which the communists seek to establish at all costs, "can arise only as the result of the smashing of the bourgeois state machine, the bourgeois army, the bourgeois bureaucratic apparatus, the bourgeois police."

One shudders to imagine the "smashing" of so many institutions, the destruction of the capitalist system itself, and the advent of a full-blown socialist dictatorship. Ask yourself: *Would America's nuclear deterrent survive such a process?* Surely, Beijing would applaud the advent of a communist regime in Washington, if only because Chinese world dominance would be assured.

It's Time to Get Out of California

09/09/2020

It's no use lying to ourselves. The state of California is no longer safe. Its government has assumed the likeness of something inimical. It is "progressive," having turned to the "left." It has put out the welcome mat for La Raza (*UnidosUS*), Antifa, and the People's Liberation Army. The state appears to be run by Marxists. Should that surprise us? California's business and political elites are tied to Beijing. San Francisco, with its many homeless encampments, is part Chinese colony and part liberal zoo. Meanwhile, Los Angeles is becoming a foreign city.

As these words are written, California burns. Outside my window ash is falling. The sky has a pinkish-orange glow because wildfires are raging across the state. Yesterday the fires knocked out our connection to the internet. The state's leading politicians blame the fires on Trump's failure to combat "global warming." But the wildfires are not due to global climate change. The fires, wrote Chuck Devore of Forbes Magazine, are the result of "decades of environmental mismanagement that has created a tinderbox of unharvested timber, dead trees, and thick underbrush."[52]

The radical leftists, who dominate California, are slowly destroying it. Their totalitarian urges have always been in evidence. If you have any doubts on the matter, consider what happened to California GOP state Senator Janet Nguyen on 23 February 2017. Following the death of Senator Tom Hayden, a pro-communist radical, Nguyen prepared a commentary on Hayden's treasonous activities during the Vietnam War. She first read her statement in Vietnamese, but as soon as she began to pronounce it in English, presiding Senator Ricardo Lara called her out-of-order, cut off her microphone and brought in the sergeant-at-arms to escort her out of the room.[53]

Even before Nguyen attempted to criticize Hayden, a Democratic staffer named Dan Reeves, working for Senate President Kevin de Leon, had emailed

52 https://www.forbes.com/sites/chuckdevore/2019/02/25/wildfires-caused-by-bad-environmental-policy-are-causing-california-forests-to-be-net-co2-emitters/?sh=37d76e25e303

53 https://www.mercurynews.com/2017/02/23/gop-state-senator-a-vietnamese-refugee-removed-from-california-senate-floor-after-criticizing-late-senator/

VIDEO: https://vimeo.com/205434558

Nguyen's staff, warning them that any statement against Senator Hayden would be a violation of Hayden's rights and "will be ruled out of order and rebuked by the [Senate] body."

Senate President Kevin de Leon took full responsibility for the action against Nguyen, finally agreeing to let her speak.[54] Yet the true feelings of de Leon are best reflected by the further statements of his staffer, Dan Reeves, who maintained that Nguyen had no right to criticize Hayden because Hayden had not criticized her. We can see, by this, the true north of the ruling Democrat's moral compass.

That sorry affair happened more than three years ago. Today the situation continues to worsen. The state government, being opposed to electricity for the sake of "the planet," didn't allow enough power plants to be built; so last month's heat wave resulted in rolling blackouts, business shut-downs and lost working hours. Last fall there were preemptive power shut-downs. Get this: The odd chance that wind might knock a tree onto a power line resulted in whole cities being deprived of power. And yet the forests and the underbrush burn anyway.

Environmentalism of the communist kind, bent on sabotaging private property, is an important aspect of California politics. Remember the spotted owl? They stopped timber falling to save the spotted owl. Now the spotted owl is burned out of his habitat because the loggers aren't clearing the dead trees and brush.

It would be wishful thinking to expect California's ruling party to change. They are not going to rebuke their radical policies. Consequently, businesses and people are leaving the state. They are voting with their feet. As a friend in San Francisco told me this morning, "People are fleeing, rents are dropping; but even with rents dropping, people don't want to live here because it has become a cesspool."

The writing is on the wall. It is time to get out of California. I am preparing to leave, too. Whatever happens, it's going to get worse in California before it gets better. The United States has tolerated treason and sedition for decades. Our collective unwillingness to identify domestic and external enemies has brought the country to a crisis. Even now, we are not facing the

54 https://www.sacbee.com/news/politics-government/capitol-alert/article135336514.html

facts. California, like New York City, is being abandoned by those who work and produce. Why? Because in the end, the Marxists are destroyers. They will destroy private property. They will end free speech. As they are emboldened, their tyranny will grow.

AMERICA'S 13TH VENDEMAIRE?

09/16/2020

We'll give them a whiff of grapeshot.

— NAPOLEON BONAPARTE

Some say the French Revolution turned a corner when Napoleon Bonaparte, on the 13th of Vendemaire (5 Oct.) 1795, ordered 40 cannons to open fire on an armed Paris mob of 30,000. The mob was coming to attack the National Convention at the Tuileries Palace. Between four hundred and a thousand "citizens" in the front ranks of the mob were mowed down by grapeshot and bullets. The mob fled in panic. Power in France remained with five men who, by 1799, gave way to one man — *Napoleon*.

In America, right now, a revolution is underway. The revolutionaries see themselves as champions of equality, anti-racism and "saving" the planet. The mentality behind today's revolution may be glimpsed in the "second tactical briefing" of Adbusters Media Foundation (regarding a 50-day siege of the White House scheduled for 17 September). According to Adbusters, America is oppressed by "dark forces," consisting of "alt-right hordes and white supremacists" allegedly aligned with President Donald Trump. To save American democracy from these "minions of evil," hundreds of thousands of "peaceful protesters" are being summoned to Washington, D.C. Their stated goal is "to remind this authoritarian regime" of the left's significance.

The Adbusters Media Foundation is based in Canada. It is not even American. Yet they have decided to intervene in *American* politics. The left is international, of course, having little regard for borders or nations. The left is also opposed to traditional religion. Their revolutionary ideology is something out of the John Lennon song, *Imagine*. Some think this song is beautiful. But on close inspection, it is a denunciation of God and country (and also, property):

Imagine there's no heaven
It's easy if you try

No hell below us
Above us only sky
Imagine all the people living for today

Imagine there's no countries
It isn't hard to do
Nothing to kill or die for
And no religion too
Imagine all the people living life in peace

You may say I'm a dreamer
But I'm not the only one
I hope some day you'll join us
And the world will be as one

Imagine no possessions
I wonder if you can
No need for greed or hunger
A brotherhood of man
Imagine all the people sharing all the world....

Coming from a super-rich rock star living under capitalism, the song is a very peculiar blend of melody and hypocrisy. If you try to "*imagine*" a world without religious faith, without nations or property, you'd better brace yourself; for people who believe in nothing are dangerous, and people who have no country are called "stateless persons," like the Jews who were gassed by Hitler. To make a republic of the whole world is to build a Tower of Babel that will collapse in civil war. And a world without property is even less pretty; for as no one owns anything, none will take care of anything. Why would anyone make something, or build something, if it cannot be sold as property to someone else? The communist values expressed in John Lennon's song are, in practice, an inversion of all those necessary things that make civilization possible in the first place. And yet, our revolutionaries, knowing neither philosophy nor history, see themselves as *philosophers* and *makers of history*.

If our young revolutionaries knew even a little history, they would know how much blood was spilled trying to build their socialist utopia in the twentieth century. If they knew a little about political science, they would know that their ideal signifies *tyranny in practice.* But they know almost nothing. That is what damns these children of revolution. Their ideals were tested in Soviet Russia and Communist China, Cuba and Venezuela — and many other places, too. The result of socialist revolutions is always civil strife, man-made famine, mass executions, secret informers, show trials, gulags and poverty.

To be so dishonest as to affirm a lie, and fight for that lie, is to renounce one's own humanity. Here is a passage into soul-rotting corruption if there ever was one. To be so careless, so thoughtless, as to unwittingly side with totalitarian "ideals," is to declare oneself the enemy of all who think, and all who truly care. This thoughtlessness is reflected in the very language of our young revolutionaries. Consider, if you will, the outrageous profanities of Black Lives Matter activist John Sullivan, who gave the following speech on August 29th to a leftist crowd in Washington, D.C.:

> …my name is John Sullivan. I'm from Salt Lake City, Utah. My group is Insurgents USA. We [are] about to burn this shit down. Fuck this shit…. Power to the people! Power to the people! Power to the people! [Crowd repeats the refrain] Damn right! We gotta fucking rip Trump out of that office over there, pulling him out of that shit. We [are] not about waiting for the next election. We [are] about to go get that motherfucker. I am about that shit. Because you know what time it is? I want you to repeat after me. It's time for revolution! It's time for revolution! It's time for revolution! [Crowd repeats the refrain.][55]

This is John Lennon's song without the prettifying tune. It is, of course, a seditious refrain — inciting rebellion against the government. As such, it is punishable by fines and imprisonment, though it is doubtful Sullivan will ever be punished. This revolutionary agitation is, on all sides, nurtured by the misguided tolerance of the state. What will come of this?

55 https://youtu.be/I8Pl564BnfA

"Ideas have consequences," noted Richard M. Weaver, in a book of the same title. Absolute truth exists; and we are obligated, as human beings, to find that truth and live by that truth. Otherwise, civilization declines or collapses; for civilization rises only so far as truth is honored. The violent revolutionary of today, however, doesn't believe in absolute truth. He may not even believe in reality. False notions, taught by socialist professors, have degraded him. The same can be said about our dreadful politicians — whose sickening fabrications are no longer endurable.

The false ideas of the left, which underlie today's revolution and may prove fatal to our country, are nurtured and transmitted by our universities. They are winked at by politicians and repeated *ad nauseam* by the media. In their present form, they demonize one man: President Donald J. Trump. As in the "second tactical briefing" of the Adbusters Media Foundation, we find Trump described as "this howling void of a president" with "sins too many to name…." But the *real* "howling void" is found on the left. The Canadian Adbusters claim to be working for "a global movement of systemic change — a Global Spring — a cultural heave towards true world order." But it's all nonsense. They wouldn't know what a "true world order" is. In the first place, if they cared about oppression, they'd be agonizing over the slave labor camps of China and North Korea. But no. They are preparing to attack the White House; and after that, the suburbs.

Who, indeed, will defend the suburbs? Which officer, assigned to defend, would say with Bonaparte, "We'll give them a whiff of grape"? Who has the nerve?

In 1850 Thomas Carlyle wrote, "The French explosion [of 1848], not anticipated by the cunningest men … [defied all] computation or control. Close following which … all Europe exploded…." He added. "Everywhere immeasurable democracy rose monstrous, loud, blatant, inarticulate as the voice of chaos." Carlyle said that civilization "was scandalously laid bare to dogs and the profane…." The kings of Europe "stared in sudden horror, the voice of the whole world bellowing in their ear, "Begone, ye imbecile hypocrites … Off with you, off!" What was most damning, thought Carlyle, was the weakness of the official response. None "stood upon his Kingship, as upon a right he could afford to die for, or to risk his skin…." Carlyle called this weak response an "alarming peculiarity." He wrote, "Democracy, on this new occasion, finds all Kings conscious that they are but Play-actors."

Today we do not have a king, but a Constitution. Is our Constitution, now, a play-acted Constitution? Will anyone seriously uphold it? For if you have pledged to defend the Constitution, what is your obligation regarding its enemies? Are you not obliged to deal with *them*? If you have pledged allegiance and you are a mayor, a governor, a president, a commanding general, *what are you waiting for*? Are you not sworn to defend the Constitution against "all enemies, foreign and domestic"? Or is it a play-acted oath that all these play-acting officials have pretended to take?

Ah, of course, they never intended to keep the oath! When they swore, they were all just *pretending*. The whole of our officialdom, then, is a fraud! Here is Carlyle's "alarming peculiarity" in our own time, in which solemnly constituted laws and forms of government are done away with by the "squeak" of Antifa's juvenile voice. Was Napoleon a butcher on 13 Vendemaire? Yes. Was it horrible? Yes. Being sworn to uphold the Constitution of France, did he have any choice? No. There was, before him, a duty to defend. Did you have the mistaken idea that *defending is nice*?

Order is a necessary thing. It is *not* to be set aside. The collapse of order, by its very nature, always signifies blood-soaked carnage. If violence is required to enforce order, then it is a *necessary* violence. Yet order cannot be established by fraudulent men sporting fraudulent ideas. That is why, at this juncture, only the *truthful* can save us. As Carlyle noted:

> A more scandalous phenomenon … never afflicted the face of the sun. Bankruptcy everywhere; foul ignominy, and the abomination of desolation, in all high places: odious to look upon, as the carnage of a battlefield on the morrow morning; — a massacre not of the innocents … but a universal tumbling of Impostors and of Impostures into the street!

The Mystery of China's Military Doctrine

09/24/2020

> In war, the subjection of the enemy is the end, and the destruction of his fighting forces the means.
>
> — CARL VON CLAUSEWITZ

Roger Cliff is the author of a recent study on the People's Liberation Army (PLA), titled *China's Military Power: Assessing Current and Future Capabilities.*[56] Cliff says that modern wars are decided by strategy and doctrine. He also says China hides its military doctrine behind disinformation and secrecy.

It should come as no surprise that Beijing keeps its military doctrine hidden. The reason is simple. The Chinese rulers have two faces: (1) a communist face; (2) a capitalist face. *Shall we guess which is their true face?*

The regime in Beijing is Marxist-Leninist. It is totalitarian and criminal. It actively suppresses dissent, murders political activists, operates reeducation labor camps, and persecutes religious believers. Add to this China's military buildup and threatening behavior toward Australia, India and Taiwan. What sense does it make to think the Chinese leaders are capitalists *who merely pretend* to be communists?

According to Roger Cliff, China's military objectives are determined by the ruling Communist Party. This party subscribes to Leninist revolutionary theory — a theory that seeks to engineer the downfall of capitalism. *Translation: Beijing is trying to defeat the United States.*

On this last point Washington and the Pentagon are confused. Occasionally they see what China is up to. But then everyone in Washington reverts back to Panda-hugging. One might ask: Why do we trade with China when Beijing uses so many unfair trade practices? Why do we tolerate their ongoing intellectual theft and political subversion?

Here we find that American policymakers also have two faces. They have a face that is indignant at Beijing's crimes, and a face that wants to do business with Beijing. Which is the true face of the American policymakers? *Shall we guess?*

56 Roger Cliff, *China's Military Power. Assessing Current and Future Capabilities*: https://www.amazon.com/dp/1107502950?tag=sa-sym-new-20&linkCode=osi&th=1&psc=1

It is time to say the truth. America's policy of trading with China is dangerous. It has to stop. We should not be sharing technology with the People's Liberation Army. We should not give Chinese communists access to our financial system. President Xi Jinping is a thug who sits atop a murderous regime, rife with corruption and primed for military aggression. Close collaboration with such a regime will get us *a knife in the back.*

It is only a question of *when* the Chinese communists decide to knife us. After all, America is the enemy the Communist Party has sworn to destroy. In Roger Cliff's book, there are several clues to China's military strategy for defeating the United States. We know that Chinese strategy emphasizes preemption, surprise and a desire for "rapid decision." Chinese texts say, "take the initiative as soon as you can." Consistent with ancient Chinese practice, these texts also emphasize avoiding a "direct engagement with enemy military forces" together with "precision strikes" and "unified leadership under centralized command."

In terms of China's military doctrine, here are the taglines for China's secret "Campaign Guidance" documents: (1) "integrated joint operations" (suggests an amphibious invasion); (2) "new domains of struggle (suggests the amphibious operation will aim at objectives outside China's sphere of influence); (3) "expansion of the scope of operations." (suggests an entirely new theater of operations). If we take the three "Campaign Guidance" concepts together, it seems the Chinese envision some kind of naval/amphibious invasion involving "new domains" by expanding the "scope of [military] operations."

More recently the PLA has issued a fourth "Campaign Guidance" concept in support of the first three: namely, "counter-terrorist operations." The Chinese apparently expect to occupy someone's territory, with attending civilian resistance (i.e., "terrorism"). Thus, "counter-terror" is required, possibly along the lines of Gen. Chi Haotian's references (in his secret speech)[57] to the killing of "women, children and prisoners of war."

Might the PLA's "Campaign Guidance" documents refer to a direct attack on U.S. territory following the collapse of the U.S. economy in a civil war scenario?

When asked by the author whether an invasion of North America had ever been contemplated by Russian or Chinese strategists, Col. Stanislav

57 See "The Secret Speech of General Chi Haotian", in the Appendix.

Lunev (a Russian defector) referred to *Operation Weserübung* — athe German invasion of Norway in 1940. He then made special mention of German infiltration troops. The role of such troops, in a Russian/Chinese invasion scenario, could be greatly enlarged for operations in North America. Troops could be infiltrated into the U.S. as tourists, students, or illegal aliens. Once inside the United States, they could pick up uniforms and weapons at secret arms caches. They could then secure key points of entry (like airfields and ports). Invading forces need not come directly from China or Russia. Lunev noted that ideas presented in the Zimmerman Telegram,[58] during World War I, were ahead of their time. In that telegram, the German Foreign Office proposed a military alliance between Mexico and Imperial Germany. Mexico, under the right circumstances, could be an important ally for an invading power. (Though Germany at that time was in no position to invade the United States or position troops in Mexico.)[59]

58 https://en.wikipedia.org/wiki/Zimmermann_Telegram

59 NOTES AND LINKS:

Viktor Suvorov, *Spetsnaz: The Inside Story of Soviet Special Forces*: https://www.amazon.com/s?k=spetsnaz&i=stripbooks&ref=nb_sb_noss_2

Huffington Post, "Putting China on Our Border": https://www.huffpost.com/entry/putting-china-on-our-bord_b_14685690

https://youtu.be/lp0eWqx6eRU

Democrat Secession Talk

09/28/2020

> Dear Red States…. We've decided we're leaving. We intend to form our own country, we're taking the other Blue States with us … that includes Hawaii, Oregon, California, New Mexico, Washington, Minnesota, Wisconsin, Michigan, Illinois, and all the Northeast.
>
> — LANNY DAVIS (*TWITTER*)

What should we think about prominent Democrats, like Lanny Davis, who want to divide America into two separate countries — along party lines?

In his Farewell Address,[60] George Washington explained that union should be regarded as "the palladium" of our "political safety and prosperity…." Union is of such benefit, and disunion so harmful, he added, "there will always be reason to distrust the patriotism of those who in any quarter may endeavor to weaken its bands."

Washington warned against those who, in seeking disunion, misrepresent the opinions and aims of others: "You cannot shield yourselves too much against the jealousies and heartburnings which spring from these misrepresentations; they tend to render alien to each other those who ought to be bound together by fraternal affection."

A government of the whole is "indispensable," said Washington, if only for reasons of national defense. He explained, "No alliance, however strict, between the parts can be an adequate substitute; they must inevitably experience the infractions and interruptions which all alliances in all times have experienced." The Constitution which unifies us under one law, "is sacredly obligatory upon all. The very idea of the power and the right of the people to establish government presupposes the duty of every individual to obey the established government."

Anything destructive of these fundamental principles, warned Washington, will have "a fatal tendency." Anything that serves to "organize faction, to

60 https://www.govinfo.gov/content/pkg/GPO-CDOC-106sdoc21/pdf/GPO-CDOC-106sdoc21.pdf

give it an artificial and extraordinary force," is to be discountenanced. Regular opposition to the acknowledged authority, and "the spirit of innovation upon its principles," should also be discountenanced. Washington considered the "spirit of party" to be the very "worst enemy" of popular government:

> The alternate domination of one faction over another, sharpened by the spirit of revenge, natural to party dissension, which in different ages and countries has perpetrated the most horrid enormities, is itself a frightful despotism.

Washington warned that party strife "agitates the community with ill-founded jealousies and false alarms, kindles animosity of one part against the other, foments occasionally riot and insurrection." More dangerous yet, Washington warned that kindling such internal animosity "opens the door to foreign influence and corruption, which finds a facilitated access to the government itself through the channels of party passions." In other words, the United States, through this process, *could become subject to a foreign power*.

Talk of secession by a prominent Democrat, like former White House Special Counsel Lanny Davis, is no joke. He displays, in various tweets, a blazing hatred of Christians and conservatives, referring to them as "crazy bastards." His high ideals amount to nothing more than bad manners, impudence, and degenerate cynicism.

You want to divide the country, Lanny? People of your ilk have been allowed to dominate our country far too long. Now *we* see what you are; that is to say, *all those things you accuse others of being*. Yes, Lanny, that's right. You are divisive little man. *A bigot*. You have no charity for your own countrymen; and you have no true intellect, being incapable of appreciating the intellectual arguments of those you have denounced. Do you really think its honest — or even intelligent — to say an unborn human child isn't human? Do you think its intelligent to suggest (by convoluted arguments) that our country shouldn't have a border? — when every other country in the world has one! Is it your position that Trump is a warmonger and a Russian stooge? Look to your clients, Mr. Davis. You want to see a stooge of Russia and China? The Clintons fit the description far better than President Trump.

Divide this country at your own peril, Mr. Davis. The Union is indivisible. Millions have fought for it and millions will fight again. And now you bare your leftist fangs, as if to impress us. Many of us already know what you are. Yes, we see you clearly: — we see your traitor's heart, your corrupt clients, your dysfunctional blue cities (like San Francisco and New York) being handed to thugs and criminals. Everything in your world smells like an open sewer. We get it. We do.

You're a subversive, Mr. Davis, and now you're an advocate of treason. So here are a few choice lines on your project from Shakespeare's *Troilus and Cressida*:

> O, when degree is shak'd,
> Which is the ladder to all high designs,
> Then enterprise is sick! How could communities,
> Degrees in schools and brotherhoods in cities,
> Peaceful commerce from dividable shores,
> The primogenity and due of birth,
> Prerogative of age, crowns, sceptres, laurels,
> But by degree away, untune that string,
> And hark what discord follows! Each thing meets
> In mere oppugnancy. The bounded waters
> Should lift their bosoms higher than the shores
> And make a sop of all this solid globe;
> Strength should be lord of imbecility,
> And the rude son should strike his father dead;
> Force should be right; or rather, right and wrong
> (Between whose endless jar justice resides)
> Should lose their names, and so should justice too.
> Then everything includes itself in power,
> Power into will, will into appetite;
> And appetite, an universal wolf,
> So doubly seconded with will and power,
> Must make perforce an universal prey,
> And last eat up himself.

Putin's Dialectic

10/09/2020

> The Democratic Party is traditionally closer to … social democratic ideas. And it was from the social democratic environment that the Communist Party evolved. After all, I was a member of the Soviet Communist Party for nearly 20 years. I was a rank-and-file member, but it can be said that I believed in the party's ideas. I still like many of these left-wing values. Equality and fraternity. What is bad about them? In fact, they are akin to Christian values.
>
> — VLADIMIR PUTIN

President Vladimir Putin of Russia gave an interview this past week in which he denied interfering in American elections. He was asked which candidate appealed to him more? — Trump or Biden? "We are onlookers," responded Putin; "we do not interfere in the process." Regarding allegations that Russia had interfered with American elections in the past, he said, "It is proof of the standard of the political culture [in America] — or the lack thereof."

Putin was mildly amused at the credit he has received (from Democrats) for manipulating the 2016 election. Referring to Trump's impeachment earlier this year, Putin noted, "when anyone tries to humiliate or insult the incumbent head of state, in this case … this actually enhances our prestige, because they are talking about our incredible influence and power. In a way, it could be said that they are playing into our hands…."

The double-edged subtlety of Putin's remarks did not stop there. Putin admitted that President Trump was interested in improving Russian-American relations. While this was certainly appreciated in Moscow, the reality of Trump's policy turns out to be negative toward Russia. According to Putin, "the greatest number of various kinds of restrictions and sanctions were introduced during the Trump presidency." Trump imposed new sanctions or extended existing sanctions 46 times and withdrew from the INF Treaty, the Russian president said.

Then Putin began to analyze the Democrats. He noted the "rather sharp anti-Russian rhetoric" of the Democrats. Yet the Democrats share European social democratic ideas, and these are also the ideas of the Communist Party Soviet Union. This was the party Putin belonged to for nearly twenty years. Putin admitted, "I believed in the party's ideas. I still like many of these left-wing values. Equality and fraternity. What is bad about them? In fact, they are akin to Christian values." Therefore, he insisted, there is "an ideological basis for developing contacts with the Democratic representative."

Then, with a wink to Black Lives Matter, Putin said: "It is a fact that African Americans constitute … one of the electorates of the Democratic Party. It is a well-known fact…. The Soviet Union also supported Africa Americans' movement for their legitimate rights." Putin added:

> Back in the 1930s, Communist International leaders wrote that both black and white workers had a common enemy — imperialism and capitalism. They also wrote that these people could become the most effective group in the future revolutionary battle. So, this is something that can be seen … as common values, if not a unifying agent for us. I am not afraid to say so. This is true. Do you remember … a time when huge portraits of Angela Davis, a member of the US Communist Party and an ardent fighter for the rights of African Americans, were on view around the Soviet Union?

The ideological comradeship between Soviet communists and American Democrats is now unmistakable, and Putin has chosen an interesting moment to wink at his American comrades. Many will feel surprise, perhaps even alarm at this sudden turnabout; but there is no turnabout at all. In general, the world has been tricked by the Russians. Putin is not a nationalist, as Russian nationalists have testified. Putin is not pro-capitalist. He still likes Marxist ideas, and so do his future partners in the Democratic Party. In fact, Putin said that Biden is "ready" to sign a "new strategic offensive reductions treaty" with Moscow.

How does Putin know what Biden is ready to agree to? Well, given Biden's past relationships with "former" Soviet officials in Ukraine and Russia, and his family's lucrative deals with communist China, the answer should be obvious.

The fun thing for the former KGB colonel is that he can *tell the truth*, plainly and simply, while many observers simply won't believe him. Meanwhile, the communists on America's streets are encouraged by such remarks. They have a powerful ally in the Kremlin, and a powerful ally in Beijing. Therefore, the time is ripe to burn more high-end stores, force suburban whites to their knees, and overthrow the government.[61]

61 https://youtu.be/4QrHzhmDme4

Two Presidents, Two Narratives

11/11/2020

> Mr. Lincoln arrived in Washington and took up the reins of control. It soon became very evident that, so far as the Republican party is concerned, secession if properly managed is rather a benefit than a misfortune.
>
> — HENRY ADAMS

In his famous essay, "The Great Secession Winter of 1860-61," Henry Adams wrote, "It appears very generally among our people that our theory of Government is a failure." This failure manifested itself on February 18, 1861 when Jefferson Davis was sworn in as Provisional President of the Confederate States of America on the steps of the Alabama State Capitol. Two weeks later Abraham Lincoln was inaugurated 16th President of the United States at the East Portico of the U.S. Capitol in Washington, D.C. At that moment, America had two presidents instead of one. Two narratives instead of one. Two opposing armies instead of one united army.

It was an error, of course, for Adams to think the division of the country was "rather a benefit than a misfortune." He did not envision battlefields strewn with corpses. He did not say how countless disputes would be resolved between North and South. Adams was then too inexperienced to see that no benefit could derive from two presidents leading two countries with two armies.

The political polarization of America, prior to 1861, was a gradual process. It took so long, and advanced with such subtlety, that Abraham Lincoln scoffed at the likelihood of Southern secession during the Republican Party's 1860 convention in Chicago. The South was bluffling, he said. Secession would never happen because the South would lose federal offices and preferments. Of course, Lincoln was wrong. Most Southern politicians didn't care about federal offices and preferments. They had other priorities. It can be said, therefore, that a long process of polarization led to a breakup of the country and to a bloody civil war.

The polarization of America, prior to 2020, has also been gradual — masked by the country's prosperity and apparent stability. The country is now divided into two camps, governed by diametrically opposing principles. The differences are now so striking, so profound, that it is inconceivable they will long tolerate one another. The violence of last summer is but a foretaste of what we should expect.

Despite what the media says, Joseph Biden has not legally won the presidency. The election is in dispute because of election "irregularities." And now, with tens of millions of mail-in ballots, a basic principle of free and fair elections has been violated; namely, the requirement that people show up in person to vote. An election with mail-in ballots, mailed by God-knows-who, was a standing invitation to fraud. And massive fraud is exactly what happened.

Voting is about government accountability. Election fraud, at its core, negates this accountability. Much of our media, and Biden's partisans, do not want to be accountable. From their lips, talk of investigating election "irregularities" produces scoffing on the one hand, and threats on the other. By various hints we are given to understand that any proper counting of votes may lead to widespread violence. The left, after all, has prepared this threat in advance (for exactly this eventuality).

Since last summer's looting and vandalism, the left has relied on violence and intimidation. Theirs is the *politics of extortion*. The left, in essence, is asking the country to forfeit election transparency to avoid violence. If America gives in, the Party of Extortion will extend its dominion over the entire country. Unchecked by police power, outrage will follow outrage. The Party of Extortion, having conquered the police, will begin to exercise police powers of its own. It will then be a question of accepting slavery or fighting a civil war.

How realistic is this scenario? An American friend in South America, who witnessed the collapse of Venezuela and the civil war in Colombia, texted me on election night. Seeing that Arizona had flipped to Biden, he sensed that the fix was in, that the election would be stolen. Having lost faith in the fairness of the process, with decades of Latin American experience behind him, he suggested that civil war would be our only way out. I was shocked. *But look at the situation from his vantage point*: America could either choose the fate of Venezuela or the fate of Colombia. In the first instance, Venezuelans acquiesced in several fraudulent elections and lost their freedom to a socialist dictatorship. In the second instance, Colombia saved itself by resisting the left in a long civil war.

This dire analysis would strike most Americans as unduly pessimistic. Election fraud, after all, is a Latin American problem and not an American problem. Yet America's elections do not follow the guidelines of our own Election Assitance Commission (EAC). Of the ten EAC requirments for a free and fair election, the United States falls short on four counts: (1) Votes were cast without proper registration; (2) tens of millions did not vote in person; (3) every ballot cast was not counted; (4) and in the cases of Detriot and Philadelphia, President Trump was not allowed to have an agent inside the polling stations.

Even if most Americans avert their gaze and pretend nothing has happened, the problem is not going away. Polarization follows a logic of its own. In 1860-61 a majority of Americans did not think the election of 1860 would lead to Southern secession followed by civil war. "Let the Southern states secede if they want," people said. "They will eventually come back into the Union." This is the kind of wishful thinking that often prevails at the outset of a crisis. But soon enough wishful thinking gives way to reality. In 1861 the Confederate attack on Fort Sumter caused a psychological shift in the North. Suddenly Southerners were viewed as "rebels" and "traitors" who made war on their own country.

In the present crisis, a similar shift in national psychology cannot be ruled out. Everything depends on how things unfold from this point forward. President Trump's lawyers *will* prove that massive election fraud has occurred. If the left and the Democratic Party refuses to accept the verdict of the courts, we will have two presidents, two narratives, and two armed camps.

It may be premature to write, at present, of "The Great Secession Winter of 2020-2021," but we are going to have to confront the erosion of the rule of law in America. This is not something we can hide from. A confrontation will come, either now or later. Meanwhile, in Beijing, the Chinese communists believe they have won two victories against America. First, by disrupting our society with a virus; and second, there is the "Biden coup."

The political process in America has become, over the years, a process of foreign subversion under the false flag of special interest politics. We have turned a blind eye to this process because we value peace and quiet. Russian dissident Natan Sharansky once said, "In dictatorships you need courage to fight *evil*; in the free world you need courage to see evil." If we are not willing to see, if we bury our heads in the sand, America won't continue as a great power. The truth is, we have been subverted, our institutions have been penetrated and compromised. Absent clearsightedness about this, we are doomed to defeat. The system of the Founding Fathers cannot make up for a lapse in courage on our part.

In 1861 Henry Adams thought America's "experiment" with republican government would fail because the Founding Fathers were themselves doubtful of its prospects. They knew there would be trouble, especially over the issue of slavery. Henry Adams wrote: "By an unfortunate necessity which has grown with its growth, the country contained in itself, at its foundation, the seeds of its future troubles." America got through those troubles, with a high cost in blood and treasure. And now we are facing worse troubles.

The new religion of socialism, which has ravaged many countries around the world, now overtakes us at home. It has grown like a cancer, inside the state, inside the culture. If the cancer of socialism continues unchecked, it will destroy the country. With Joe Biden in the White House, the socialists will close in for the kill. Representative Alexandria Ocasio-Cortez and others are already talking about making lists of Trump supporters for the sake of future reprisals.

It takes courage to see evil, as Sharansky said. And courage is what we must pray for. We cannot be afraid of two presidents with two narratives and two armed camps; for if we do not confront evil, it will destroy us. In that event there will be no president and no country.[62]

62 NOTES AND LINKS

Notes on election fraud by my friend, Allan Dos Santos:

Trump was warned in 2012 about voter fraud, saying (https://twitter.com/realdonaldtrump/status/256063573669855232?s=21):

"It doesn't matter who you vote for — it matters who is counting the votes." Be careful of voter fraud!

Latin America is fully of stories involving fraud, as it follows:

Study casting doubt on Bolivian election fraud triggers controversy: https://www.reuters.com/article/us-bolivia-politics-idUSKBN20O2BT

After lots of fraud accusations linked to Smartmatic, Brazilian Supreme Court says printing electronic votes is inconstitucional, even after a Constitutional amendment aprove by the Congress:

https://www.correiobraziliense.com.br/politica/2020/09/4875485-stf-decide-que-voto-impresso-e-inconstitucional.html

Well, CUI BONO? Who is Smartmatic's owner? Lord Mark Malloch-Brown, also a board-member of Open Society Foundation:

https://www.smartmatic.com/pt/sobre-nos/nossa-equipe/detalhe/lord-mark-malloch-brown

Smartmatic was close to Chavez and active in Brazil: https://veja.abril.com.br/mundo/smartmatic-era-proxima-do-chavismo-e-atuou-no-brasil/

Venezuela poll turnout figures 'manipulated by at least 1m votes': https://www.theguardian.com/world/2017/aug/02/venezuela-poll-turnout-figures-manipulated-by-at-least-1m-votes

Founded in Venezuela, the company – that today is headquartered in London – was accused of having direct ties to Hugo Chávez: https://www.bbc.com/portuguese/internacional-40807344

Between 2004 and 2015, Smartmatic participated in 14 elections in Venezuela. More than half a million voting machines and 377 million votes processed, according to the company itself.

A BBC story in Portuguese from 2017 (https://www.bbc.com/portuguese/internacional-40807344) says Smartmatic started in Venezuela, although its oficial website says otherwise: "Smartmatic was founded in Palm Beach County, Florida, USA", in 2000. Curiously, same year and same state where Al Gore and Bush battled back the election time.

In 2020, more than 1.6 million residents of Los Angeles County participate in the first-ever vote using the Voting Solutions for All People (VSAP) system designed by Smartmatic.

Smartmatic joined the United States Department of Homeland Security's Sector Coordinating Council, (SCC) for the Election Infrastructure Subsector in 2018.

Brazil, Sierra Leone, Oman, Armenia, Philippines, Argentina AND VENEZUELA use SMARTMATIC. Today Smartmatic is know as DOMINION: Michigan and many other states use voting machines supplied by Dominion Voting Systems, which is basically Smartmatic International Corp (https://law.justia.com/cases/delaware/court-of-chancery/2013/ca-7844-vcp.html).

One more thing to add: Opal Tometi https://twitter.com/opalayo/status/648910802687262720?s=21 is shameless known as a Maduro's supporter https://m.huffpost.com/us/entry/us_560a836fe4b0af3706ddc573?guccounter=1 a point of being invited as honorable Watcher in 2015 Venezuelan election. She described Venezuela saying that: "in a place where there is intelligent political discourse." Link: https://www.dailyherald.com/article/20151206/news/312069960

Willful Blindness

11/20/2020

> Think about the global interests behind your own news organizations. Think about the pressure being brought to bear from the social media companies to shut down free speech on any challenge to the election. This is a massive, well-funded, coordinated effort to deprive 'we the people of the United States' of our most fundamental right under the Constitution to preserve this Republic that we all cherish.... It is the 1775 of our generation and beyond.
>
> — SIDNEY POWELL, 19 NOVEMBER 2020
> WHITE HOUSE LAWYERS'
> PRESS CONFERENCE ON ELECTION FRAUD

The election fraud on November 3rd was significant. Evidence for fraud was presented yesterday at a press conference led by Rudy Giuliani and Sidney Powell. The question is: Will we reinstate the values of the American Revolution, or will we embrace the values of the Bolshevik Revolution? Are we ready for hard truths? Or do we prefer willful blindness? Here is the heart of the matter. Civilization is an ethical proposition. And ethics are rooted in truth — not blindness.

During an interview with Sydney Powell on Fox Business, Lou Dobbs lamented that the Department of Justice (DOJ) was "slow to move" on election irregularities. Powell objected. The trouble with the DOJ was not slowness, said Powell. "They have adopted a position of willful blindness to this massive corruption across the country...."

Willful blindness, in this case, is the result of ideological commitments; specifically, *socialist* commitments. As Benjamin Gitlow pointed out nine decades ago, America's socialists were corrupted after the success of the Bolshevik Revolution by Lenin's teaching that the ends justifies the means. A cynical disregard for honest dealing and truth became fashionable on the radical left. And now we see how this plays out, as noted by Sidney Powell during Thursday's press conference of White House lawyers. She spoke of a "massive attack on the integrity of the voting system…." She said, "They have trashed the right to vote…. And there is no doubt about it. This is a plan. You'd have to be a fool not to realize it." Powell spoke of "the massive influence of communist money through Venezuela, Cuba, and likely China" in our election.

How did the communists do it? A variety of methods were used. The method with the greatest impact allegedly involved the use of vote-altering computer software.

According to Powell, they used the "Dominion voting systems, the Smartmatic technology software, and the software that goes into other computerized voting systems." These were "created in Venezeula at the direction of Hugo Chavez to make sure he never lost an election…." Powell spoke of a "very strong witness who explained how it works."

Chavez, of course, was a communist. He died in communist Cuba before passing power to Nicholas Maduro, the current dictator of Venezuela. The communists have kept power in Venezuela by fraudulent elections. And now they've exported this method of taking and holding power to the United States.

You might ask: How did this happen? And why didn't the Justice Department intervene to protect the integrity of our election system? And why has the justice system allowed corrupt election practices to flourish?

This is what you probably missed: Communists got into our justice system after taking over various law schools. Under the Clintons and Obama they poured into government, infecting the Justice Department with "willful blindness." Former DOJ official J. Christian Adams[63] explained the situation as follows: "In effect, the precise institution designed to protect our rights is populated by people who believe some of us aren't worthy of protection." Adams went on to explain,

> The DOJ already had its share of leftwing radicals during the Bush administration, but their skullduggery was counter-balanced by the professionalism of newly hired, non-ideological attorneys and by the political leadership. Later, under the Obama administration,

63 https://www.amazon.com/dp/B005QBKXSM/ref=dp-kindle-redirect?_encoding=UTF8&btkr=1

> I saw what happens when every part of the bureaucratic machinery resists doing the right thing....

According to Adams, "the DOJ is now staffed with far more extremists than ever before. The prospect that these are the precise individuals who will be enforcing election laws... should keep every law-abiding American awake at night."

And now we have arrived. The left is attempting to steal an election. If they succeed, they will begin to exercise a new kind of power. Here is the context for understanding Powell's statement to Lou Dobbs. She knows that the left is ideologically committed to replacing our constitutional system with a socialist system. They intend to use the ongoing pandemic as leverage. Unless they are stopped, the United States may be politically and militarily weakened past the point of recovery.

Nothing about our stolen election ought to surprise us. We were warned about vote fraud for many years. Journalists from South America, like Allan Dos Santos,[64] tried to warn us. Members of Congress tried to warn us. Powell quoted from a 2006 letter written to Hank Paulson from Congresswoman Carolyn B. Maloney warning of foreign actors, hiding behind various coporate names, becoming part of American computer voting systems. Referring to the Smartmatic voting software, the letter affirmed that a Venezuelan businessman owned a "controlling interest" in Smartmatic. The other owners are "hidden through a web of offshore private entities."

Two U.S. Senators raised concerns about the integrity of our voting machines last year, noted Powell. "Why our government has not taken them seriously is beyond my comprehension," Powell added.

What about the foreign-connected perpetrators of the election fraud? Powell made the following observation, which is worth quoting: "the Dominion executives are nowhere to be found now. They are moving their offices overnight to different places. Their office in Toronto [Canada] was shared with one of the Soros entities." (*Of course.*)

As an aside, persons associated with the development of the Smartmatic software have made some curious statements. According to Powell,

64 https://www.ntd.com/allan-dos-santos-us-election-problems-mirror-vote-rigging-in-latin-america_525377.html

> Speaking of Smartmatic's leadership, one of the Smartmatic patent-holders, Eric Coomer[65] I believe his name is, is on the web as being recorded in a conversation with Antifa members, saying that he had the election rigged for Biden, 'Nothing to worry about here.' And they were going to 'F Trump.' His social media is filled with hatred for the president and for the United States of America as a whole, as are the social media accounts of many other Smartmatic people.

Powell then stated that this corrupt computerized vote-counting system (associated with Smartmatic) was "used in two thousand jurisdictions and thirty states." Widespread use of the software defies expert warnings that the software is highly vulnerable to manipulation. "People can literally go in and change what they want," noted Powell.

Powell and Giuliani spoke at length during the White House Lawyers' Press Conference. They are both noteworthy for their courage and public service. Lawyers involved in this process have been physically threatened and harrassed. These are not stupid people, but highly professional people. Attempts to ridicule them will, in the end, backfire. Citizens are beginning to speak out. Consider the recent presentation by actor Jon Voight, who made a very strong statement:

VIDEO: "*...this ballot count is corruption, like they are...* "[66]

This is a message that resonates with millions of Americans, and it is going to grow. Why will it grow? Because the militant left has become a cancer on the Republic — a cancer of corruption that now threatens our liberty.

Giuliani said during the Thursday press conference, "Our country has had it's ballots counted — calculated and manipulated — in a foreign country with a company controlled by friends of an enemy of the United States." That is quite a summary.

65 https://www.bing.com/news/search?q=Eric+Coomer&qpvt=eric+coomer&FORM=EWRE

66 https://youtu.be/k1jcy17vThA

Powell was right when she warned that it's 1775 all over again. The people of this country have a real grievance. If it is not taken seriously there is going to be a breakdown in the country's political system. "Americans are fed up with the corruption from the lowest level to the highest level of our government," said Powell, "and we are going to take this country back. We are not going to be intimidated. We are not going to back down."[67]

67 https://youtu.be/akqeL9AtJYI

A Disturbing Little Book

11/24/2020

> Whoever argues for a restoration of values is sooner or later met with the objection that one cannot return, or as the phrase is likely to be, 'you can't turn the clock back.' By thus assuming that we are prisoners of the moment, the objection well reveals the philosophic position of modernism.
>
> — RICHARD M. WEAVER

Richard M. Weaver was born on March 3, 1910 and died on April 1, 1963. He was a scholar and author whose work remains relevant today. Had he lived to the end of the Cold War, he would not have congratulated America on its supposed victory. Communism, he knew, was part of a deeper problem; that is, a philosophical and moral problem. The West was sliding into decadence. It was spiritually disintegrating. "Every man participating in a culture has three levels of conscious reflection," noted Weaver: "his specific ideas about things, his general beliefs or convictions, and his metaphysical dream of the world."

Western man has lost his metaphysical dream of the world. According to Weaver, our intuitive feeling about the nature of reality is the key. As he explained, "this is the sanction to which both ideas and beliefs are ultimately referred to for verification." And as we are about to find out in the midst of a disputed election, "Without [this] metaphysical dream it is impossible to think of men living together harmoniously over an extent of time." The dream binds us into a spiritual community. It orients us to the world and each other. But now, as recent events indicate, there is no "metaphysical dream of the world." There appears in its place the serial stupidities of ideology.

I am, of course, drawing quotes from a disturbing little book, written by Weaver in 1948, titled *Ideas Have Consequences*. The book offers dark prophecies supported by metaphysical arguments (like the one above). The West, Weaver predicted, would attempt to win the Cold War by living more comfortably than the East. The communists, he noted, believe in struggle.

Therefore, Weaver hinted, communism was likely to prevail. All our economic and technological advantages would prove irrelevant in stopping communism. In fact, these advantages would bind us in a cocoon of illusion.

Even those conservatives who praise Weaver today, who echo many of his insights, are bound by this cocoon of illusion. For example, Roger Kimball's foreword to the new expanded edition of Weaver's book is a case in point. While praising Weaver as one of our "half-forgotten conservative sages," Kimball remains evasively dubious with regard to Weaver's anti-modernism. Weaver, after all, held that equality between the sexes was "decadent." He thought modern technology was stupefying and degrading. Kimball dares not affirm these points. He does not think, as Weaver, that modernity is damned. Science, says Kimball, has shaped our world. Kimball then asks: Is it not hubris, on Weaver's part, to "think we could dispense with that world in an effort to live 'strenuously, or romantically'?"

But Weaver is not arguing that we should "dispense with that world." He is saying that *world* will dispense with itself. Ideas, after all, have consequences. Therefore, Kimball misses the point of Weaver's disturbing little book. Modernity's "spiritual disintegration" is not occurring in some remote madhouse. It is all around us, in politics and the marketplace. It permeates everything and its destructive effects are inescapable. Weaver says that a decadent civilization may appear to prosper, but we shouldn't be fooled by appearances. *Civilization is going away.*

Weaver knows that modernity is going to implode. We are going to be forced to live strenuously whether we want to or not. It is not a question of volunteering to give up our distracting technologies, our decadence, and the comfortable lies that rule over us. In the long run, we will have no choice. We will have to give it up.

At the same time, no political program could have arrested the moral and cultural decline of the last seven decades. Ours is a culture that denies its decadence. Look at the chicanery on every side. For every problem we have a false solution. Stewed in lies as we are, the rule of law is breaking down. We are now passing from an era of prosperity based on borrowed money to an era of outright spoliation.

Weaver's little book is disturbing because he knew all this was coming. He foresaw that all our pundits, our political fixit men, would be deadenders.

We lack the grit to confront our problems. Inevitably, however, our problems will force us back to the truth. Weaver knew that a culture built on false notions must collapse. After all, we have been organizing our own collapse for many years. Yet, even so, there will be survivors. There will be a future. And in that future, men will live *more strenuously*.

It is odd, is it not, that those who deny the permanent things – who deny the primacy of spirit – should imagine that the world of science and technology is permanent. But nothing here, in the material world, is permanent. And as modernity is based on the most material of all material conceptions of existence, it is the least permanent thing of all. To say, as Kimball does, that Weaver's imagined world is "an uninhabitable domicile" is therefore an odd inversion; for Kimball's "world shaped by science" is a runaway train, going faster and faster – either jumping the tracks or smashing up at the end of the line.

Weaver introduces *Ideas of Have Consequences* with the following sentence: "This is another book about the dissolution of the West." We are inclined to pass over the word "dissolution" because we don't want to go there. We cannot imagine that this world of ours, "made by science" as Kimball says, is doomed to fail. We believe too fondly in modern man's "successes." Yet a spiritual collapse has already occurred. We are already going backward, blunder by blunder – and we are likely to go all the way back to the Middle Ages if not to the Dark Ages.

Why are we going back? Because civilization is an ethical proposition and moral nihilism has overtaken us. Our problem, says Weaver "is getting men to distinguish between better and worse." This is not a problem we can solve with smartphones. We cannot fix it through social media. These technologies would hardly impress Weaver, who wrote, "There is ground for declaring that modern man has become a moral idiot."

How did this come to pass? Weaver has a remarkably concise answer. Around the late fourteenth century Western Man abandoned belief in the existence of transcendentals; that is, we abandoned our belief in truth, beauty and goodness. This came about through a "seemingly innocent form of attack upon universals." The result was a creeping subjectivism that would lead us to moral anarchy. At the same time, a process of de-spiritualization began. Finally, during the last century, man turned to politics for salvation by way of liberalism, communism and National Socialism. But there is no salvation in political ideologies.

According to Weaver, the denial of universals leads to the cult of empiricism. It leads to the denial of truth and to a general intellectual breakdown. Our intellectuals, in fact, are incredibly corrupt. Even science has been corrupted by them; for science is now the province of political hacks who do not know what the word "science" means. Worse yet, language itself has begun to break down.

"The practical result," argued Weaver, "is to banish the reality which is perceived by the intellect and to posit as reality that which is perceived by the senses. With this change in the affirmation of what is real, the whole orientation of culture takes a turn…." Goodbye truth, Beauty and goodness. Everything that is "higher," everything that is noble, is debunked.

After this fashion modern man was reduced to an abysmal state. And that is where we are today. Man craves truth, noted Weaver, yet he is told to live "experimentally" (without a moral compass). This has led us to "a long series of abdications." Here is the acme of our decadence, attended by denials and self-congratulations — with lies on top of lies. "To establish the fact of decadence," wrote Weaver, "is the most pressing duty of our time because, until we have demonstrated that cultural decline is a historical fact … we cannot combat those who have fallen prey to hysterical optimism."

Hysterical optimism? Do you want to convince me that things are getting better, not worse? Consider how ready we are to blot out the truth: (1) by denouncing truth as "pessimism"; or (2) by denouncing the truth as "impractical"; or (3) by dismissing the truth because it doesn't do that kissy-kissy thing that tickles your ego.

What Weaver is saying, in the end, is that truth is our only source of salvation, though we are ready to revolt against it. The most important truths come as warnings. "It is when the first faint warnings come that one has the best chance to save himself," noted Weaver. If we miss the chance then presented, our self-imposed blindness will paralyze us. "Thus in the face of the enormous brutality of our age we [will] seem unable to make appropriate response to perversions of truth and acts of bestiality."

Look at what is happening in our country. We have seen illegalities ignored, lies embraced as truth, criminals rewarded and the righteous denounced.

An election has been stolen. The Constitution is no longer the Supreme Law of the Land. Civilization, noted Weaver, “has been an intermittent phenomenon; to this truth we have allowed ourselves to be blinded by the insolence of material success.”

Weaver’s disturbing little book can be read in a few hours. It offers us a more realistic glimpse at our situation. It challenges our false optimism. It points to our philosophical mistakes. Here is an intellectual corrective. Here is medicine for the soul. Here is clarity.

On Choosing the Right Side

12/17/2020

When you drive your car, do you drive in the middle of the road? This seems a silly question to ask because you don't, of course, if you want to stay alive and get somewhere.

But a lot of people have been sold on the idea that the middle of the road is the safest place in politics on all sorts of controversial questions. They have been led to believe that in the middle position you are out of harm's way and you are more likely to be right than those who are on either side of a question. A little thought will show that this idea is born not of wisdom but of confusion or fear or both.

RICHARD M. WEAVER
"THE MIDDLE OF THE ROAD: WHERE IT LEADS", 1956

Machiavelli warned that neutrality is more dangerous than taking sides; for if you fail to take a side, both sides will despise you. Playing both ends against the middle is also dangerous, since you prove to be a false friend to all. And being everyone's friend will not work if each side represents diametrically opposing principles. The right camp is never found in splitting the difference between two opposing camps. Conservative philosopher Richard M. Weaver pointed out in 1956, "middle-of-the-roadism is not a political philosophy at all. It is rather the absence of a philosophy or an attempt to evade having a philosophy."

In the great and perpetual struggle that is history, to strive mightily without principles is to strive in vain. Even if you manage to win, nothing is affirmed. Nothing is advanced. As time stretches out before us, *something will be affirmed. Something will be advanced. Somebody's philosophic principles are going to prevail.* Will those principles be good or evil? Will they sustain civilization or destroy it?

If your principles are good, would you be willing to compromise them for expediency's sake? Weaver asked his readers, "Try imagining the figure that Washington would cut in history today if he had decided on a compromise settlement with the British." Weaver saw the emerging Republican establishment of the post-McCarthy period, under President Dwight Eisenhower, as representing the opposite of Washington's example: "The prophets of the New Republicanism ... insist that the Republican Party keep moving to the left behind (but not too far behind) the Democratic Party."

Has anything changed in the last 64 years?

Where did the Republican Party under Eisenhower and Nixon think it was going? Where does the Republican Party, before and after Trump, think it is going? Weaver noted: "They do not bother to ask whether the leftward drift is not toward something essentially bad...." Weaver called this "a curious piece of political servility and blindness." He characterized the emerging Republican establishment of the post-McCarthy period as "a typical product of the 'operational thinker,' who does not really 'think.' Instead, he 'senses,'" like "an insect with its antennae," detecting "the drift of things." The question, noted Weaver, is whether the operational thinker "can ever be anything more than an insect...."

Thomas Carlyle, who spent his literary career describing heroes and great men, said that a great man is someone who sees the truth others are afraid to see. A hero takes a stand when others will not. Carlyle suggested the mediocre man – the "insect" – cannot see truth or stand by it. Instead of taking a stand, the mediocre man attempts a compromise. He falsifies reality. He temporizes. He forges an imaginary middle path between irreconcilable opposites. He imagines this is a safe bet. Of course, it is not safe. As Weaver explained, "a position half way between right and wrong is not a sound position. It only postpones and makes more difficult the eventual decision."

This is where we are today. Our Constitutional system has been compromised. Our elections have been compromised. Our courts have been compromised. We are told to close our eyes and pretend everything is fine. That is what many of our authorities are doing. They pretend there is no fraud, which is yet another kind of fraud.

In principle, there should be no compromises when it comes to corruption. There should be no compromises when it comes to truth. And yet, that is all we are given to expect. Men imagine they will gain by this; but in the end everyone will lose. History offers us a choice of *either/or.* It does not offer us *either and or.*

"The great causes which have triumphed and the leaders which have led them have never been found in the middle of the road," noted Weaver, who described the Whig Party of the early-to-mid-nineteenth century and its leader, Henry Clay, as making "the fatal mistake of trying to straddle the fence on major issues that were in conflict." As a result, Clay did not go to the White House. It was the "hard-hitting" Andrew Jackson who became President. We can see, from this, that history has recently repeated itself. The middle-of-the-road Jeb Bush did not go to the White House, but the hard-hitting Donald J. Trump is sitting in the White House as these words are written.

Another historical example, Weaver noted, is the British Liberal Party. This party neutered itself by taking a middle position between the Conservative Party and the Labor Party. By doing this the Liberal Party destroyed its position in British politics. "All great political parties owe their vitality to the importance of the principles they stand for," wrote Weaver. The middle-of-the-road, therefore, is not the path of political success because it is not a path of principle. According to Weaver, "A beaten party with a real issue has an excellent chance of coming back. A beaten party without an issue is a dead duck." He added, "Dodging issues and watering down solutions is not merely the way to failure; it is the way to extinction."

Why should the consequences of dodging issues and watering down solutions be so dire? "There is one group," wrote Weaver, "not clearly distinguished by a party name, but quite definite about what it wants and expects to bring about in this nation." This is a group that works "on various fronts and under various labels, but there is no need to be confused about its objectives. It wants an America, new-modeled according to the Soviet Union." This group operates by two main ideas: (1) atheistic materialism; and (2) a state supremacy that "crushes the individual." To compromise with this group is, indeed, "the way to extinction."

"You would think that in this great country of ours," wrote Weaver, "with its heritage and its achievements, there would be a tremendous outcry and opposition to anything so one-sided [as collectivism] in its interpretation of … man's nature and so chilling to human instincts." But many of our leaders, said

Weaver, "have adopted the policy of appeasement. Instead of issuing a direct challenge in terms of principle, they have tried to see how many concessions they could make without being accused of surrender." He added, "They have tried to see how closely they could approach the position of collectivism while still paying lip service to what they are supposed to be defending."

Weaver argued, there is no viable middle position "between militant collectivism and our tradition of freedom and individualism." He continued, "Historical examples show that the next step is capitulation, or liquidation of the party which is so cowardly." If the collectivists win, wrote Weaver, "it will certainly be recorded by history that no people ever gave up so much for so little."

This is how Weaver saw the situation in 1956. And here we are, 64 years later, without free and fair elections, without investigations into treason and subversion, without any redress of many serious grievances, without protection from corruption and fraud, without a legal way to fight back. "There is little doubt that the middle of the road leads in this direction," wrote Weaver. "The radicals know what they want; too many of the rest of us only temporize and hope."

What is needed? "The need of the time is for a leadership willing to face facts," said Weaver. We do not need leaders or political parties predicated on "self-defeat through compromise." Many of us want to know when things are going to change. Who is willing to act? Who will take on the collectivists and call them to account?

The hour is late. Our fair goal is justice. The problem, wrote Weaver in *Ideas Have Consequences*, is that modern man "is a moral idiot." Toward the end of the book Weaver added, "modern man is a parricide" who has "taken up arms against … what former men have regarded with filial veneration." Think of how love of country is now vilified as white nationalism. Even the existence of America's border is "racist." Family and tradition have been traduced as gender bigotry. This "idiocy" rules over us. It corrupts us as it swindles us.

The time to organize opposition to this "idiocy" is now. We must stand up for the country. We must stand up for posterity. This may be our last chance to choose the right side.

A Momentous Day

01/06/2021

> It is precisely because Marxism is not a lifeless dogma, not a completed, ready-made, immutable doctrine, but a living guide to action, that it was bound to reflect the astonishingly abrupt change in the conditions of social life.
>
> — VLADIMIR LENIN

The hour is very late. The country has been asleep for decades. But now, it seems, the country is beginning to wake up. The real question is whether our leaders are ready for the task at hand. We have some smart people in government; but do they understand the enemy we are facing? Are they prepared to battle that enemy in the midst of so much confusion and misinformation?

This morning I saw a Breitbart headline about China: "Xi Jinping orders Chinese army to prepare for war 'at any second.'"[68] Here is our enemy, positioning himself to strike. There is no other way to read it. If we consider the timing of this threat, it's clear what they want us to do. After all, they have much to gain if Biden becomes president. And besides, they are not so careless as to let their prey escape.

As we watch what happens in today's joint session of Congress, I am reminded of Stalin's question, set down in his book, *Foundations of Leninism*: "Does not the history of the revolutionary movement show that the parliamentary form of struggle is only a school for, and an auxiliary in organizing the extra-parliamentary struggle?"

Marx, Engels and Lenin were opposed to the "opportunism" of those who wanted to work within the capitalist system for peaceful change. The whole point of Marxism is to make a revolution. The Second International, according to Lenin, was dominated by opponents of revolution. He called them "opportunists." Such people weren't real Marxists. "Instead of revolutionary

68 *"Xi Jinping Orders Chinese Army to Prepare for War 'at Any Second"*: https://www.breitbart.com/asia/2021/01/05/xi-jinping-orders-pla-prepare-war-any-second/

policy," wrote Stalin, "there was flabby philistinism and sordid political bargaining, parliamentary diplomacy and parliamentary scheming...."

"A revolution is not a dinner party," snarled Mao Zedong, "or writing an essay, or painting a picture, or doing embroidery; it cannot be so refined, so leisurely and gentle, so temperate, kind, courteous, restrained and magnanimous. A revolution is an insurrection, an act of violence by which one class overthrows another."

Americans may not fully understand what lies in store for them. A communist revolution, said Friedrich Engels, requires the annihilation of whole races and classes of people. It is in this sense that America is the target of a communist revolution. In this context Joe Biden may seem quite harmless, but his Chinese communist backers are murderers. If Biden assumes power, the government will devolve into a one-party state. He will kowtow to China. There will be no more U.S. nuclear deterrent. The country's economy will be damaged. A process of weakening, of stripping out defenses, will accelerate. The communists in Beijing know that America cannot be made into a communist country. The American people would violently turn against the government. To use an old Soviet expression, America is "irredeemably bourgeois." In other words, Engels was right. A communist revolution requires the annihilation of whole races and classes of people. Most of all, it requires the annihilation of the Americans.

This aspect of communism is not even understood by most communists. After all, very few of them have actually read Marx or Engels. That kind of study is reserved for people at the top of the communist hierarchy. The Americans also never understood communism, because it was too boring to bother with. The conservatives, who pretended to understand communism as an "ideology" of mass murder actually didn't understand it at all; that is to say, they never got to know communism in depth. They knew it was murderous, yet they never saw the method in its madness. What they saw disgusted and horrified them, so they didn't want to get any closer and learn what it actually was.

Marxist leaders are *not* normal people. When Lenin assailed the "opportunists" of the Second International, the first thing he mocked was their bourgeois inclinations; that is, he criticized them for being normal. These fake Marxists, he said, wouldn't make a revolution because they didn't have the majority on their side. They wouldn't make a revolution because they lacked trained cadres. They wouldn't make a revolution through a "general strike" because parliamentary politics was more effective. Lenin said their Marxism was hooey. You don't need a majority, said Lenin. You don't wait to take power because you lack trained cadres. First take power, then train the cadres. And who cares about the anarchist concept of the "general strike"? Marxism is a more focused, tightly and intelligently controlled form of violence.

The key, of course, is always violence; but violence with craft and cunning behind it. There is no dogma in Marxism about having a majority, or having elite cadres, or launching a general strike. Lenin said "revolutionary theory is not a dogma," and that it "assumes final shape only in close connection with practical activity of a truly mass and truly revolutionary movement…." (See *"Left-Wing" Communism: An Infantile Disorder* for details).

Now that we're watching a communist revolution unfold here in the United States, we ought to get a little more familiar with Marxism-Leninism as a "thesis" and not as a "dogma." It is something that our conservatives long refused to do; and this refusal is exactly why they went running like dogs to lick Mr. Gorbachev's face three decades ago. You will always hear conservatives refer to "communist ideology" and its "failures," as if communism actually represented an economic doctrine. But there is no economic system propounded by Marx. For his part, Lenin retreated into state capitalism after the Russian Civil War. And Stalin's collectivization of farming was a political measure rather than an economic one. If he had not impoverished the farmers, the farmers would have overthrown him.

The whole course of Marxism-Leninism has been misunderstood, from first to last. Our great historians and conservative thinkers had all the facts. But they never really read Marx or Lenin or Stalin. They never quite understood the motivation, the strategy, the brainpower. And so, they mistook Marxism for an ideology when Marxism was never an ideology. Marx defined "ideology" as the "false consciousness" of a ruling class in a society in which ruling ideas are represented as "universal truth." You see, Marxists don't believe in universal truth at all.

Stalin said Marxism had two elements: (1) a materialist "outlook" and (2) a dialectical method. Everything followed from these two things. Many people who are not communists believe that a materialist outlook is the most common-sense view available to modern man. Here we begin to see why communism has been so difficult to oppose. After all, many of our non-communists have no problem with its central proposition.

The Marxist, noted Stalin, is opposed to "idealism" which "regards the world as the embodiment of an 'absolute idea,' a 'universal spirit,' 'consciousness'…." Stalin explained that "the world is by its very nature material, that the multifold phenomena of the world constitute different forms of matter in motion, that … the world develops in accordance with the laws of movement and matter and stands in no need of a 'universal spirit.'" (That is, no need of God.)

As you can see, this is not an "ideology." This is something broader and more fundamental. It is one of two possible cosmologies: (a) one that tends toward the supernatural, and (b) one that tends toward the natural. What makes Marxism different, and more effective as a weapon against supernaturalism, is its reliance on dialectics. "Contrary to metaphysics," wrote Stalin, "Dialectics does not regard nature as an accidental agglomeration of things, of phenomena, unconnected with, isolated from, and independent of, each other, but as a connected and integral whole, in which things … are organically connected with … and determined by, each other." What that means is not at all clear, and it is no accident that Marxists look back fondly to the pre-Socratic philosopher Heraclitus who was also known as Heraclitus "the obscure." Stalin quoted Heraclitus to the effect that "the world, the all in one, was not created by any God or any man, but was, is and ever will be a living flame, systematically flaring up and systematically dying down…." Lenin called this, "A very good exposition of the rudiments of dialectical materialism."

Heraclitus taught that the universe was continually changing. "Contrary to metaphysics," noted Stalin, "dialectics holds that nature is not a state of rest and immobility, stagnation and immutability, but a state of continuous movement and change, of continuous renewal and development, where something is always arising and developing, and something is always disintegrating and dying away."

This is where the revolution comes in. The communist's simple insight is that the existing order (capitalism) and its attending Christian civilization is "disintegrating and dying away." Nietzsche was not the only nineteenth century thinker to suppose that "God is dead." The Marxist is that clever species of legacy-hunter who goes to the funeral of the "dead God" expecting to steal something; that is to say, the legacy of Western civilization.

One of the reasons that Marxism has been so successful, is the way it plausibly exploits the superficial assumptions of modern man. Another reason is Marxism's strategic and tactical flexibility. When you draw your inspiration from an obscure Greek philosopher whose utterances were as dubious as the Delphic Oracle, and you claim to be "scientific" in your approach, it is given that your theses will change with time. And this is exactly what has happened. Those academic pedants who see in Marxism a set of rigid doctrines discredited by history have missed the whole point of Marx's writings. Every failed Marxist thesis paves the way for a new thesis. That is, after all, the scientific method. If something fails, you return to the drawing board; for Marxism is not about believing. Marxism is about doing. It is about the "science of revolution," as Stalin said. And this science, at the time of Marx, was only in its infancy. Today it has reached its full destructive maturity. Please note with what sophistication Marxism commands events, dominates media, dictates the principles of education, destroys the careers of its opponents, co-opts liberals and pretends to fight climate change. There is so much more that could be added here.

It is true, of course, that the Marxists have gotten a great deal of power by peddling several false doctrines and leftist dogmas: homosexual marriage, transgenderism, critical race theory, global warming, etc. But none of these are Marxist in the true sense. These "dogmas" are merely tools of Marxism – tools in the scientific toolbox of revolution. In his essay, "Certain Features of the Historical Development of Marxism," Lenin explained that Marxism "is not a dogma, but a guide to action." Lenin continued, "This classical statement stresses with remarkable force and expressiveness that aspect of Marxism which is very often lost sight of. And by losing sight of it, we turn Marxism into something one-sided, distorted and lifeless; we deprive it of its life blood; we undermine its basic theoretical foundations – dialectics, the doctrine of historical development, all-embracing and full of contradictions; we undermine its connection with the definite practical tasks of the epoch, which may change with every new turn of history." (p. 248, *V.I. Lenin: Marx, Engels, Marxism*, Eighth Revised Edition, Progress Publishers, Moscow, 1968).[69]

Imagine the flexibility of a science that "may change with every new turn of history." This is why George Orwell was so frightened by the Marxists; why

69 *V. I. Lenin: Marx, Engels, Marxism*, 8th rev. ed., Progress Publishers, Moscow, 1968, p. 248.

the socialist regime in his novel, 1984, was described as a boot stomping on a human face, "forever." He didn't see how Marxism would ever lose. Those who said the Marxists would fail because they never understood human nature were wrong. Marx understood human nature perfectly. His adepts could not have lasted in power so long – in China and, dare I say, in Russia too, where they were flexible enough to give up the communist label while retaining the essentials of the communist system. Those families that ruled Soviet Russia – *the Central Committee families* – yet remain in control. The old Soviet oligarchy hides behind the fake "capitalist" NEP-men of the Gorbachev-Yeltsin-Putin New Economic Policy (NEP). The whole thing is right out of Lenin's playbook. (And that is what flexibility has to offer.)

You might ask why Marxism is so keen on revolution? Why does dialectical materialism require revolution? The answer to this question is simple. All the Marxist arguments for revolution are not scientific. They are window-dressing. The reason for the revolution will never be stated publicly by Marxist-Leninist theoreticians or leaders. This is the part where you have to study biography; where you have to look at the psychology of Marxist revolutionaries. Think, if you can, what follows from a cynical human being like Marx, who doesn't believe in God or an afterlife. Cut off from all hope of spiritual salvation, the only thing left for such a person is political power; that is to say, the only real power a materialist can believe in. The salvation found here is that of becoming a God through the politics of revolution. Here we draw closer to the real Marx, and the real Lenin, and – undeniably – the real Stalin; for the Marxist dictators have indeed achieved a godlike status for themselves.

So, as we live through this momentous day we ought to reflect on what it will take to defeat Marxism. If you think we face an uphill battle now, you haven't seen anything yet. I do not believe we really know our enemy. I also do not believe we know ourselves; yet today may be a good day to begin learning.

Inauguration Day: Utopia Limited or the Flowers of Regression

01/21/2021

> Hitherto the question has always stood: What is God? – and German philosophy has resolved it as follows: God is man.... Man must now arrange the world in a truly human way, according to the demands of his nature.
>
> — FRIEDRICH ENGELS

Several decades after the devil's own Friedrich Engels wrote that man "must now arrange the world," Leon Trotsky argued that the Revolution must make the "collective man" into the "sole master" of all.[70] And now, nearly a century after Trotsky made that pronouncement, we arrive at the inauguration of Joseph Biden. Look at him, before the Capitol, stepping into the shoes of George Washington. Behold this fraud, on old knees, personifying the "sole master" and "collective man," with his dyslexic malapropisms and lapses of memory. Behind Mr. Biden, the eyeballs of Vice President Kamala Harris are excitedly glued to a banana peel under his left shoe. One thinks of Joseph Stalin and the ailing Lenin in 1922. If we listen, we may hear the mocking voice of Karl Marx citing Hegel's comment that "all facts and personages of great importance in world history occur, as it were, twice."[71] Hegel forgot to add, "the first time as tragedy, the second as farce."

And what a farce! For Kerensky, we have Trump; for the Kadets, we have the Republicans; for the storming of the Winter Palace, the storming of the Capitol; for Fanny Kaplan, we have two guardsmen with militia ties; for Felix Dzerzhinsky we have Gen. Stanley McChrystal; for the Red Terror we have a new domestic Terror Bill. As Marx wrote, "Men make their own history, but they do not make it just as they please; they do not make it under circumstances chosen by themselves, but under circumstances directly encountered, given and transmitted from the past."

70 https://www.marxists.org/archive/trotsky/1924/lit_revo/intro.htm

71 Karl Marx, *The 18th Brumaire of Louis Bonaparte, I.*

The past is something we cannot escape, even if we do not remember it. Marx thought it a bad thing that the "tradition of all the dead generations weighs like a nightmare on the brain of the living." If only Marx's "philosophy" had not destroyed our regard for the past, if only we had kept memory alive, perhaps this shameful moment would not have come. *But come it has*, with a clown's multi-colored finger-prints marking an over-reaction that might have been less ridiculous had the Capitol suffered the fate of the burning Reichstag of 1933.

Unfortunately for Mr. Biden, our erstwhile right-wing baddies were too busy taking selfies and forgot their gasoline cans. But one may, with help from an ever bloviating media, make a Himilayan mountain range out of a road apple. And now, with 30,000 troops swarming the Capitol, and the FBI declaring a massive conspiracy against the government, Biden takes the Oath of Office to defend the Constitution against all enemies, *imaginary and domestic.*

What absurdities will he pronounce in his inaugural address? Marx wrote that men cannot resist conjuring up "the spirits of the past to their service," adopting battle cries and battle flags from bygone wars. "Thus Luther donned the mask of the Apostle Paul, the Revolution of 1789 to 1814 draped itself alternately as the Roman republic and the Roman empire…." What pose will Biden strike? Whose words will he borrow? Will he mimic Lincoln? Will he borrow a line from FDR? How about a line or two from Hitler's Enabling Act of 1933? But no, this is not the end of the Weimar Republic. It is a farce, and nothing but. Already the Biden administration is a parody of oppression, set on by intelligence agencies of the Maxwell Smart variety; all of them eagerly promising, *"Don't worry chief, it won't happen again."* (Or, in the case of Russia-gate, *"Missed it by that much!"*)

At the other end of the parody, we find the brainless efficiency of Facebook, Apple and Twitter, moving against the state's newly declared enemies: Donald Trump, Parler and free speech. What do these social media buffoons know of our great traditions of free discourse? They prattle on about the first amendment as if that's what everything is based upon. Oh no, you historical illiterates. Long before the First Amendment said "Congress shall make no law … abridging the freedom of speech, or of the press," we had John Milton's *Areopagitica.* The great poet inveighed against those who vainly held "that none must be heard but whom they like....”[72] It is by such persons that “knowledge is kept at a distance from us.” Yes, that’s exactly right. By stopping free speech you stop the free flow of thought and you stop the engine that made America great. But of course, you all hate the idea of American greatness. So now you stop America’s brain, its creativity, even though it is your own life blood. You cut off your own customers and destroy the basis of your own “information economy.” There are no words for you. There is only the suicide you have procured by blocking your only path to correction and reform. “For when God shakes a kingdom with strong and healthful commotions to a general reforming,” wrote Milton, “God then raises to his own work men of rare abilities, and more than common industry, not only to look back, and revise what hath been taught before, but to gain further, and go on some new enlightened steps in the discovery of truth.”

And what truth will we find by blocking all criticism of political correctness? How shall we then escape the left’s intolerant mantras on tolerance, or the invidious demagoguery of declaring persons equal in a world where *none are* equal? How will we, then, preserve what is best against the foul negating spirit of cancel culture as it brings our traditions of free speech to an end? Will we allow these hyenas, yapping their stale stupidities, to dictate *our* speech, *our* social discourse? Will we be dictated to by these leftist automata, with their lobotomized brains in formaldehyde jars labeled with university credentials so obtained?

How have yapping hyenas and leftist automata come to be so prominent in our media, in our large corporations and government? It is but testimony to the intellectual bankruptcy of this pitiful country. We are an impossibly stupid society, having stored up for ourselves and our children a chastizement of Biblical proportions; for we have already been stifling speech in the universities, in our centers of learning, for an entire generation. And so, a time of spoliation and destruction and murder far exceeding our worst imaginings is on its way. For what is the true promise of those who are now taking office in Washington? Is it the promise of strength against foreign enemies? Are we getting persons honorable and trustworthy? When Biden slips on that banana peel it will be President Harris — as genuine as a three dollar bill, as empty

72 John Milton, *Areopagitica*.

as the U.S. Treasury, as incapable as she is faithless. History is not kind when countries are governed by the likes of Kamala Harris.

In aspiring to become gods of the human hive, these ambitious nobodies can destroy our liberty, our prosperity, and the country itself; first, because their intentions are not benevolent; second, because their ambitions are inappropriate to who they are; third, because they are weak and foolish and Godless.

All these bright-eyed young people, eager for the world of equality and tolerance they've been taught about in school, won't find salvation in Biden or Harris. The left deludes itself that the imminent failure of the Biden/Harris administration shall owe everything to the wicked machinations of the right, rearing its ugly head and blocking the path to utopia. But this is stupid. There is no path to utopia here. If the right didn't exist, and if THE BAD ORANGE MAN disappeared altogether, their utopia would still fail. It could not happen otherwise; for there is no utopia. Man cannot save himself through politics. To think so is the essence of historical illiteracy.

The beautiful world of bliss which awaits, after Biden's inauguration, will resemble the very Fascism the left supposedly detests. Only it will be a ridiculous kind of Fascism, made doubly ridiculous by its subservience to Beijing. The Chinese communists know that a true socialist Revolution cannot be realized by an inauguration alone. Real socialism requires violence and compulsion. It must signify the end of freedom and the end of prosperity. With Biden and Harris tottering irresolutely on the shoulders of Marx and Engels, with China moving in from behind, America's elites are committing group suicide. A sane man doesn't stand beneath a structure that is about to collapse. He runs as far as he can from ground zero. Meanwhile, the government can mass all the troops they want in the capital, as a show of force. The American people are not threatening them. The real threat is a nuclear bomb from China, or Russia, or North Korea, or Iran. But even as our new rulers glower at America's patriots, they will be clinking glasses with the Chinese. This we can count on.

> Whoever digs a pit will fall into it, and a stone will come back on him who starts it rolling.
>
> PROVERBS 26:27

ANNEX

The Secret Speech of General Chi Haotian

In 2005, *The Epoch Times* acquired a secret speech given by Defense Minister Chi Haotian to high-level Communist Party Cadres sometime before his retirement in 2003. Details given in Chi's speech coincide with previously unpublished defector testimony on Sino-Russian military plans.

The speech follows:

"Comrades,

I'm very excited today, because the large-scale online survey sina.com that was done for us showed that our next generation is quite promising and our party's cause will be carried on. In answering the question, "Will you shoot at women, children and prisoners of war," more than 80 percent of the respondents answered in the affirmative, exceeding by far our expectations.

Today I'd like to focus on why we asked sina.com to conduct this online survey among our people. My speech today is a sequel to my speech last time, during which I started with a discussion of the issue of the three islands, [where I] mentioned that 20 years of the idyllic theme of "peace and development" had come to an end, and concluded that modernization under the saber is the only option for China's next phase. I also mention we have a vital stake overseas. Today, I'll speak more specifically on these two issues.

The central issue of this survey appears to be whether one should shoot at women, children and prisoners of war, but its real significance goes far beyond that. Ostensibly, our intention is mainly to figure out what the Chinese people's attitude toward war is: If these future soldiers do not hesitate to kill even non-combatants, they'll naturally be doubly ready and ruthless in killing combatants. Therefore, the responses to the survey questions may reflect the general attitude people have towards war.

Actually, however, this is not our genuine intention. The purpose of the CCP Central Committee in conducting this survey is to probe people's minds.

We wanted to know: If China's global development will necessitate massive deaths in enemy countries, will our people endorse that scenario? Will they be for or against it?

As everybody knows, the essence of Comrade Xiaoping's thinking is "development is the hard truth." And Comrade Jintao, has also pointed out repeatedly and emphatically that "development is our top priority," which should not be neglected for even a moment. But many comrades tend to understand "development" in its narrow sense, assuming it to be limited to domestic development. The fact is, our "development" refers to the great revitalization of the Chinese nation, which, of course, is not limited to the land we have now but also includes the whole world.

Why do I put it this way?

Both Comrade Liu Huaquing, one of the leaders of the old generation in our Party, and Comrade He Xin, a young strategist of our Party, have repeatedly stressed the theory regarding the shift of the center of World Civilization. Our slogan of "revitalizing China" has this way of thinking as its basis. You may look into the newspapers and magazines published in recent years or go online to do some research to find out who raised the slogan of national revitalization first. It was Comrade He Xin. Do you know who He Xin is? He may look aggressive and despicable when he speaks in public, with his sleeves and pants all rolled up, but his historical vision is a treasure our Party should cherish.

In discussing this issue, let us start from the beginning.

As everybody knows, according to the views propagated by Western scholars, humanity as a whole originated from one single mother in Africa. Therefore, no race can claim racial superiority. However, according to the research conducted by most Chinese scholars, the Chinese are different from other races on earth. We did not originate in Africa. Instead, we originated independently in the land of China. The Peking Man at Zhoukoudian that we are all familiar with represents a phase of our ancestors' evolution. "The Project of Searching for the Origins of the Chinese Civilization" currently undertaken in our country is aimed at a more comprehensive and systematic research on the origin, process and development of the ancient Chinese civilization. We use to say, "Chinese civilization has had a history of five thousand years." But now, many experts engaged in research in varied fields including archeology, ethnic cultures, and regional cultures have reached consensus that the new discoveries such as the Hongshan Culture in the northeast, the Liangahn Cutlure in Zhejiang province, the Jinsha Ruins in Sichuan province, and the Yongzhou Shun Emperor Cultural Site in Hunan province are all compelling evidence of the exitence of China's early civilizations, and they prove that China's rice-growing agricultural history alone can be traced back as far as 8,000 to 10,000 years. This refutes the concept of "five thousand years of Chinese civilization."

Therefore, we can assert that we are the product of cultural roots of more than a million years, and a single Chinese entity of two thousand years. This is the Chinese entity of two thousand years. This is the Chinese nation that calls itself, "descendants of Yan and Huang," the Chinese nation that we are so proud of. Hitler's Germany had once bragged that the German race was the most superior race on earth, but the fact is, our nation is far superior to the Germans.

During our long history, our people have disseminated throughout the Americas and the regions along the Pacific Rim, and they became Indians in the Americas and the East Asian ethnic groups in the South Pacific.

We all know that on account of our national superiority, during the thriving and prosperous Tang Dynasty our civilization was at the peak of the world. We were the center of the world civilization, and no other civilization in the world was comparable to ours. Later on, because of our complacency, narrow-mindedness, and the self-enclosure of our own country, we were surpassed by Western civilization, and the center of the world shifted to the West.

In reviewing history, one may ask: Will the center of the world civilization shift back to China?

Comrade He Xin put it in his report to the Central Committee in 1988: If the fact is that the center of leadership of the world was located in Europe as of the 18th Century, and later shifted to the United States in the mid-20th century the center of leadership of the world will shift to the East of our planet. And, "the East" of course mainly refers to China.

Actually, Comrade Lui Huaquing made similar points in the 1980s. Based on an historical analysis, he pointed out that the center of world civilization is shifting. It shifted from the East to Western Europe and later to the United States; now it is shifting back to the East. Therefore, if we refer to the

19th century as the British century, and the 20th century as the American century, then the 21st century will be the Chinese century.

To understand conscientiously this historical law and to greet the advent of the Chinese Century is the historical mission of our Party. As we all know, at the end of the last century, we built the Altar to the Chinese Century in Beijing.

At the very moment of the arrival of the new millennium, the collective leadership of the Party Central Committee gathered there for a rally, upholding the torches of Zhoukoudian, to pledge themselves to get ready to greet the arrival of the Chinese Century. We were doing this to follow the historical law and setting the realization of the Chinese century as the goal of our Party's endeavors.

Later, in the political report of our Party's Sixteenth National Congress, we established that national revitalization should be our great objective and explicitly specified in our new Party Constitution that our Party is the pioneer of the Chinese people. All these steps marked a major development in Marxism, reflecting our Party's courage and wisdom. As we all know, Marx and his followers have never referred to any communist party as a pioneer of a certain people; neither did they say that national revitalization could be used as a slogan of a communist party. Even Comrade Mao Zedong, a courageous national hero, only raised high the banner of "the global proletarian revolution," but even he did not have the courage to give the loudest publicity to the slogan of national revitalization.

We must greet the arrival of the Chinese Century by raising high the banner of national revitalization. How should we fight for the realization of the Chinese Century? We must borrow the precious experiences in human history by taking advantage of the outstanding fruition of human civilization and drawing lessons from what happened to other ethnic groups.

The lessons include the collapse of communism in the former Soviet Union and Eastern Europe, as well as the defeats of Germany and Japan in the past. Recently there has been much discussion of the lessons of the collapse of communism in the former Soviet Union and Eastern European countries, so I will not dwell on them here. Today I'd like to talk about the lessons of Germany and Japan.

As we all know, Nazi Germany also placed much emphasis on the education of the people, especially the younger generation. The Nazi Party and government organized and established various propaganda and educational institutions such as the "Guiding Bureau of National Propaganda," "Department of National Education and Propaganda," "Supervising Bureau of Worldview Study and Education," and "Information Office," all aimed at instilling into the people's minds, from elementary schools to colleges, the idea that German people are superior, and convincing people that the historical mission of the Aryan people is to become the "lords of the earth" whose right it is to "rule over the world." Back then the German people were much more united than we are today.

Nonetheless, Germany was defeated in utter shame, along with its ally, Japan. Why? We reached some conclusions at the study meetings of the Politburo, in which we were searching for the laws that governed the vicissitudes of the big powers, and trying to analyze Germany and Japan's rapid growth. When we decide to revitalize based on the German model, we must not repeat the mistakes they made.

Specifically, the following are the fundamental causes for their defeat: First, they had too many enemies all at once, as they did not adhere to the principle of eliminating enemies one at a time; second, they were too impetuous, lacking the patience and perseverance required for great accomplishments; third, when the time came for them to be ruthless, they turned out to be too soft, therefore leaving troubles that resurfaced later on.

Let's presume that back then Germany and Japan had been able to keep the United States neutral and had fought a protracted war step by step on the Soviet front. If they had adopted this approach, gained some time to advance their research, eventually succeeded in obtaining the technology of nuclear weapons and missiles, and launched surprise attacks against the United States and the Soviet Union using them, then the United States and the Soviet Union would not have been able to defend themselves and would have had to surrender. Little Japan, in particular, made an egregious mistake in launching the sneak attack on Pearl Harbor. This attack did not hit the vital parts of the United States. Instead, it dragged the United States into the war, into the ranks of the gravediggers that eventually buried the German and Japanese fascists.

Of course, if they had not made these three mistakes and won the war, history would have been written in a different fashion. If that had been the case, China would not be in our hands. Japan might have relocated their capital to China and ruled over China. Afterwards, China and the whole of Asia under Japan's command would have brought into full play the oriental wisdom, conquered the West ruled by Germany and unified the whole world. This is irrelevant, of course. No more digressions.

So, the fundamental reason for the defeats of Germany and Japan is that history did not arrange them to be the "lords of the earth," for they are, after all, not the most superior race.

Ostensibly, in comparison, today's China is alarmingly similar to Germany back then. Both of them regard themselves as the most superior races; both of them have a history of being exploited by foreign powers and are therefore vindictive; both of them have the tradition of worshipping their own authorities; both of them feel that they have seriously insufficient living space; both of them raise high the two banners of nationalism and socialism and label themselves as "national socialism"; both of them worship "one state, one party, one leader, and one doctrine."

And yet, if we really are to make a comparison between Germany and China, then, as Comrade Jiang Zemin put it, Germany belongs to "pediatrics" – too trivial to be compared. How large is Germany's population? How big is its territory? And how long is its history? We eliminated eight million nationalist troops in only three years. How many enemies did Germany kill? They were in power for a transient period of little more than a dozen years before they perished, while we are still energetic after being around for more than eighty years. Our theory of the shifting center of civilization is of course more profound than Hitler's theory of "the lords of the earth." Our civilization is profound and broad, which has determined that we are so much wiser than they were.

Our Chinese people are wiser than the Germans because, fundamentally, our race is superior to theirs. As a result, we have a longer history, more people, and larger land area. On this basis our ancestors left us with the two most essential heritages, which are atheism and great unity. It was Confucius, the founder of our Chinese culture, who gave us these heritages.

This heritage determined that we have a stronger ability to survive than the West. That is why the Chinese race has been able to prosper for so long. We are destined "not to be buried by either heaven or earth" no matter how severe the natural, man-made, and national disasters. This is our advantage.

Take response to war as an example. The reason that the United States remains today is that it has never seen war on its mainland. Once its enemies aim at the mainland, these enemies would reach Washington before its congress finishes debating and authorizes the president to declare war. But for us, we don't waste time on these trivial things. Comrade Deng Xiaoping once said, "The Party's leadership is prompt in making decisions. Once a decision is made, it is immediately implemented. There's no wasting time on trivial things like in capitalist countries. This is our advantage! Our Party's democratic centralism is built on the tradition of great unity. Although fascist Germany also stressed high-level centralism, they only focused on power of the top leader, but ignored the collective leadership of the central group. That's why Hitler was betrayed by many later in his life, which fundamentally depleted the Nazis of their war capacity.

What makes us different from Germany is that we are complete atheists, while Germany was primarily a Catholic and Protestant country. Hitler was only half atheist. Although Hitler also believed that ordinary citizens had low intelligence, and that leaders should therefore make decisions, and although German people worshipped Hitler back then, Germany did not have the tradition of worshipping sages on a broad basis. Our Chinese society has always worshipped sages, and that is because we don't worship any God. Once you worship a god, you can't worship a person at the same time, unless you recognize the person as the god's representative like they do in Middle Eastern countries. On the other hand, once you recognize a person as a sage, of course you will want him to be your leader.... This is the foundation of our democratic centralism.

The bottom line is, only China is a reliable force in resisting the Western parliament-based democratic system. Hitler's dictatorship in Germany was perhaps but a momentary mistake in history.

Maybe you have now come to understand why we recently decided to further promulgate atheism. If we let theology from the West into China and empty us from the inside, if we let all Chinese people listen to God and follow

God, who will obediently listen to us and follow us? If the common people don't believe Comrade Hu Jintao is a qualified leader, question his authority, and want to monitor him, if the religious followers in our society question why we are leaving God in churches, can our Party continue to rule China?

Germany's dream to be the "lord of the earth" failed, because ultimately, history did not bestow this great mission upon them. But the three lessons Germany learned from experience are what we ought to remember as we complete our historic mission and revitalize our race. The three lessons are: Firmly grasp the country's living space; firmly grasp the Party's control over the nation; and firmly grasp the general direction toward becoming the "lord of the earth."

Next, I'd like to address these three issues.

The first issue is living space. This is the biggest focus of the revitalization of the Chinese race. In my last speech, I said that the fight over basic living resources (including land and ocean) is the source of the vast majority of wars in history. This may change in the information age, but not fundamentally. Our per capita resources are much less than those of Germany's back then. In addition, economic development in the last twenty-plus years had a negative impact, and climates are rapidly changing for the worse. Our resources are in very short supply. The environment is severely polluted, especially that of soil, water, and air. Not only our ability to sustain and develop our race, but even its survival is gravely threatened, to a degree much greater than faced by Germany back then.

Anybody who has been to Western countries knows that their living space is much better than ours. They have forests alongside the highways, while we hardly have any trees by our streets. Their sky is often blue with white clouds, while our sky is covered by a layer of dark haze. Their tap water is clean enough for drinking, while even our ground water is so polluted that it can't be drunk without filtering. They have few people in the streets, and two or three people can occupy a small residential building; in contrast, our streets are always crawling with people, and several people have to share one room.

Many years ago, there was a book titled Yellow Catastrophes. It said that, due to our following the American style of consumption, our limited resources would not long support the population and society would collapse, once our population reaches 1.3 billion. Now our population has already exceeded this limit, and we are now relying on imports to sustain our nation. It's not that we haven't paid attention to this issue. The Ministry of Land Resources is specialized in this issue.

But the term 'living space' (lebensraum) is too closely related to Nazi Germany. The reason we don't want to discuss this too openly is to avoid the West's association of us with Nazi Germany, which could in turn reinforce the view that China is a threat. Therefore, in our emphasis on He Xin's new theory, "Human rights are just living rights," we only talk about "living," but not "space," so as to avoid using the term "living space." From the perspective of history, the reason that China is faced with the issue of living space is because Western countries established colonies ahead of Eastern countries. Western countries established colonies all around the world, therefore giving themselves an advantage on the issue of living space. To solve this problem, we must lead the Chinese people outside of China, so that they could develop outside of China.

The second issue is our focus on the leadership capacity of the ruling party. We've done better on this than their party. Although the Nazis spread their power to every aspect of the German national government, they did not stress their absolute leadership position like we have. They did not take the issue of managing the power of the party as first priority, which we have. When Comrade Mao Zedong summarized the "three treasures" of our party's victory in conquering the country, he considered the most important "treasure" to be developing the Chinese Communist Party (CCP) and strengthening its leadership position.

We have to focus on two points to fortify our leadership position and improve our leadership capacity.

The first is to promote the "Three Represents" theory, stressing that our Party is the pioneer of the Chinese race, in addition to being the pioneer of the proletariat. Many citizens say in private, "We never voted for you, the Communist Party, to represent us. How can you claim to be our representatives?"

There's no need to worry about this issue. Comrade Mao Zedong said that if we could lead the Chinese people outside of China, resolving the lack of living space in China, the Chinese people will support us. At that time, we don't' have to worry about the labels of "totalitarianism" or "dictatorship." Whether we can forever represent the Chinese people depends on whether we can succeed in leading the Chinese people out of China.

The second point, whether we can lead the Chinese people out of China, is the most important determinant of the CCP's leadership position.

Why do I say this?

Everyone knows that without the leadership of our Party, China would not exist today. Therefore, our highest principle is to forever protect our Party's leadership position. Before June 4, we realized vaguely that as long as China's economy is developed, people would support and love the Communist Party. Therefore we had to use several decades of peacetime to develop China's economy. No matter what-isms, whether it is a white cat or a black at, it is a good cat if it can develop China's economy. But at that time, we did not have mature ideas about how China would deal with international disputes after its economy becomes developed.

Comrade Xiaoping said then that the main themes in the world were peace and development. But the June 4 riot gave our Party a warning and gave us a lesson that is still fresh.

The pressure of China's peaceful evolution makes us reconsider of these two main themes of our time. We see that neither of these two issues, peace and development, have been resolved. The western oppositional forces always change the world according to their own visions; they want to change China and use peaceful evolution to overturn the leadership of our Communist Party. Therefore, if we only develop the economy, we still face the possibility of losing control.

The June 4 riot almost succeeded in bringing a peaceful transition; if it were not for the fact that a large number of veteran comrades were still alive and at a crucial moment they removed Zhao Ziyang and his followers, then we all would have been put in prison. After death we would have been too ashamed to report to Marx. Although we have passed the test of June 4, after our group of senior comrades pass away, without our control, peaceful evolution may still come to China like it did to the former Soviet Union. In 1956, they suppressed the Hungarian incident and defeated the attacks by Tito's revisionists of Yugoslavia, but they could not withstand Gorbachev thirty some years later. Once those pioneering senior comrades died, the power of the Communist Party was taken away by peaceful evolution.

After the June 4 riot was suppressed, we have been thinking about how to prevent China from peaceful evolution and how to maintain the Communist

Party's leadership. We thought it over and over but did not come up with any good ideas. If we do not have good ideas, China will inevitably change peacefully, and we will all become criminals in history. After some deep pondering, we finally come to this conclusion: Only by turning our developed national strength into the force of a first striking outward – only by leading people to go out – can we win forever the Chinese people's support and love for the Communist Party. Our party will then stand on invincible ground, and the Chinese people will have to depend on the Communist Party. They will forever follow the Communist Party with their hearts and minds, as was written in a couplet frequently seen in the countryside some years ago: "Listen to Chairman Mao, follow the Communist Party!" Therefore, the June 4 riot made us realize that we must combine economic development with preparation for war and leading the people to go out! Therefore, since then, our national defence policy has taken a 180 degree turn and we have since emphasized more and more "combining peace and war." Our economic development is all about preparing for the needs of war! Publicly we still emphasize economic development as our center, but in reality, economic development has war as its center! We have made a tremendous effort to construct "The Great Wall Project" to build up, along our coastal and land frontiers as well as around large and medium-sized cities, a solid underground "Great Wall" that can withstand a nuclear war. We are also storing all necessary war materials. Therefore, we will not hesitate to fight a Third World War, so as to lead the people to go out and to ensure the Party's leadership position. In any event, we, the CCP, will never step down from the stage of history! We'd rather have the whole world, or even the entire globe, share life and death with us than step down from the stage of history! Isn't there a "nuclear bondage" theory? It means that since nuclear wepaons have bound the security of the entire world, all will die together if death is inevitable. In my view, there is another kind of bondage, and that is, the fate of our Party is tied up with that of the whole world. If we, the CCP, are finished, China will be finished, and the world will be finished.

Our Party's historical mission is to lead the Chinese people to go out. If we take the long view, we will see that history led us on this path. First, China's long history has resulted in the world's largest population, including Chinese in China as well as overseas. Second, once we open our doors, the profit-seeking western capitalists will invest capital and technology in China to assist our development, so that they can occupy the biggest market in the world. Third, our numerous overseas Chinese help us create the most favorable environment for the introduction of foreign capital, foreign technology, and advanced experience into China. Thus, it is guaranteed that our reform and open-door policy will achieve tremendous success. Fourth, China's great economic expansion will inevitably lead to the shrinkage of per-capita living space for the Chinese people, and this will encourage China to turn outward in search for new living space. Fifth, China's great economic expansion will inevitably come with significant development in our military forces, creating conditions for our expansion overseas. Ever since Napoleon's time, the West has been alert for the possible awakening of the sleeping lion that is China. Now, the sleeping lion is standing up and advancing into the world, and has become unstoppable!

What is the third issue we should clinch firmly in order to accomplish our historical mission of national renaissance? It is to hold firmly onto the big "issue of America."

This appears to be shocking, but the logic is actually very simple.

Comrade He Xin put forward a very fundamental judgment that is very reasonable. He asserted in his report to the Party Central Committee: The renaissance of China is in fundamental conflict with the Western strategic interest, and therefore will inevitably be obstructed by the western countries doing everything they can. So, Only by breaking the blockade formed by the western countries headed by the United States can China grow and move toward the world!

Would the United States allow us to go out to gain new living space? First, if the United States is firm in blocking us, it is hard for us to do anything significant to Taiwan, Vietnam, India, or even Japan, [so] how much more living space can we get? Very trivial! Only countries like the United States, Canada and Australia have the vast land to serve our need for mass colonization.

Therefore, solving the "issue of America" is the key to solving all other issues. First, this makes it possible for us to have many people migrate there and even establish another China under the same leadership of the CCP. America was originally discovered by the ancestors of the yellow race, but Columbus gave credit to the white race. We the descendants of the Chinese nation are entitled to the possession of the land! It is said that the residents of the yellow race have a very low social status in the United States. We need to liberate them.

Second, after solving the "issue of America," the western countries of Europe would bow to us, not to mention Taiwan, Japan and other small countries. Therefore, solving the "issue of America" is the mission assigned to the CCP members by history.

I sometimes think how cruel it is for China and the United States to be enemies that are bound to meet on a narrow road! Do you remember a movie about Liberation Army Troops led by Liu Bocheng and Deng Xiaoping? The title is something like "Decisive Battle on the Central Plains." There is a famous remark in the movie that is full of power and grandeur: "The enemies are bound to meet on a narrow road, only the brave will win!" It is this kind of fighting to win or die spirit that enabled us to seize power in Mainland China. It is historical destiny that China and the United States will come to unavoidable confrontation on a narrow path and fight each other! The United States, unlike Russia and Japan, has never occupied and hurt China, and also assisted China in its battle against the Japanese. But, it will certainly be an obstruction, and the biggest obstruction! In the long run, the relationship of China and the United States is one of a life-and-death struggle.

One time, some Americans came to visit and tried to convince us that the relationship between China and the United States is one of interdependence. Comrade Xiaoping replied in a polite manner: "Go tell your government, China and the United States do not have such a relationship that is interdependent and mutually reliant." Actually, Comrade Xiaoping was being too polite, he could have been more frank, "The relationship between China and the United States is one of life-and-death struggle." Of course, right now it is not the time to openly break up with them yet. Our reform and opening to the outside world still rely on their capital and technology, we still need America. Therefore, we must do everything we can to promote our relationship with America, learn from America in all aspects and use America as an example to reconstruct our country.

How have we managed our foreign affairs in these years? Even if we had to put on a smiling face in order to please them, even if we have to give them the right cheek after they had hit our left cheek, we still must endure in order to further our relationship with the United States. Do you remember the character of Wuxun in the movie the "Story of Wuxun"? In order to accomplish his mission, he endured so much pain and suffered so much beating and kicking! The United States is the most successful country in the world today. Only after we have learned all of its useful experiences can we replace it in the future. Even though we are presently imitating the American tone "China and the United States rely on each other and share honor and disgrace," we must not forget that the history of our civilization repeatedly has taught us that one mountain does not allow two tigers to live together.

We also must never forget what Comrade Xiaoping emphasized: "Refrain from revealing ambitions and put others off the track." The hidden message is: we must put up with America; we must conceal our ultimate goals, hide our capabilities, and await the opportunity. In this way, our mind is clear. Why have we not updated our national anthem with something peaceful? Why did we not change the anthem's theme of war? Instead, when revising the Constitution this time, for the first time we clearly specified "March of the Volunteers" is our national anthem. Thus we will understand why we constantly talk loudly about the "Taiwan issue" but not the "American issue." We all know the principle of "doing one thing under the cover of another." If ordinary people can only see the small island of Taiwan in their eyes, then you as the elite of our country should be able to see the whole picture of our cause. Over these years, according to Comrade Xiaoping's arrangement, a large piece of our territory in the North has been given up to Russia; do you really think our Party Committee is a fool?

To resolve the issue of America we must be able to transcend conventions and restrictions. In history, when a country defeated another country or occupied another country, it could not kill all the people in the conquered land because back then you could not kill people effectively with sabers or long spears, or even with rifles or machine guns. Therefore, it was impossible to gain a stretch of land without keeping the people on that land. However, if we conquered America in this fashion, we would not be able to make many people migrate there.

Only by using special means to "clean up" America will we be able to lead the Chinese people there. This is the only choice left for us. This is not a matter of whether we are willing to do it or not. What kind of special means is there available for us to "clean up America"?

Conventional weapons such as fighters, canons, missiles and battleships won't do; neither will highly destructive weapons such as nuclear weapons. We are not as foolish as to want to perish together with America by using nuclear weapons, despite the fact that we have been exclaiming that we will have the Taiwan issue resolved at whatever cost. Only by using non-destructive weapons that can kill many people will we be able to reserve America for ourselves. There has been rapid development of modern biological technology, and new bio-weapons have been invented one after another. Of course, we have not been idle, in the past years we have seized the opportunity to master weapons of this kind. We are capable of achieving our purpose of "cleaning up" America all of a sudden. When Comrade Xiaoping was still with us, the Party Central Committee had the perspicacity to make the right decision not to develop aircraft carrier groups and focus instead on developing lethal weapons that can eliminate mass populations of the enemy country.

From a humanitarian perspective, we should issue a warning to the American people and persuade them to leave America and leave the land they have lived in to the Chinese people. Or at least they should leave half of the United States to be China's colony, because America was first discovered by the Chinese. But would this work? If this strategy does not work, then there is only one choice left to us. That is, use decisive means to "clean up" America and reserve America for our use in a moment. Our historical experience has proven that as long as we make it happen, nobody in the world can do anything about us. Furthermore, if the United States as the leader is gone, then other enemies have to surrender to us.

Biological weapons are unprecedented in their ruthlessness, but if the Americans do not die then the Chinese have to die. If the Chinese people are strapped to the present land, a total societal collapse is bound to take place. According to the computation of the author of Yellow Peril, more than half of the Chinese will die, and that figure would be more than 800 million people! Just after the liberation, our yellow land supported nearly 500 million people, while today the official figure of the population is more than 1.3 billion. This yellow land has reached the limit of its capacity. One day, who knows how soon it will come, the great collapse will occur any time and more than half the population will have to go.

We must prepare ourselves for two scenarios. If our biological weapons succeed in the surprise attack, the Chinese people will be able to keep their losses at a minimum in the fight against the United States. If, however, the attack fails and triggers a nuclear retaliation from the United States, China would perhaps suffer a catastrophe in which more than half of its population would perish. That is why we need to be ready with air defense systems for our big and medium-sized cities. Whatever the case may be, we can only move forward fearlessly, for the sake of our Party and State and our nation's future, regardless of the hardships we have to face and the sacrifices we have to make. The population, even if more than half dies, can be reproduced. But if the Party falls, everything is gone, and forever gone.

In Chinese history, in the replacement of dynasties, the ruthless have always won and the benevolent have always failed. The most typical example involved Xiang Yu the King of Chu, who, after defeating Liu Bang, failed to continue to chase after him and eliminate his forces, and his leniency resulted in Xiang Yu's death and Liu's victory… Therefore, we must emphasize the importance of adopting resolute measures. In the future, the two rivals, China and the United States, will eventually meet each other in a narrow road, and our leniency to the Americans will mean cruelty toward the Chinese people. Here some people may want to ask me: What about the several millions of our compatriots in the United States? They may ask: aren't we against Chinese killing other Chinese?

These comrades are too pedantic; they are not pragmatic enough. If we had insisted on the principle that the Chinese should not kill other Chinese, would we have liberated China? As for the several million Chinese living in the United States, this is of course a big issue. Therefore, in recent years, we have been conducting research on genetic weapons, i.e., those weapons that do not kill yellow people. But producing a result with this kind of research is extremely difficult.

Of the research done on genetic weapons throughout the world, Israel is the most advanced. Their genetic weapons are designed to target Arabs and protect the Israelis. But even they have not reached the stage of actual deployment. We have cooperated with Israel on some research. Perhaps we can introduce some of the technologies used to protect Israelis and remold these technologies to protect the yellow people. But their technologies are not mature yet, and it is difficult for us to surpass them in a few years. If it has to be five or ten years before some breakthrough can be achieved in genetic weapons, we cannot afford to wait any longer.

Old comrades like us cannot afford to wait that long, for we don't have that much time to live. Old soldiers of my age may be able to wait for five or ten more years, but those from the period of the anti-Japanese War or the few old Red Army soldiers cannot wait any longer.

Therefore, we have to give up our expectations about genetic weapons. Of course, from another perspective, the majority of those Chinese living in the United States have become our burden, because they have been corrupted by the bourgeois liberal values for a long time and it would be difficult for them to accept our Party's leadership. If they survived the war, we would have to launch campaigns in the future to deal with them, to reform them. Do you still remember that when we had just defeated the Koumintang (KMT) and liberated Mainland China, so many people from the bourgeois class and intellectuals welcomed us so very warmly, but later we had to launch campaigns such as the "suppression of the reactionaries" and "Anti-Rightist Movement" to clean them up and reform them? Some of them were in hiding for a long time and were not exposed until the Cultural Revolution. History has proved that any social turmoil is likely to involve many deaths.

Maybe we can put it this way: death is the engine that moves history forward. During the period of the three kingdoms, how many people died? When Genghis Khan conquered Eurasia, how many people died? When Manchu invaded the interior of China, how many people died? Not many people died during the 1911 Revolution, but when we overthrew the Three Great Mountains, and during the political campaigns such as "suppression of the reactionaries," "Three-Anti-Campaign," and "Five-Anti-Campaign," at least 20 million people died. We were apprehensive that some young people today would be trembling with fear when they hear about wars and people dying.

During wartime, we were used to seeing dead people. Blood and flesh were flying everywhere, corpses were lying in heaps on the fields, and blood ran like rivers. We saw it all. On the battlefields, everybody's eyes turned red with killing because it was a life-and-death struggle and only the brave would survive.

It is indeed brutal to kill one or two hundred million Americans. But that is the only path that will secure a Chinese century in which the CCP leads the world. We, as revolutionary humanitarians, do not want deaths. But if history confronts us with a choice between deaths of Chinese and those of Americans, we'd have to pick the latter, as, for us, it is more important to safeguard the lives of the Chinese people and the life of our Party. That is because, after all, we are Chinese and members of the CCP. Since the day we joined the CCP, the Party, life has always been above all else! History will prove that we made the right choice.

Now, when I am about to finish my speech, you probably understand why we wanted to know, whether the people would rise against us if one day we secretly adopt resolute means to "clean up" America. For over twenty years, China has been enjoying peace, and a whole generation has not been tested by war. In particular, since the end of World War II, there have been many changes in the formats of war, the concept of war and the ethics of war. Especially since the collapse of the former Soviet Union and Eastern European Communist states, the ideology of the West has come to dominate the world as a whole, and the Western theory of human nature and western view of human rights have increasingly been disseminated among the young people in China. Therefore, we were not very sure about the people's attitude. If our people are fundamentally opposed to "cleaning up" America, we will, of course, have to adopt corresponding measures.

Why didn't we conduct the survey through administrative means instead of through the web? We did what we did for a good reason.

First of all, we did it to reduce artificial inference and to make sure that we got the true thoughts of the people. In addition, it is more confidential and won't reveal the true purpose of our survey. But what is most important is the fact that most of the people who are able to respond to the questions online are from social groups that are relatively well-educated and intelligent. They are the hard-core and leading groups that play a decisive role among our people. If they support us, then the people as a whole will follow us. If they oppose us, they will play the dangerous role of inciting people and creating social disturbance.

What turned out to be very comforting is they did not turn in a blank test paper. In fact, they turned in a test paper with a score of over 80. This is the excellent fruition of our Party's work in propaganda and education over the past few decades.

Of course, a few people under western influence have objected to shooting at prisoners of war and women and children. Is everybody crazy? Some others said, "The Chinese love to label themselves as a peace-loving people, but actually they are the most ruthless people. The comments are resonant of killing and murdering, sending chills to my heart."

Although there are not too many people holding this kind of viewpoint and they will not affect the overall situation in any significant way, but we still need to strengthen the propaganda to respond to this kind of argument.

That is to vigorously propagate Comrade He Xin's latest article, which has already been reported to the central government. You may look it up on the website.

If you get on the website using key words to search, you will find out that a while ago comrade He Xin pointed out to the Hong Kong Business News during an interview that: "The U.S. has a shocking conspiracy." According to what he had in hand, from September 27 to October 1, 1995, the Mikhail Sergeevich Gorbachev Foundation, funded by the United States, gathered 500 of the world's most important statesmen, economic leaders and scientists, including George W. Bush (he was not the U.S. president at the time), the Baroness Thatcher, Tony Blair, Zbigniew Brzezinski, as well as George Soros, Bill Gates, futurist John Naisbitt, etc., all of the world's most popular characters, in the San Francisco Fairmont hotel for a high-level roundtable conference, discussing problems about globalization and how to guide humanity to move forward into the 21st century. According to what He Xin had in hand, the outstanding people of the world in attendance thought that in the 21st century a mere 20 percent of the world's population will be sufficient to maintain the world's economy and prosperity, the other 80 percent or 4/5ths of the world's population will be human garbage unable to produce new values. The people in attendance thought that this excess 80 percent population would be a trash population and "high-tech" means should be used to eliminate them gradually.

Since the enemies are secretly planning to eliminate our population, we certainly cannot be infinitely merciful and compassionate to them. Comrade He Xin's article came out at the right time, it has proven the correctness of our tit for tat battle approach ... [and] Comrade Deng Xiaoping's great foresight to deploy against the United States military strategy.

Certainly, in spreading Comrade He Xin's views, we cannot publish the article in the Party newspapers, in order to avoid raising the enemy's vigilance. He Xin's conversation may remind the enemy that we have grasped the modern science and technology, including "clean" nuclear technology as well as biological weapons technology, and we can use powerful measures to eliminate their population on a large scale.

The last problem I want to talk about is of firmly seizing the preparations for military battle.

Currently, we are at the crossroad of moving forward or backward. Some comrades saw problems flooding everywhere in our country – the corruption problem, the state-owned enterprise problem, the bank's bad accounts problem, environmental problems, society security problems, education problems, the AIDS problem, various appeals problems, even the riots problem. These comrades vacillated in the determination to prepare for military battles. They thought: they should first grab the political reform problem, that is, our own political reform comes first. After resolving the domestic problems, we can then deal with the foreign military battle problem.

This reminds me of the crucial period in 1948 in the Chinese Revolution. At that time the People's Liberation Army's "horses were drinking water" in the Yangtze River, but they faced extremely complex situations and difficult problems everywhere in the liberated areas, and the central authority received emergency reports daily. What to do? Should we stop to manage rear areas and internal matters first before moving forward, or press on to pass the Yangtze River with one vigorous effort? Chairman Mao, with his extraordinary wisdom and mettle gave the marching order "Carry on the revolution to the end," and liberated all of China. The previously thought "serious" conflicting problems were all resolved in this great forward moving revolutionary wave.

Now, it seems like we are in the same critical period as the "horses were drinking water" in the Yangtze River days in the revolutionary era, as long as we resolve the United States problem at one blow, our domestic problems will all be readily solved. Therefore, our military battle preparation appears to aim at Taiwan but in fact is aimed at the United States, and the preparation is far beyond the scope of attacking aircraft carriers or satellites.

Marxism pointed out that violence is the midwife for the birth of China's century. As war approaches, I am full of hope for our next generation."

The Lies We Believe In

China, Russia and the communist revolution in America

Printed in the USA
CPSIA information can be obtained
at www.ICGtesting.com
LVHW070159100524
779894LV00004B/16

9 786588 248218